APPROACHES TO THE HISTORY OF THE MIDDLE EAST: INTERVIEWS WITH LEADING MIDDLE EAST HISTORIANS

APPROACHES TO THE HISTORY OF THE MIDDLE EAST: INTERVIEWS WITH LEADING MIDDLE EAST HISTORIANS

Edited by Nancy Elizabeth Gallagher

First Edition

ISBN 0 86372 185 0

British Library Cataloguing-in-Publication Data.
A catalogue record for this book is available from the British Library.

Jacket design by Mark Slader
Typeset by Columns Design & Production Ltd, Reading
Printed in Lebanon

Ithaca Press is an imprint of Garnet Publishing Ltd,
8 Southern Court, South Street, Reading RG1 4QS UK.

For Albert Hourani

CONTENTS

PREFACE

I embarked on this book because I have often wanted an introduction to Middle Eastern historiography that would be lively, engaging, and accessible to students. I wanted a book that would humanize the discipline and that would demystify the academic life, and set out to fill that need. To this end, I settled on the methods of oral history. I found that the spontaneity and liveliness of the oral interview imparted a conversational style and sense of immediacy quite different from that of the written word. The interviewer can ask the narrator to expand on certain points, to return to matters of interest to readers, and, for comparative purposes, to address questions asked of other narrators.

For this study, I interviewed eight senior historians who are pioneers in their respective fields, who have lived through and participated in the major historical and historiographical transitions of the post-World War II era, and who have influenced English-speaking students. Many additional scholars could have been included, of course, but time and space did not permit. I should mention that one or two scholars were unable to participate for various reasons.

I was acquainted to varying degrees with all eight historians before the interviews. In the 1970s, I studied Middle Eastern history with Afaf Lutfi al-Sayyid Marsot, who directed my dissertation, and with Nikki Keddie, at the University of California, Los Angeles, and have been in frequent contact with both professors in subsequent years. I spent a year (1975-6) studying with Albert Hourani at St Antony's College, Oxford. Like many others, I continued to correspond with and visit Mr Hourani until his much-lamented death in 1993. I had briefly met or had heard lectures by Charles Issawi, André Raymond, Maxime Rodinson, Halil Inalcik, and Abdul-Karim Rafeq. I had, of course, read the principal scholarly works of all eight historians.

Each interview in this book began with a discussion of the scholar's formation, that is, family background, childhood experiences, early and later education, and the influences of persons and events. I then asked what led to their interest in Middle Eastern history and how their research methods, underlying assumptions, theoretical frameworks, and philosophies of history evolved over time. I asked about the influence of the Annales school, the orientalist debate, the current state of the narrator's field, and the study of women in Middle Eastern history. Finally, I asked what advice the narrator had for students. All of the interviews were in English except those of Maxime Rodinson and André Raymond which were in French. I then transcribed, edited, and in the case of the latter two, translated the interviews, and submitted them to the eight narrators for review. The final versions were then prepared according to their corrections and comments.

An oral history such as this could not have been conceived in the pre-World War II era. In the words of one historian interviewed for this study, "A generation ago, one did not feel it necessary to think about what one did. One just did it." Placing one's methodological and philosophical approaches to the study of history in the context of one's life is not easy, and I am very grateful to the eight historians who participated in this project. Without exception, they were gracious, kind, and helpful at all times. Ralph Jaeckel thoughtfully discussed the entire manuscript with me at various stages of its preparation. Farzaneh Milani conducted the first half of two of the interviews. May Seikaly read the manuscript and offered insightful comments. Adel Kamal, editor of Ithaca Press, and Sue Coll of the Editorial Department, gave their expert attention to the manuscript. The study was partially funded by the Academic Senate of the University of California, Santa Barbara. My husband, Tony Gardner, was always helpful. My children, Lisa and Karina, kept me company while I was working on the manuscript.

Department of History
University of California
Santa Barbara

INTRODUCTION

In this book, eight senior historians explain how their approaches to the writing of history have evolved in the wider context of their lives. All, whether of Western or Middle Eastern origin, have been influenced by Western historical methods and are well-known to English-speaking specialists in Middle Eastern history in the West and in the Middle East. Taken together, their works represent the central historiographical transitions of the post-World War II era. This era has witnessed a vast increase in interest in the history of the Middle East. Many more books and articles have been written, library collections have been expanded, universities have introduced or expanded programmes in Middle Eastern history, numerous students have entered the field, professional organizations have grown, and governmental and non-governmental research institutes have been established. The media regularly feature stories on the Middle East. There are more sophisticated theoretical and methodological approaches. Scholars use a wider variety of sources, and the origins of the scholars themselves are far more diverse. Most importantly for our purposes, the scholarly approach generally termed "orientalism" has yielded in part to an historical approach informed by the methods of sociology, anthropology, political science, economics, and other disciplines.[1]

Orientalism, the study of Eastern civilizations, developed in eighteenth- and nineteenth-century Europe along with increased interest in Biblical studies, in ancient and medieval history, in the sciences and philosophy, and in the non-European regions of the world. The training of orientalist scholars centred on the study of religions and on the philological examination of manuscripts and the languages in which they were written. Orientalist scholars sought to discover, through the study of religions and language, the unique characteristics and essential nature of Islamic civilization.[2] An orientalist who wanted to know more about "the Islamic city," for example, might study the classic texts for more information on cities in the Islamic world, seeking to discover the "essential character" that differentiates them from cities of other civilizations. Such a scholar might begin by noting that the Arabic word for city is *madina*, a word derived from the Arabic word for religion, *din*, and then surmise that the Islamic city originated as a centre of religion.

Partly because of the long years required to learn the languages of the region, partly because of their methodological training, many European orientalists tended to work in isolation from their colleagues in other fields who were asking new questions and working out new scholarly methods for studying the past.

These new questions and methods evolved largely out of the political and social movements of the early twentieth century. In the years following the Russian Revolution of 1917, for example, the Soviet Union became an inspiration for millions, a source of hope that the age-old social injustices of humanity could be ended by a revolutionary process. In the Soviet Union, Western Europe, the United States, China, India, and every part of the world, intellectuals studied the works of Marx, Lenin, Trotsky, and other leading Marxists and began to ask new questions about the role of economics in history, and in particular about class struggle. Numerous scholars were influenced by Marxist ideals, by Marxist analytical frameworks, and by Marxism's scientific guidelines for ending social and economic exploitation and for creating egalitarian, classless, non-racist, non-sexist, and non-élitist societies.

The discipline of history in particular appealed to Marxist and other leftist intellectuals because it dealt with change over time and with broad political and social transformations. Many leftist historians were influenced by the discipline of anthropology, which was oriented toward the study of non-Western societies and cultures, and by sociology, which focused on Western, often urban, social groupings. With these interdisciplinary influences, leftist historians began to study class struggles and popular movements over long periods of time in Western and non-Western societies.

In the late 1920s, a small group of scholars, mostly French, steeped in Weberian and Marxist political theories, influenced by the methods of anthropology, sociology, geography, economics, linguistics, and other disciplines, began to work out new approaches to the study of the past. By concentrating on long periods of time (*la longue durée*) rather than on discrete events, they sought to locate the underlying structures that govern historical evolution. They studied social and economic history, often quantitatively, focusing on the activities of ordinary people rather than on major political events. Such historians came to be known as the "Annales school". The term derives from the journal first entitled *Annales d'histoire économique et sociale*, which was founded in Strasbourg in 1929 by Lucien Febvre (1878–1956) and Marc Bloch (1886–1944) to publish studies focusing on their kind of social history.[3]

This post-World War I intellectual context slowly influenced the study of Middle Eastern and North African history. Charles-André Julien's *Histoire de l'Afrique du Nord*, a two-volume study published in 1931, was influenced by Marxist historiography and to a lesser extent by the ideas of the Annales scholars. It was a far broader work than earlier histories by European scholars because it included the economic, social, and cultural dimensions of North African history, and because it did not centre on the European conquest and colonization of the region.[4]

The methodological advances continued, notably in two dissertations published in 1940. The first was by Claude Cahen (1909–91), a French historian of medieval Islam, and was entitled *La Syrie du Nord à l'époque des croisades et la principauté franque d'Antioche*.[5] The other was by Bernard Lewis (1916–), a British historian of medieval Islam and Ottoman history, and was entitled *The Origins of Ismailism*.[6] Both studies demonstrated that the history of the medieval Middle East could be studied with the same methods of analysis as the history of medieval Europe. Both Cahen and Lewis skilfully combined the methods of orientalism and the newer historical methods in their pioneering studies. Unlike Lewis, Cahen was deeply influenced by Marxist historiography and was to introduce it nearly single-handedly into the study of the medieval Middle East.

Historical methodology evolved rapidly following World War II, when Fernand Braudel (1902–85), a student of Marc Bloch and Lucien Febvre, became the central figure in French historiographical circles. Braudel's massive French doctoral thesis, *La Méditerranée et le monde méditerranéen à l'époque de Philippe II*, published in 1949, introduced new concepts to students of history.[7] Braudel, like most other Annales scholars, took great pains to explain his basic paradigms and methodological approaches. The first part, as Braudel carefully explained, dealt with the relation of human evolution to geography and climate. The second part dealt with the history of social forms and different human groupings. The third part related the history of events to the underlying foundations of history he had established in the first two parts. In contrast to the orientalists, who often focused on Islamic civilization as an analytical unit, Braudel focused on a geographical unit, that is, on European, Ottoman, North African, and Levantine societies bordering on the Mediterranean Sea.[8]

By the late 1940s scholars throughout the continent and in Britain were becoming increasingly interested in social and economic history.

At the School of Oriental and African Studies in London, for example, Ann Lambton (1912–), a British scholar specializing in modern Iran, published her ground-breaking study, *Landlord and Peasant in Persia*, one of the first books to concentrate on the rural society and economy of the Middle East.[9] Lambton, who carried out her research in Iran in the 1940s, dealt extensively with rural social and economic relations in modern Iran.

Meanwhile, increasing numbers of scholars from the Middle East were studying in Western universities, continuing a trend that had begun in the nineteenth century. In 1934, Charles Issawi (1916–), an economist and historian of Syrian origin, for example, had left Egypt to study in Oxford. In 1949, Halil Inalcik (*ca* 1916–), a Turkish historian specializing in Ottoman history, travelled to London to study at the School of Oriental and African Studies (SOAS). In 1955 Afaf Lutfi al-Sayyid Marsot (1933–), an Egyptian historian specializing in the history of modern Egypt, left Cairo for Stanford University. She later studied at Oxford University. In 1958 Abdel-Karim Rafeq (1931–), a Syrian historian specializing in the Arab provinces under Ottoman rule, was sent to London where he studied at SOAS. These four only exemplify the diversity of the many hundreds of students from the Middle East who studied history in universities throughout Europe and North America. The scholars of Middle Eastern origin were eager to utilize the new scholarly methods described above in order to study their nations' history and to correct the distortions of earlier historical accounts.

Partly in response to the new trends in history, a few European orientalists were becoming dissatisfied with their field. Sir Hamilton Gibb (1895–1971), the Laudian professor of Arabic language and literature and Islamic studies at Oxford and author of *Modern Trends in Islam* (1947) and *Mohammedanism* (1949), for example, often expressed his desire to have closer contact with history and the social sciences than his position as professor of Arabic language and literature allowed him.[10] He was not alone.

In 1954, at a conference of the Congress of Orientalists in Cambridge, England, all participants received a brochure entitled "Orientalism and History". The brochure recommended that orientalists learn to place their fields of study in "their proper place in general history."[11] The five essays in the brochure – on the ancient Near East, Islam, India and its cultural empire, China, and Central Eurasia – demonstrated the influence these civilizations had had on world history. Bernard Lewis began his essay by saying: "It has been remarked that the history of the Arabs has been written in Europe chiefly by historians who knew no Arabic, or by Arabists who knew no history."[12] In his article Lewis called for the increased use of Ottoman and other Middle Eastern archival materials and for "the integration of the history of Islam into the study of the general history of humanity."[13] The brochure, which set the tone for the conference, did not call for a break with orientalist scholarship, but rather for a new direction for it.

Claude Cahen, a participant at the conference, later commented that Lewis's whimsical opening statement accurately summarized the general unhappiness with both orientalists' and historians' approaches to the study of the Middle East. In his influential article entitled "L'histoire économique et sociale de l'orient musulman médiéval" (The economic and social history of the medieval Muslim Orient), Cahen lamented the lack of interest in social and economic history on the part of orientalists.[14] He complained that the first edition of the *Encyclopaedia of Islam* contained next to nothing on rural life and only "occasional bits and snippets on artisanal and commercial life ..."[15] He then called for the study of fiscal institutions, land taxes, the social categories of landowners, the economic and technical forms of culture, the history of cities, and the professions and patterns of work and commerce. He argued that the upheavals in Muslim societies in the medieval era must have at least partly originated in contradictions in their economic and social structures. He added that studying economic and social history would reveal internal conflicts and antagonisms and perhaps a kind of class struggle. He insisted that the sources for such historical inquiry were not plentiful but could nevertheless be found.[16] Cahen's influential article, "Mouvements populaires et autonomisme urbain dans l'Asie musulman du moyen âge" (Popular movements and urban autonomy in Muslim Asia in the Middle Ages), published in 1958–9, for example, demonstrated that popular movements in Muslim societies could be understood within a Marxist analytical framework.[17]

Cahen was unhappy with much of orientalist scholarship because it ignored the competition of groups struggling against one another for wealth and power. The social and economic studies of Lambton, Inalcik, and others, were a start, but much more, he believed, remained to be done.

In a direct response to the sentiments expressed at the Cambridge conference, the *Journal of the Economic and Social History of the Orient* was founded in 1957. Claude Cahen and Gustave von Grunebaum (1909–72), an orientalist trained in Austria who had emigrated to the United States in 1938, were among the first seven editorial board members. The introduction to the first issue stated that "While the study of the economic and social history of Europe and America attracts steadily growing attention, many economic and social aspects of the history of the East remain by comparison neglected."[18]

Specialized monographs and extended studies of social and

economic topics soon followed the publication of this journal. In 1962
Gabriel Baer, an Israeli historian specializing in the modern Middle
East, published his *History of Land Ownership in Modern Egypt*, a study
focusing on land tenure in nineteenth-century Egypt.[19] New attention
to economic analysis can be seen in *Islam and Capitalism*, a study by
Maxime Rodinson (1915–) published in 1966.[20] As the title suggests,
the study combined the approaches of orientalist and Marxist
scholarship in that it focused on both "Islam" and an economic
question. In response to those who claimed that European (Protestant) civilization was, unlike Islamic civilization, uniquely hospitable to
capitalism, Rodinson demonstrated that there was nothing unique to
Islam that hindered the development of capitalism. He argued that
Islamic societies, like other societies worldwide, simply set aside or
reformulated theological guidelines when they impeded economic
interests.

At about the same time, still other approaches to the history of the
Middle East were being worked out by scholars of widely varying
backgrounds, many of whom had not been trained as orientalists.
Albert Hourani (1915–93), a British scholar of Lebanese origin who
had studied European philosophy and intellectual history at Oxford,
was able to identify with Arab culture and to convey his ideas to
Western readers in a way that was entirely unprecedented. In *Arabic
Thought in the Liberal Age, 1798–1939*, published in 1962, Hourani
analysed the ways in which Muslim and Christian thinkers of the
Middle East reacted to and modified Western thought.[21] The book
focused on fifteen thinkers in depth, and on others more briefly,
explaining their views to Western readers in the context of the
Western political and economic expansion in the Middle East. For the
first time the ideas of Arab teachers, intellectuals, politicians, and
administrators were made accessible to Western readers.

Unlike the social histories of the Annales scholars, Hourani's study
centred on the educated élite. The author himself later remarked that
he "said little in the book about the connection between the
movements of thought which were its subject and the movements of
social and political change with which they were connected" or about
trends in Islamic thought that were not influenced by European
ideas.[22] Nevertheless, the book, like his later writings, brought a
certain "understanding from within" to the study of the Middle East
that was in itself a new approach.

The use of new sources, the asking of new questions, and the
interest in new types of Middle Eastern history continued. In the
mid-1960s, Charles Issawi began publishing his series of economic
histories of the Middle East. Issawi's studies were based nearly entirely
on contemporary commercial, banking, and financial records. Issawi,

who was already well known for studies such as *Egypt: An Economic and Social Analysis* (1941) and *The Economics of Middle Eastern Oil* (1962), did not concentrate on "Islamic civilization" but rather on secular economic forms and relationships in his historical studies.

By the 1960s many orientalists had been influenced by the methods of cultural anthropology, as evidenced by the writings of Gustave von Grunebaum. Trained as an orientalist and little influenced by Marxist ideas, von Grunebaum acquired a deep interest in cultural anthropology while at the University of Chicago. At the time, the University of Chicago was a centre of innovative anthropological research and of historical scholarship that was strongly influenced by the Annales school. In 1957 von Grunebaum came to the University of California, Los Angeles, to establish the Center of Near Eastern Studies. While organizing and administering a large and active centre, he continued his interest in cultural anthropology. In writing about Islamic civilization he used both philological and anthropological methods to understand medieval and modern Islamic culture and civilization.[23] At the time of his death in 1972 he was interested in epistemological questions emerging from disciplines from anthropology to psychology, even the study of dreams. He did not isolate himself from other colleagues or from criticism. On the contrary, when his methods or conclusions, such as his observations that medieval and modern Islamic ideologies were essentially pre-modern, were criticized, his reaction was to invite his critics to his university to teach and to engage in scholarly discourse with him.

Meanwhile, the new approaches to history were greatly facilitated by the availability of new archival sources as Middle Eastern governments began to make their archival collections available to Western scholars. Egypt had begun to make its archives available in the 1930s. Between 1949 and 1956, the Turkish government opened the vast Ottoman archival materials to Western scholars, although Turkish historians of great distinction had already begun to utilize them.[24] Bernard Lewis was one of the first among Western scholars to use the Ottoman archives. Other archival collections, in Lebanon, Tunisia, Morocco, Iran, and elsewhere, were also opened. In Syria, Abdul-Karim Rafeq began working on the Syrian court records.

Middle Eastern governments were eager to sponsor the archival collections because they had come to believe that historical distortions and biases were far more likely if scholars were forced to rely exclusively on Western source materials. While limited resources and bureaucratic difficulties often made the research process a nightmare for archivists and scholars alike, more and more materials were eventually added to inventories, and scholars could soon find in the local source materials new information on the social and economic history of the Middle East just as their colleagues were able to do in Europe. This in turn led to new directions in historical research and to new methodological advances.

The Geniza documents, a depository maintained by notables of the Jewish community of Egypt, made famous by Shlomo Goitein (1900–85), a Jewish–Palestinian scholar of German origin, shed new light on the medieval Egyptian–Jewish community and trade relations, commercial patterns and everyday life of the wider society. Using fragments of commercial and shipping records, personal correspondence, and other documents dating from the eleventh to the thirteenth centuries, Goitein was able to reconstruct aspects of medieval Jewish society: family life, daily activities, commerce and finance, travel, seafaring, communal organization, and even the "mentality" of the era. In studying the Geniza documents, he combined the philological methods of the orientalist, the newer focus on social and economic history and on everyday life, and the use of rich local historical sources. This combination of old and new methods was evident throughout Goitein's five-volume *A Mediterranean Society* (1967–88).[25]

Goitein was deeply interested in the relationship between the historian and his or her work. In the introduction, he states that "much depends on the mind and life experience of the historian . . . The diversity of my own life experience helped me in understanding the Geniza world."[26] He did not, however, explain in detail how his formation and life experience had shaped his interpretation of the source materials.

The partial transition in historical method can be dated from the mid-1950s to the mid-1960s. Before that time, as mentioned above, an orientalist studying, for example, the "Islamic city" might look for its essential character. In the introduction to *The Islamic City*, a book that contained papers given at a colloquium held in 1965 by the "Near Eastern History Group" of All Souls College in Oxford, Albert Hourani asked if there was such as thing as an "Islamic city". While he and all of the authors more or less agreed that there was indeed such a thing, a certain hesitancy runs through the Introduction and the book itself, as though the authors were arguing with unseen opponents who were suggesting otherwise.[27] Significantly, we are cautioned at the outset of the introduction that the Islamic city cannot be studied in isolation from its wider context, and that Islamic cities (like other cities) differed widely according to time and place.[28] Gone was the earlier tendency to study topics in isolation from their wider historical contexts. And unspoken perhaps was the knowledge that historians of Europe would be very unlikely to call a conference on the "Christian city".

By the end of the 1960s, the orientalist approach was no longer evident in certain major studies. André Raymond (1925–), a French historian specializing in the Middle East and North Africa, did not use "Islam" or "Islamic civilization" – central foci of orientalism – as analytical categories to explain the Ottoman administrative and fiscal system in his *Artisans et commerçants au Caire au XVIIIième siècle* (Artisans and merchants in eighteenth-century Cairo).[29] Raymond sought to learn more about Cairo and other Middle Eastern cities through the study of a city's material evidence and from local and foreign archival records. Raymond asked about the political, social, and economic roles of Middle Eastern cities and how these roles changed over time. Scholars such as Raymond were usually trained first in the disciplines such as history, sociology, and anthropology, second in Middle Eastern languages, and not at all in philology, often to their regret.

The new methods can be seen in many genres of history. In biographical history, the focus was no longer on the subject but on the wider historical context in which the subject was situated. In 1972, for example, Nikki Keddie (1930–) published a biography of Jamal al-Din al-Afghani (1839–97), the Islamic philosopher and activist-reformer, taking care to describe the political and social climate in which he lived.[30] Scholars also began to subordinate their biographical studies to the wider historical context. In 1984, for example, Afaf Lutfi al-Sayyid Marsot studied the political, economic, and social transformation of nineteenth-century Egypt through the life of Muhammad Ali (ruled 1805–48).[31] Under the influence of "the new social history", narrative biography itself fell out of favour.

Meanwhile, a few Western scholars, influenced by the new methods, by the critical spirit of scholars such as Cahen, by the entry of Middle Eastern scholars into the field, and by changing political realities, had begun to question the basic assumptions of certain orientalists. In 1962, in a landmark study entitled *Islam dans le miroir de l'Occident* (Islam in the Mirror of the West), Jacques Waardenburg, a Dutch historian of religion, showed how the formations, philosophical precommitments, and academic and non-academic interests of five major orientalists, of different backgrounds, nationalities, and religious affiliations – Ignaz Goldziher (1850–1921), C. Snouk Hurgronje (1857–1936), Carl H. Becker (1876–1933), Duncan MacDonald (1863–1943), and Louis Massignon (1883–1962) – shaped their views on Islam.[32] Waardenburg argued that the personal beliefs of these scholars resulted in valid though incomplete scholarship. He hoped that future scholars would recognize and come to terms with the influence of their own background on their scholarly work.[33]

Waardenburg's ideas were of great interest to Marshall Hodgson (1921–68), an American-born historian at the University of Chicago.

Hodgson included a section entitled "On scholarly precommitments" in the introduction to his influential three-volume study, *The Venture of Islam: Conscience and History in a World Civilization* written in the 1950s and 1960s and published in 1974.[34] After citing Waardenburg's study, which he had reviewed for the *Journal of Asian Studies*, Hodgson emphasized the influence of personal commitments in shaping historians' perspectives, particularly in Islamic studies: "On the most serious levels of historical scholarship – where the human relevance of major cultural traditions is at issue, such as that of religious or artistic or legal or governmental traditions, or even that of whole civilizations – historical judgement cannot be entirely disengaged from the basic precommitments of inquirers."[35] He believed that only the deeply committed historian would even raise such important issues, and that bias, once self-acknowledged, could be guarded against. He further argued that the consciously committed were more likely to be aware of, to analyse, and to control the influence of their precommitments on their work than those not consciously committed, who because they were not aware of the inevitable influence of their partisan views on their work, made no effort to control it.[36] He did not explain his own precommitments in his introduction to *The Venture of Islam*, but he may have been intending to: his career was brought to a close by his untimely death at the age of 47.

If Hodgson had chosen to tell his academic life story, it would have been characteristic of the environment in which he worked. At the University of Chicago there was a general climate of thought in which historians were expected to explain themselves. In the early 1970s, for example, William McNeill (1917–), an American historian of modern Europe and a colleague of Hodgson, asked Fernand Braudel to tell his life story and how he was "shaped as a historian". In response, Braudel traced his life from his early years to maturity and analysed his scholarly formation, his work on the *Annales* journal, and his historical writings. The article was published in *The Journal of Modern History*, of which McNeill was editor.[37]

The idea that a scholar might be expected to "explain himself" took on new meaning when a number of scholars of Middle Eastern origin, trained in Western methods of historical research, often politically active and influenced by leftist and nationalist ideologies, began to question the methods and assumptions of Western orientalism. The Middle Eastern scholars had experienced political realities very different from those of their Western counterparts, and while appreciative of Western methods of scholarship, many came to believe that the works of the major Western orientalists distorted Middle Eastern history to justify Western domination.

In 1963, for example, Anouar Abdel-Malek (1924–), an Egyptian scholar and Marxist thinker residing in Paris, categorically stated that "it is urgent to undertake a revision, a critical re-evaluation of the general conception, the methods and the implements for the understanding of the Orient that have been used by the West, notably from the beginning of the last century, on all levels and in all fields."[38] He charged that the orientalists portrayed the Middle East as unchanging and bound in the metaphysical essentialism of the classical religious and historical texts and that this portrayal enabled European imperial governments to justify their domination of the region. Abdel-Malek hoped that the paradigms and methods of orientalism would be replaced by those of disciplines such as history, sociology, anthropology, and political science, and that the study of the Middle East would then become liberated from Eurocentrism just as the colonies had been liberated from European domination. He called for "intellectual liberation" from the domination of orientalists.

Abdel-Malek forced orientalists to examine their own presuppositions, if only to defend themselves. His arguments were at once a continuation of Cahen's socio-economic approach and the beginning of a new direction of political protest in which scholars of Middle Eastern origin played a prominent role.

Middle Eastern scholars soon made other criticisms of Western orientalists that led to further self-examination. In 1964, just a year after Abdel-Malek's article appeared, A. L. Tibawi (1910–81), a Palestinian historian then at Harvard's Center for Middle Eastern Studies, published a critique entitled "English-speaking Orientalists."[39] Tibawi complained that Western scholars of Islam and of Arab nationalism contained an unconscious urge to fit them into "Christian, or, rather, Western moulds".[40] Some, for example, assumed that Islam would and should go through a Protestant reformation as had Christianity. This, to Tibawi, was the inappropriate imposition of a Western model on the Middle East. Like Abdel-Malek, he called upon Western scholars to examine their basic assumptions because, he thought, they would find that what they had accepted as common sense would prove, upon careful examination, to be highly subjective value judgements. He asked Western scholars "to show, within the bounds of scholarship, more concern for human relations, more sympathy in handling controversial subjects, and more courtesy in the use of language".[41] Tibawi was perhaps over-confident in his belief that greater sympathy and tact could get around the influence of unequal political power on historical writing, but he had underscored an important point about the basic assumptions underlying Western studies of the Middle East.

Soon younger scholars of Western origin were calling into question the presuppositions of orientalism. Roger Owen (1935–), a British

scholar specializing in the economic history of the Middle East, in a
review published in 1973 of *The Cambridge History of Islam*, wrote that
nearly the entire book suffered from the weaknesses of orientalist
scholarship.[42] In particular he mentioned its isolation from the
methodological advances of other fields and its élitist tendency to
dismiss criticism from outsiders on the grounds that they lacked the
necessary linguistic expertise to judge the orientalists' work. He
further lamented the "general sense of omniscience which pervades
the . . . two volumes" and added, "The majority of contributors seem
very much at ease in giving confident answers to large, general
questions . . . There is also a general unwillingness to question, or
even to examine, any of the basic presuppositions which underlie the
study of Islamic history."[43] In particular he criticized the presuppositions that Islamic civilization was the basic unit of study and that Islam
was the essential determinant in societies from Africa to Asia. For
Owen and many other scholars, the "motors of history" should be
sought in economic processes, social struggles, advances in scientific
and technological knowledge, and demographic and environmental
changes rather than in "Islam".

The critics of orientalism became much more overtly political when
Edward W. Said (1935–), a Palestinian–American professor of
English literature, published his controversial book, *Orientalism*
(1978).[44] In the introduction to the book, Said carefully emphasized
the importance of coming to terms with "the personal dimension" of
scholarship.[45] In it he quoted Antonio Gramsci (1891–1937), the
famous Italian cultural Marxist: "The starting-point of critical
elaboration is the consciousness of what one really is, and is 'knowing
thyself' as a product of the historical process to date, which has
deposited in you an infinity of traces, without leaving an inventory . . .
therefore it is imperative at the outset to compile such an
inventory."[46] He then remarked: "Much of the personal investment in
this study derives from my awareness of being an 'Oriental' as a child
growing up in two British colonies. All of my education, in those
colonies (Palestine and Egypt) and in the United States, has been
Western, and yet that deep early awareness has persisted. In many ways
my study of Orientalism has been an attempt to inventory the traces
upon me, the Oriental subject, of the culture whose domination has
been so powerful a factor in the life of all Orientals."[47] He stated that
in his study he had tried to "maintain a critical consciousness" and to
carefully employ scholarly methods of research.[48]

Said asserted that the orientalists had perhaps unintentionally
created the "oriental", the dehumanized "other", who thereby became
suitable for domination by Europeans. He implicitly criticized the
approach of orientalists for their focus on the study of civilizations,

the study of classic texts in isolation from their historical contexts, and the reductionist search for cultural essences and ideal types applicable in all times and places.

In the concluding remarks to his book, however, Said offered a cautiously optimistic assessment of the future of Middle East studies. Like Hodgson, he argued that a solution to the problems he had identified lay in bringing a "methodological self-consciousness" to the study of the Middle East. He concluded by saying:

> Scholars and critics who are trained in the traditional Orientalist disciplines are perfectly capable of freeing themselves from the old ideological straitjacket. Jacques Berque's [1910–] and Maxime Rodinson's training ranks with the most rigorous available, but what invigorates their investigations even of traditional problems is their methodological self-consciousness. For if Orientalism has historically been too smug, too insulated, too positivistically confident in its ways and its premises, then one way of opening oneself to what one studies in or about the Orient is reflexively to submit one's method to critical scrutiny.[49]

Said believed that orientalists were limited by their political and scholarly ideologies and by their old-fashioned and flawed method-ologies, but that by becoming critically conscious of them and by carefully controlling them, by learning from the methodological advances of other disciplines, and by becoming aware of contem-porary political realities, they could surmount their limitations.

Said's negative views of orientalism differed from those of Maxime Rodinson, a French scholar of the Islamic world, who offered his own critique of orientalism and suggested new approaches to the study of the Middle East in his book, *La Fascination d'Islam*, published in French in 1980 and in English translation as *Europe and the Mystique of Islam* in 1988.[50] Rodinson's book contained two essays, one entitled "Western views of the Muslim world", first written in 1964 for an earlier edition of *The Legacy of Islam*, in which it appeared in condensed form, and the other entitled "A new approach to Arab and Islamic studies", an updated version of a lecture given in Leiden in 1976.[51] In the first essay, Rodinson traced the evolution of Western views of the Muslim world and the development of traditional orientalism. In the second, he analysed the present "state of the craft" and suggested new approaches to Arab and Islamic studies. In this latter section he pleaded that the knowledge accumulated by orientalist scholars during the past two centuries not be forgotten or ignored. He urged that scholars strive for objectivity though the goal was ultimately unattainable, and that they should carry out long and tedious research before attempting to form solid theories. To avoid the tendency towards Eurocentrism, he recommended that Western and indigenous scholars collaborate. Like the other critics of orientalism, he urged students to study non-classical periods and popular attitudes and customs (*histoire des mentalités*) and to integrate current events and developments into the mainstream of Islamic studies within the framework of contemporary global history, sociology, and anthropology.[52] He then proclaimed that there was no such thing as the "orient" or the "east", but rather only large numbers of diverse people.

The strength of Rodinson's arguments lay in his ability to reach a compromise. He managed to support the revisionist arguments both methodologically and politically, but at the same time maintained great respect for the works of the orientalists. Significantly, he concluded his book with the observation that one's images of other societies pass through a "prism of ideological formation and evolution" and that "this process represents a vast field of inquiry whose study has scarcely begun".[53]

Since Rodinson published his book, a few such studies have appeared. Jacques Berque, the French historian of North Africa and Egypt, was extensively interviewed in *Arabies: entretiens avec Mirese Akar*, published in 1978 and expanded in 1980; M'Hammed Sabour discussed Arab academics in *Homo academicus arabicus*, published in 1983; Soraya Altorki and Camillia Fawzi El-Solh edited *Arab Women in the Field: Studying Your Own Society*, consisting of personal accounts of Arab women who have carried out field research in the Middle East, published in 1988, and Thomas Naff edited *Paths to the Middle East: Ten Scholars Look Back*, a study containing autobiographies of senior scholars of several disciplines, published in 1993.[54] This book, unlike earlier studies, focuses only on the discipline of history and on the comparative study of Middle East historiography in the past half-century.

In recent years, new methods and approaches in post-modernist and feminist historiography have been transforming once again the study of the Middle East. In the future, I hope that these and other methodological approaches will be placed in the context of historians' lives to further our understanding of historiographical evolution.

Notes

1. Orientalists (orient = east, occident = west) study the Middle East and what is now called "Asia", including India, China, and Japan. According to Maxime Rodinson, "The term *orientalist* appeared in English around 1779 and in

French in 1799. The French form, *orientalisme*, found a place in the *Dictionnaire de l'Académie Française* of 1838" (Maxime Rodinson, *Europe and the Mystique of Islam* [Seattle: University of Washington Press, 1987], p. 57; translation of *La fascination de l'Islam* [Paris: Librairie François Maspero, 1980]).

2. Rodinson, *Mystique of Islam*, p. 61.
3. In 1939 the journal was retitled *Annales d'Histoire Sociale*. In 1942 it became *Mélanges d'Histoire Sociale*. In 1945 it was again *Annales d'Histoire Sociale*, and from 1946 to the present, *Annales: Économies, Sociétés, Civilisations*. Marc Bloch's views on historical scholarship can be found in his *The Historian's Craft* (New York: Knopf, 1953), the English translation of *Apologie pour l'histoire: ou, métier d'historien* (Paris: A. Colin, 1949). See also Carole Fink, *Marc Bloch: A Life in History* (New York and Cambridge: Cambridge University Press, 1989). For information on Lucien Febvre's historical approach, see Peter Burke (ed.), *A New Kind of History: From the Writings of Febvre* (New York: Harper & Row, 1973).
4. Charles-André Julien, *History of North Africa: Tunisia, Algeria, Morocco, from the Arab Conquest to 1830*, translated from the French (London: Routledge & Kegan Paul, 1970).
5. Claude Cahen, *La Syrie du Nord à l'époque des croisades et la principauté franque d'Antioche* (Paris: P. Geuthner, 1940).
6. Bernard Lewis, *The Origins of Ismaīīlism: A Study of the Historical Background of the Fatimid Caliphate* (Cambridge, England: W. Heffer & Sons, 1940).
7. Fernand Braudel, *La Méditerranée et le monde méditerranéen à l'époque de Philippe II* (Paris: Colin, 1949) translated as *The Mediterranean and the Mediterranean World in the Age of Philip II* (New York: Harper & Row, 1972). For a summary of the Annales approach see *A History of Civilizations* (New York: Allen Lane and Penguin, 1993).
8. ——, "The Mediterranean and the Mediterranean World in the Age of Philip II: Extract from the Preface", in Braudel, *On History* (Chicago: University of Chicago Press, 1980), pp. 3–5, translation of Braudel, *Ecrits sur l'histoire* (Paris: Flamarion, 1969).
9. Ann K. S. Lambton, *Landlord and Peasant in Persia: A Study of Land Tenure and Land Revenue Administration* (New York and London: Oxford University Press, 1953).
10. H. A. R. Gibb, *Modern Trends in Islam* (Chicago: University of Chicago Press, 1947) and *Mohammedanism: An Historical Survey* (New York and London: Oxford University Press, 1949).
11. Denis Sinor (ed.), *Orientalism and History* (Cambridge: W. Heffer & Sons, 1954).
12. Bernard Lewis, "Islam", in ibid., p. 16.
13. Ibid., p. 32.
14. Claude Cahen, "L'histoire économique et sociale de l'orient musulman médiéval" (The economic and social history of the medieval Muslim world), *Studia Islamica*, 3 (1955), pp. 93–115.
15. Ibid., p. 96.
16. Ibid., pp. 112–13.
17. Claude Cahen, "Mouvements populaires et autonomisme urbain dans l'Asie musulman du moyen âge" (Popular and autonomist urban movements in medieval Muslim Asia), *Arabica*, 5 (1958), pp. 225–50, (1959), pp. 25–6.
18. *Journal of the Economic and Social History of the Orient*, 1, Part 1 (August 1957), p. 1.

19. Gabriel Baer, *A History of Landownership in Modern Egypt, 1800–1950* (New York and London: Oxford University Press, 1962).

20. Maxime Rodinson, *Islam et capitalisme* (Paris: Edition du Seuil, 1966), translated as *Islam and Capitalism* (New York: Pantheon Books, 1974).

21. Albert Hourani, *Arabic Thought in the Liberal Age, 1798–1939* (New York and London: Oxford University Press, 1962).

22. Quoted in Donald M. Reid, "*Arabic Thought in the Liberal Age* Twenty Years After", *International Journal of Middle East Studies*, 14 (1982), p. 551.

23. See, for example, G. von Grunebaum's *Medieval Islam: A Study in Cultural Orientation* (Chicago: Chicago University Press, 1946) and *Islam: Essays in the Nature and Growth of a Cultural Tradition* (New York: Barnes and Noble, 1961); also his *Modern Islam: The Search for Cultural Identity* (Berkeley: University of California Press, 1962).

24. See, for example, M. Fuad Köprülü, *The Origins of the Ottoman Empire*, published in French in 1935, translated from the Turkish edition (1959) and edited by Gary Leiser (Ithaca: State University of New York Press, 1992).

25. S. D. Goitein, *A Mediterranean Society: The Jewish Communities of the Arab World as Portrayed by the Documents of the Cairo Geniza* (5 vols., Berkeley: University of California Press, 1967–88).

26. Quoted by A. Udovitch in ibid., vol. 5, p. xiii.

27. Albert Hourani and S. M. Stern, *The Islamic City* (Philadelphia: University of Pennsylvania Press, 1970). See, for example, pp. 23–4.

28. Ibid., pp. 10–16.

29. André Raymond, *Artisans et commerçants du Caire au XVIIIième siècle* (Artisans and merchants in eighteenth-century Cairo) (Damascus: Institut français de Damas, 1973–4).

30. Nikki Keddie, *Sayyid Jamal ad-Din "al-Afghani": A Political Biography* (Berkeley: University of California Press, 1972).

31. Afaf Lutfi al-Sayyid Marsot, *Egypt in the Reign of Muhammad Ali* (New York and Cambridge: Cambridge University Press, 1984).

32. Jean-Jacques Waardenburg, *L'Islam dans le miroir de l'Occident: comment quelques orientalistes occidentaux se sont penchés sur l'Islam et se sont formés une image de cette religion* (Paris: Mouton, 1963).

33. Scholars are increasingly interested in studying how our images of other societies are formed. See for example R. W. Southern, *Western Views of Islam in the Middle Ages* (Cambridge, Mass.: Harvard University Press, 1962); Norman Daniel, *Islam and the West: the Making of an Image* (Edinburgh: Edinburgh University Press, 1960) and *The Arabs and Medieval Europe* (London: Longman Group, 1975); Albert Hourani, *Europe and the Middle East* (London: Macmillan, 1980) and *Islam in European Thought* (New York: Cambridge University Press, 1991); Hichem Djait, *L'Europe et l'Islam* (Paris: Seuil, 1978), English translation, *Europe and Islam* (Berkeley and Los Angeles: University of California Press, 1985); Bernard Lewis, *The Muslim Discovery of Europe* (New York and London: W. W. Norton & Company, 1982). A few have studied the lives of noted scholars. See for example: A. J. Arberry, *British Orientalists* (London: Collins, 1943) and *Oriental Essays: Portraits of Seven Scholars* (London: George Allen & Unwin, 1960). Note Arberry's "Self Portrait", pp. 233–56; Albert Hourani, "Sir Hamilton Gibb", *Proceedings of the British Academy*, 58 (London: published for the British Academy by Oxford University Press), pp. 493–521; Raphael Patai, *Ignaz Goldziher and His Oriental Diary* (Detroit: Wayne State University Press, 1987); Robert Simon, *Ignaz Goldziher: His Life and Scholarship as Reflected in his Works and Correspondence*

(Leiden, E. J. Brill, 1986); Bernard Lewis and P. M. Holt (eds.), *Historians of the Middle East* (New York and London: Oxford University Press, 1962).

34. Marshall Hodgson, *The Venture of Islam: Conscience and History in a World Civilization* (3 vols., Chicago: The University of Chicago Press, 1974). For an extended discussion of this study see Edmund Burke, III, "Islamic history as world history: Marshall Hodgson, 'The Venture of Islam'", *International Journal of Middle East Studies*, 10 (1979), pp. 241–64; Albert Hourani, "The Venture of Islam", *Journal of Near Eastern Studies*, 37 (1978), pp. 53–62; Edmund Burke, III, "Islam and world history: the contribution of Marshall Hodgson", *Radical History Review*, 39 (September 1987), pp. 117–23.

35. Hodgson, *Venture*, vol. I, pp. 27–8. See also his review of *L'Islam dans le miroir de l'Occident*, in *Journal of Asian Studies*, 64 (1964), pp. 642–3.

36. Ibid., p. 39.

37. Fernand Braudel, "Personal testimony", *The Journal of Modern History*, 44, 4 (December, 1972), pp. 448–67.

38. Anouar Abdel-Malek, "Orientalism in crisis", *Diogenes*, 44 (Winter 1963), p. 103.

39. A. L. Tibawi, "English-speaking orientalists: a critique of their approach to Islam and Arab nationalism", *Islamic Quarterly*, 8, 1–2 (1964), pp. 25–45, and vol. 8, 3–4, pp. 73–88.

40. Ibid., p. 80.

41. Ibid., p. 88.

42. Roger Owen, "Studying Islamic history", *Journal of Interdisciplinary History*, 4, 2 (Autumn 1973), pp. 287–98.

43. Ibid., p. 291.

44. Edward W. Said, *Orientalism* (New York: Pantheon Books, 1978).

45. Ibid., p. 25.

46. Ibid.

47. Ibid.

48. Ibid., p. 26. Said was greatly influenced by the ideas of Michel Foucault (1926–84). For more on Foucault, see David Macey, *The Lives of Michel Foucault* (New York: Pantheon; London: Hutchinson, 1993).

49. Ibid., pp. 326–7.

50. Rodinson, *Mystique of Islam*.

51. Joseph Schacht (ed.), *The Legacy of Islam* (Oxford: Clarendon Press, 1974).

52. Rodinson, *Mystique of Islam*, pp. 111–13.

53. Ibid., p. 129.

54. Jacques Berque, *Arabies: entretiens avec Mirese Akar* (Paris: Stock, 1978, Stock Plus, 1980); M'Hammed Sabour, *Homo academicus arabicus* (Joensuu, Finland: University of Joensuu, 1988); Soraya Altorki and Camillia Fawzi El-Solh (eds.), *Arab Women in the Field: Studying Your Own Society* (Syracuse: Syracuse University Press, 1988); Thomas Naff (ed.), *Paths to the Middle East: Ten Scholars Look Back* (Albany: State University of New York Press, 1993). See also MARHO (The Mid-Atlantic Radical Historians' Organization), *Visions of History*, ed. Henry Abelove *et al.* (New York: Pantheon Books, 1976) and Bennet M. Berger (ed.), *Authors of Their Own Lives: Intellectual Autobiographies by Twenty American Sociologists* (Berkeley: University of California Press, 1990).

CHAPTER ONE

ALBERT HOURANI

ALBERT HABIB HOURANI (1915–93), born in Manchester, was a historian of the modern Arab world. He studied philosophy, politics, and economics (PPE) at Oxford and taught modern Middle Eastern history and English literature at the American University in Beirut. During World War II he worked in the Middle Eastern section of the Foreign Office research department. He then held a fellowship at Magdalen College, Oxford, and taught the modern history of the Middle East in the Faculty of Oriental Studies. In 1958 he became director of the Middle East Centre at St Antony's College, Oxford. He also taught at the University of Chicago and at Harvard. He trained generations of students of Middle Eastern history who are now teaching and working throughout Western Europe, North America, and the Middle East. His students continued their relationship with him for many years via letter, telephone, and frequent visits; he was consistently generous with his time and advice. His home in Oxford was an intellectual and moral centre for many in the field. He was recipient of numerous awards and honours including the Order of the British Empire, the Commander of the British Empire and the Giorgio Levi Della Vida award. He was Emeritus Fellow of St Antony's College and Honorary Fellow, Magdalen College, Oxford. After retirement he and his wife, Odile, moved to London where he continued to receive students and scholars from all over the world.

Interviewed at his home in London on 25 and 26 August 1988, by Nancy Gallagher.

NEG: Could we begin with your formative years?
HOURANI: I was brought up in south Manchester; my parents were Lebanese. My father, an orphan, had been taken in by the American missionaries and educated at the Syrian Protestant College. Having graduated, he attended the wedding of a cousin of his who was a cotton exporter. He read a poem at the wedding, and it pleased the cousin so much that he invited him to join him in his family business

in Manchester. So in 1891 at the age of eighteen or nineteen my father came to Manchester and remained there more or less for the rest of his life. He first of all worked for his cousin and then had his own business, which had ups and downs, exporting Manchester cotton, first of all to Beirut, then in the 1910s and 1920s to Brazil through the network of Lebanese merchants, and then in the 1930s, 40s, and 50s to West Africa, again through a network of Lebanese merchants.

Mine was a typical upbringing of the immigrant community, with which you are very familiar, coming from America. We lived very much in a Middle Eastern ghetto in south Manchester where I was brought up. There were communities of Syrian and Lebanese Christians, a few Muslims who were mostly Moroccan merchants from Fez, Oriental Jews, Armenians, and Greeks. Talking later with somebody who had the same upbringing, Haim Nahmad, whose father was the leader of the Syrian Jewish community, we agreed that we had been brought up as if we were in the Ottoman Empire, in our own communities. On feast days, my father would put on his best clothes and pay a visit to Nahmad's father who would in turn visit him. Our fathers would meet with British merchants, but we would rarely go to their houses or invite them to our homes. People met at the market place and were separated in their homes. We agreed that the only difference between that and the Ottoman Empire was that the English were the Muslims. They were the majority whom you treated with respect, with whom you did business, but you kept your distance and were a bit frightened of them.

Our upbringing was different from that of immigrant communities in the United States in two different ways: first, we were much nearer to Lebanon: my father went back twenty-four times. He made a certain amount of money though he was never very rich, and he was the benefactor of his village. Every time he went back, he would call people together and organize something. First of all, he built a cemetery. Then he brought fresh water from Mt Hermon, later he helped the village to get electricity; finally, he founded a secondary school which is still there; it is flourishing. It is one of the very good secondary schools in Lebanon. My father was a highly educated and cultivated man. He had been taught Arabic by a son of the famous writer and scholar, Nasif al-Yaziji. He had a deep knowledge of Arabic literature and also a deep knowledge of English literature. He learned English early in life. When Marwan Buheiry, a professor at American University in Beirut, was a graduate student at Princeton, he found a bound volume called *Essays by Syrian Boys* in the library of the Princeton Theological Seminary. The essays were written by boys in the preparatory school at Syrian Protestant College. Their English teacher had collected them, and there were five essays by my father written in very good English. They must have had extremely good methods of teaching English in those days. My father was very much at home in both languages; he was a very cultivated man who cared for literature. He took quite a part in municipal life in Manchester, he knew a lot of people, responded very much to the culture of his adopted country, but he never forgot his own country. There was never any question of turning his back on the old country. In that way I think it was rather different from the typical experience of a Lebanese–American or a Greek–American who turns his back on the old country and makes a new life. In some curious way, my father, although he was deeply rooted in Manchester, always thought of himself as still belonging to the world from which he had come.

NEG: Did your father intend to go back to Lebanon?
HOURANI: He never intended to settle there, no.

NEG: And he did not intend for any of his sons or daughters to go back either?
HOURANI: No, but we all did go back, sooner or later, though not all permanently. I was the fifth of six. There were first of all three girls, then three sons. My eldest sister, Salwa, went when she was young to Beirut and met there a young man from Haifa and married him. My second sister went to Beirut, met the son of a professor at AUB [American University in Beirut], married him and lived there for the rest of her life. My third sister went there when she was young, didn't like it, returned to Manchester, and never went again in later life. My eldest brother, George, taught for nine years at the Government Arab College in Jerusalem and married an Egyptian Copt. My younger brother, Cecil, married a girl who was partly Turkish, partly Persian, and partly Arab. In fact, my father was torn by the question of our identity. He wanted us to be assimilated into English life, but at the same time he didn't. He didn't wish us to reject the world from which he had come. He was rather pleased that we always had a very great interest in it. I am the only one in the family who married a native [Englishwoman] so to speak, but Odile was on extremely good terms with my father. In many ways she understood him well. So that was the way we were brought up.

NEG: Your father sent you to an English school?
HOURANI: Where we were living, there was not a really good preparatory school, a school for ages six to thirteen, that would accept foreign boys. There was a sort of prejudice. So my father founded a preparatory school. There were quite a number of boys of Lebanese

and Syrian origin who attended the school, and then there were some Jewish boys, including the present head of Marks and Spencer's, Marcus Sieff, Lord Sieff, who was my classmate. At the age of thirteen I was sent to a nonconformist boarding school in North London. "Nonconformist" means neither Catholic nor a member of the Church of England, but rather a member of what are called the free churches: Presbyterians, Methodists, Baptists, and so on. This school had been founded at the time when those who were not members of the Church of England would not have been accepted by the big schools. So another school had been founded in the nineteenth century and we went there. At that time, of the three brothers, I was the one who was least interested in things Middle Eastern. I just wasn't interested. George and Cecil were always passionately interested. My great interests at that time were English history and literature, and I got a scholarship to Oxford, to Magdalen College, as a historian.

NEG: The girls went to a similar school?
HOURANI: The girls went to a private school in Manchester, not a boarding school.

NEG. Your father must have been delighted when you won the scholarship.
HOURANI: My father was delighted that we all won scholarships. He used to boast about it; he was a boastful man – we were embarrassed by that. At all occasions he would boast about his sons, not his daughters. I feel more kindly to him now because I can barely refrain from boasting about my daughter, Susanna. So I went to Oxford where instead of doing history, I switched to PPE. One does all three subjects and specializes in one of them. I specialized in philosophy. Philosophy became my dominant interest at Oxford. I did my special subject on Immanuel Kant. I read a great deal of him, of eighteenth- and nineteenth-century philosophy, metaphysics, ethics, a great deal of modern history, international history, not very much economics, I didn't take kindly to it. I was there for three years. All through that period until the very end I was not the slightest bit interested in the Middle East. I had one Middle Eastern friend, Charles Issawi, who is my oldest friend, one year junior to me. He was the first Middle Eastern friend I ever had, the first person to whom I ever talked about these things.

In 1936 three different things happened. First of all, Palestine. I began to read the newspapers and I became passionately interested almost overnight.

Second, Philip Hitti came to stay with us for three or four days after he had delivered the manuscript of his *History of the Arabs* to Macmillan's. He was a friend of my father. He was a few years younger than my father so they had not been boys together. In New York he lived near my uncle and aunt; they were neighbours. His conversations touched my imagination. His books are rather dull, but he was not at all a dull man. He was a man full of life. I don't think he was a deep historian in the sense that he had an understanding of the connections; in his books one thing happens after another. He took trouble with my brothers and me and sat down and talked to us. I suddenly became interested. I even contributed one thing to his *History of the Arabs*. There is a photograph somewhere in it of an early English coin, struck by King Offa of Mercia, with an Arabic inscription copied from an Umayyad dinar. I had happened to have seen it in the British museum so I drew his attention to it, and it is there in his book: my first contribution to scholarship.

Third, I had a crisis of identity, which very often comes to people in their adolescence. One began to ask questions, who am I? What is this thing which I don't know about which lies in the background? My parents talked Arabic to each other and to their friends. We were brought up knowing Arabic passively, not very well. It was always very familiar and in a way strange. There was something unexplained. I then decided to do a D.Phil. which was very unusual at that time. I was going to do a thesis about British undertakings during World War I, this network of promises and agreements. Nobody had written much about it. It seems very old hat now, but it was before George Antonius wrote his book [see below]. One could find occasional references in the newspapers. I registered for the D.Phil. which I didn't carry further because there was no money for graduate studies. I had done well in my B.A., and Magdalen, being a rich college, collected a hundred pounds for me and said that is all we have. And so, very sensibly I think, I spent the hundred pounds on going to the Middle East for the first time. I went to Beirut, where I stayed with my aunt who was married to a professor at AUB. I went up to our village, which was very exciting. My brother George and all the older ones, all my sisters, had been taken there as children, but Cecil and I had never gone, partly, I think, because my father lost his money in the depression, partly because his mother had died and he could not bear to go back for a time. So I went.

At my first sight of the Mediterranean world I realized that I had never known light before. I was from the world of darkness. London was not so bad, but the light of the northwest is a very dull light. The light of the Mediterranean held my eyes so I decided to stay for a time. I happened to ask Professor Soltau, a professor of politics at AUB, if he had a job. As it happened he was going on leave and asked me to teach a couple of courses. And so I taught at AUB. This was a formative experience. I discovered that I liked teaching. I taught

English history and even English literature for English examinations. I taught the history of international relations, always keeping one lecture ahead of my students. It was very enjoyable. It was a time when AUB was dominated by Arab nationalists. I made great friends. In my first class there were various people: Nadim Dimechkie, who was later Lebanese ambassador in Washington and London, a sort of elder statesman, Ismail Khalidi, Rashid Khalidi's father, and others. I found myself very much involved in the Palestine problem. One lived it, there were demonstrations, one heard stories of Arabs being arrested and tortured by the British. I went to Jerusalem . . . Charles Malik [d. 1987], was a Lebanese who had just gone back to Beirut after studying philosophy at Harvard with Whitehead. He later had a very distinguished career: he was foreign minister of Lebanon, president of the United Nations General Assembly [1959–60], and held various other posts. I held learned more from Charles Malik than from any of my Oxford teachers of philosophy. He never wrote very much; he got lost in politics. My mind was formed in a way more by Charles than by anybody else. We had a reading group with weekly meetings.

I stayed two and a half years at AUB. I came home for summer vacation when the war broke out and was asked to work for the research department of the Royal Institute of International Affairs. Arnold Toynbee ran the research department and H. A. R. Gibb was the head of the Middle Eastern section. I worked very closely with Toynbee and Gibb who were the other great influences in my life.

NEG: What was Toynbee like?
HOURANI: Difficult to say. He was warm, a mixture of warmth and distance, his mind was always far away thinking great thoughts of the history of the world. One couldn't get really close to him unless one knew him very well which I didn't. He was an extremely kind and attractive man who always had a special interest in the Middle East. Gibb was the one with whom I worked closely. I worked with him in the Middle Eastern section, and with Harold Beeley, who later became British ambassador to Cairo. Gibb was the first orientalist, the first Arabic and Islamic scholar, whom I had ever known well. Through being there, listening to him, and reading what he wrote, I absorbed something of orientalist scholarship, but I had no training at all as an orientalist. I was not a Middle Eastern specialist, but to work closely with Gibb was something.

NEG: Did the Foreign Office send you to the Middle East to write your reports?
HOURANI: In 1942 I felt I no longer knew what was happening. It was very frustrating in the middle of the war to be cut off from the Middle East so I decided that I ought to resign and join the army. Then the

Foreign Office Research Department very kindly said, "Go to the Middle East for a few months, travel around, meet younger people, the younger nationalists, and write a report. We'd like to know what they are thinking." So I went, and I spent some time in Cairo, Beirut, Damascus, Baghdad, and Jerusalem, and met a lot of people. I was treated very kindly by everybody. This was during a turning-point in 1942–3 when, among other things, the Arab nationalists decided that Britain was going to win the war rather than the Germans and there was suddenly an opening up. I was summoned by Shukri al-Quwwatli, who was to be the first president of independent Syria, to talk to him. He had had almost no conversations with any British officials. That was very interesting indeed. He talked of his hopes and fears, about solutions to the Palestine conflict, the Syrian problem, a possible agreement with the Arabs. Jerusalem was particularly interesting, because at that time there was a kind of political truce when anyone could talk to anyone else. It was just as easy to talk to Zionists as to Arabs or British. I saw Ben Gurion whom I liked enormously. He invited me to spend most of an afternoon talking to him. He talked expansively with great vision of the future. I have never thought badly of him since then. I had the impression of a man of integrity. You always knew where you stood with him. You may not like where you stood, but at least you knew. And so, after a few months, I wrote my report which is somewhere in the recesses of the Public Record Office on "Great Britain and Arab Nationalism". It was well received; many of the FO officials read it, taking the line that, "All this is very well but what can we do?" Then I returned to work for the Foreign Office Research Department. The section had been in Oxford in the first two years of the war, but it had moved to London by the time I returned so I worked there.

Then in 1943 I suddenly got a request from the Office of the Minister of State in Cairo. That was the British ministerial office which had been established in 1942 to coordinate British policy in the Middle East and political–military relations. They had read my report and liked it and said, "Would I come out to act as an assistant to the Adviser of Arab Affairs?"

NEG: Who was the Adviser?
HOURANI: Ilryd Clayton, the younger brother of Sir Gilbert Clayton. Gilbert had been the head of British military intelligence in Cairo during World War I and was the founder of the Arab Bureau. He is mentioned in *Seven Pillars of Wisdom.* Later he was Civil Secretary for the Palestine government and British High Commissioner in Iraq. Ilryd had much of the same qualities of wisdom, insight, and detachment but was not as forceful a man as his older brother.

NEG: Where was the Adviser of Arab Affairs' office located in Cairo?
HOURANI: In Garden City, near GHQ. It has vanished now without a trace. Wartime GHQ took lots of buildings in Garden City and we were in one of them. I was a liaison officer with the younger Arab nationalists, Clayton was always interested in them, liked to talk with them. He had been British political officer in Damascus in 1918–20, had seen the whole process of the British withdrawal and the French occupation, and had experienced Faisal's rule in Damascus. The nationalists of that generation were his close friends, so through him I came to know something about British policy and about the Arab nationalists.

NEG: So you continued to write Foreign Office reports?
HOURANI: Yes, though I've never again come across one. Philip Khoury [professor of Middle Eastern History at Massachusetts Institute of Technology and former student of Mr Hourani] came across one or two in the Foreign Office. I wouldn't like to read them in cold blood now. I formed part of the reports I wrote during the war into the book on Syria and Lebanon.[1] I am not very fond of it now. I have not read it again in at least thirty to forty years. The factual basis is quite flimsy, because it is surprising how little there was to go on at that time. Where could one get information? There were a few French books, all of which I used, virtually nothing in Arabic. The literature on Arab nationalism scarcely existed. I got a lot of information from the Italian journal, *Oriente Moderno*, which is still by far the best factual source on the history of that period. There was, I think, something of some value in that book, that is, all the documents that I translated and reproduced.

I also wrote a little book on minorities which has come back into fashion now that the whole question of ethnicity has come up again. The book is just a collection of facts, a collection of another series of papers. At that time I was very much criticized by Arab nationalists who said, "You ought not to be writing about this, you are dividing the people. This is a time when you ought to talk about unity, not about division." The general feeling was that I ought not to have written it.

Then in 1945 the war ended and I was still in the Office of the Minister of State and there was nothing really for me to do. Musa Alami, the Palestinian leader and philanthropist, who was a friend of Clayton, asked if I could be released to go out to work for him. He had got some money from the Iraqi government to establish Arab offices to state the Palestinian Arab case. That was the time when the Anglo-American Committee had been formed and I was to help to prepare the case. I wrote some of the documents. I even gave evidence.

NEG: Where are the Anglo-American Committee documents now?
HOURANI: You will find them all in the collection of private papers of the Middle East Centre at Oxford. One of the members of the Anglo-Arab Committee, Richard Crossman, gave his set of them. The short version – there were various versions including a full report with documentation – has been published in the Laqueur *Arab–Israel Reader*,[2] not under my name, but under the name of the Arab Office. There you will find the documents used by the Arab Office; in fact I wrote them.

After the Anglo-American Committee meeting I came to London, to the Arab Office, where I stayed for a few months. There were three offices, Jerusalem, Washington, and London. Alami was the director in Jerusalem, my brother Cecil was the director of the American office, I was not the director of the London office; the director had to be from the Husseini family for political reasons. I was a kind of adviser. Edward Atiyah, the novelist and historian, was secretary. Everybody had to be involved, they didn't do very much but they had to be involved. The other person who did a lot of work was Wasfi Tal, later the prime minister of Jordan. He had very unusual qualities. His father was a bedouin, but he was very well-educated, he read Dostoevsky, he listened to Beethoven. He was a highly cultivated man, very well organized; he was somebody who could really work. In 1970 he was assassinated outside the Sheraton Hotel in Cairo by Palestinians because he was thought to be partly responsible for Black September. So I was there for a few months, but I couldn't go on with it. I am not adapted to political propaganda, the endless repetition and the endless suppression of things which are inconvenient to talk about. You cannot state what is on your mind. And I found this impossible, so I left. Also by that time I was rather out of sympathy, not in the sense that I did not believe in the cause of the Palestinian Arabs, but I had gradually and reluctantly come to believe that by asking for too much they were going to get nothing and that some kind of partition was the only solution. I couldn't take the official line that there must be an Arab state in the whole of Palestine, because obviously there wasn't going to be one. So the best thing was to withdraw.

At the very beginning of 1948 I returned to Oxford where I had been elected to a research fellowship in my old college, Magdalen. That was a stroke of luck because I hadn't applied to it. It happened by accident. On the one hand, Magdalen had saved some money during the war and they were offering a few five-year research fellowships. I had done my undergraduate studies there and had got on well, my tutors remembered me, and I'd published a book by then. On the other hand, Gibb had got some money to expand Middle

Eastern Studies under the Scarborough scheme. This was based on a government report which recommended that certain centres of Asian and African studies be expanded. Oxford was going to be one of the centres of Middle Eastern Studies.[3] Gibb was given money for five or six posts. So I was given the research fellowship with the understanding that I would prepare myself to teach the modern history of the Middle East. At the same time I agreed to write a book in the series started by Gibb and Bowen, *Islamic Society and the West*.[4] The series arose when Toynbee was writing his study of history and became interested in the contacts between civilizations. He persuaded Chatham House to apply for a grant, I think from the Rockefeller Foundation, for a series of studies on various Asian societies and the West. There were to be four studies: on Islam, India, China, and one on Japan. The only ones which were ever finished were the Gibb and Bowen, the first two volumes dealing with the Ottoman Empire as it was just before the Western expansion, which were supposed to be the introduction to the longer book. The longer book was to be about Islamic society and the West. Gibb was to be the general editor, though by that time it was clear that it was too large for him. I was going to do the volume on the Arab provinces as my research project. So I spent the first two years, 1948 to 1950, reading in general whatever there was to read. It is surprising how little there was about the modern Middle East at that time. I could rely on Volume I of Gibb and Bowen, Volume II was not yet published. It was finished in 1939 but then Bowen fell and broke his back, and never corrected the proofs. Virtually everything that has been written in a scholarly way about the modern history of the Middle East has been written since then. I had as my bibles: Gibb and Bowen's *Islamic Society and the West*, George Antonius's *The Arab Awakening*, and two books by Toynbee which were of great importance to me.[5] One was the volume on the Middle East after the Peace Conference, which is part of the survey of international affairs for 1925.[6] It still is a masterpiece, based partly upon newspapers and to a great extent upon his own recollections when he was an official in the Foreign Office. He had had a similar office in the Foreign Office during World War I, so he had seen a lot of documents. He may not have referred to them directly but he knew them. The book is a masterly survey of the Muslim world as it was, as it emerged from the First World War. There was another one which is almost forgotten called *The Western Question in Greece and Turkey* which is about the Greek–Turkish War after World War I.[7] Toynbee had been sent by the *Manchester Guardian* to cover it. The *Guardian* thought that he would denounce Turkish atrocities. In fact, he found the Greeks were committing atrocities, and so he denounced the Greek atrocities and he was deprived of his professorship at King's College, London, which had been subsidized by the Greek community in London. He only had a temporary post and they refused to prolong it. The book is a masterly analysis of the very complex relations between great powers and nation states and nationalist movements, each thinking it was making use of the other. Apart from that, what could one read? This was a time before we began using Middle Eastern archives. They just were not open. Bernard Lewis had been given permission to work in the Ottoman archives around 1950 and he published two or three articles, but they were not open to most of us. I learned some Turkish to do so, but I was refused permission. The Egyptian archives had been used mainly by Asad Rustum, a professor at AUB who published a whole series of documents. He was the first person to have full access and to make direct use of the Egyptian archives for the history of Syria. By the time I was ready to work in them I was refused permission and never got into them. I did quite a lot of work in the Public Record Office reading enough consular reports and diplomatic reports to see that by using them alone one could never get inside what was happening in society. That is one reason I never wrote this book. It had become clear to me that the whole project was premature. I was not in a position to write it. So from 1948 to 1950 I was at Magdalen simply reading in general around the subject.

In 1951 I went out to Cairo for six months which I very much enjoyed. I had been in Cairo during the war with the Office of the Minister of State, but it was nice to be in Cairo to have time to read and write. That is when I read Jabarti's history, very thoroughly, from beginning to end. In October 1951 I began teaching at Oxford. I was appointed to a lectureship in the Modern History of the Middle East and my fellowship at Magdalen was prolonged for another term. I remained there as lecturer and as fellow at Magdalen until 1958.

NEG: When did the teaching of the modern Middle East as an academic subject start in England?
HOURANI: My post was the first one in Oxford. There was a post in modern Middle East history at SOAS [School of Oriental and African Studies] at that time; Bernard Lewis was a reader and then professor of Middle Eastern history. About 1950 they created the second post at SOAS which they offered to me, but I was then committed to Oxford. I think my post was the first one created specifically for the modern history of the Middle East.

I still remember my first lecture because nobody came. Under the Oxford system you advertise your lecture. You put an advertisement in the University Gazette which comes out at every term. For some reason they lost my advertisement, my notice. I remember the odd experience of going there dressed in my gown, the first lecture written, and waiting, and nobody came at all. The second time it was all right. It just got sorted out and a small class of eight or ten came. Under the Oxford system anybody can come who wants, but you never know how many people. Individual reading is done with tutors or supervisors, so I lectured and gave suggestions for reading, and I remained around to talk to whom ever wished to come. I was luckier than most lecturers because I had the fellowship at Magdalen and could lecture there. The Oriental Institute had not yet been built and there were people who had to lecture in their rooms, in their homes. The next few years the really important things were not so much the lectures but graduate supervision which began very soon.

My first student who was very frightening indeed was André Raymond who came in 1952. Gibb said simply, "Would you supervise him?" A rather shy, formal French student turned up, who preferred at that time to speak French, although he learned English very well and later lectured in it; he even preferred to write his thesis in French and then translated it. In fact, he was already fully trained as an historian. He is always extremely kind to me and about me, but I only taught him how to prepare a thesis for Oxford and something of the Ottoman system of government. I taught him the technical terms of the Ottoman administration, which I had got very largely from Gibb and Bowen. So he was my first student. I didn't learn much from him at that time; I wasn't ready for the kind of things he was interested in. He had been trained by Charles André Julien. André at that time had not discovered the subject of social history. He was mainly a political historian working on North Africa. His Oxford thesis, which has never been published, was on Anglo-French relations in Tunisia from 1833 to 1881. It was a rather brilliant piece of diplomatic history. He published articles from it. In a way we were far apart as historians, but we got on very well.

NEG: Why did André Raymond come?
HOURANI: He came for a very simple reason. St Antony's College was founded by a Frenchman, Antonein Besse, and there was a preference for French students. When the college was founded it wrote to Charles André Julien and said, "Can you send us some good students?" He said, "I'll send you my best student." And since André wanted to do a subject on diplomatic history, Gibb sent him to me.

There was another early student of mine, Jamal Ahmad, a Sudanese who later became foreign minister of the Sudan. He wrote a thesis with me on the intellectual origins of Egyptian nationalism which has been published by the Oxford University Press. It is a rather good little book based very largely on conversations with Ahmad Lutfi al-Sayyid. I later wrote an article called "Wednesday afternoons remembered" because he used to come and see me every Wednesday afternoon and we would talk.[8] So those were the two students I knew best.

What was more important for me at that time was working with two sorts of colleagues. At Magdalen there was nobody at all interested in the Middle East apart from the president, Tom Boase. But I found myself plunged into the general intellectual life of Oxford. I got to know some people very well, A. J. P. Taylor, C. S. Lewis. They were the people with whom one had breakfast and lunch, silent breakfasts in the Magdalen spirit, no talk at all. There was another group at Oxford who were teaching oriental studies. This was the time when Gibb had been given money to turn Oxford into one of the centres of Middle Eastern studies, and the person I worked most closely with was Gibb himself. I had worked with him during the war and got to know him well as I saw him every day, but now I got to know him academically. I never taught with him in a seminar, I never went to his classes, but we talked frequently and he always gave me books to read. In a subtle way I think he saw that I wasn't fully trained. The other was Richard Walzer, whose main interest was the impact of Greek philosophy upon Arab–Islamic thought.[9] His specialty was uncovering lost works of Greek thought in Arabic translations. He had discovered quite a lot of works of Galen and of the late Aristotelians of which the originals were lost. I learned from him about the German tradition of scholarship. At that time there was no Middle East Centre. It was the Faculty of Oriental Studies. Although my formal position was in history, I only had a formal relationship to the history department.

During that period, from 1951 to 1958, I made two trips to the Middle East. I spent several months in 1953–54 travelling around buying books, quite a good way to get to know people. I got married in February 1955 and we spent the 1956–57 academic year at AUB. In this period my own ideas about the writing of history changed. I had become rather bored with political history. The last extended thing I wrote about politics was a series of two essays called, "The Decline of the West in the Middle East", in which I gave vent to everything I thought about Middle East policy, really quite violently.[10] It caused quite a scandal. It was published in *International Affairs* which is the organ for the Royal Institute of International Affairs, and they were quite upset. They said, well, we will publish it, but we will get a reply. So they got Stephen Longrigg to reply. He wrote a rather civil reply, but he didn't see the point. The point I was making was how the relationship of power affects every relationship in life. Between the powerful and the powerless there cannot be an easy relationship of friendship. Having power is quite different from the experience of being under somebody else's power, which is a far deeper experience, just as victory is a much less profound experience than defeat. In 1953 most people in England were used to power; it seemed a natural course of events.

One thing which made me write the article was an experience I had in 1951 when I was asked to take part in a BBC programme, a radio discussion. At that time there were the troubles in the Canal Zone in Egypt. In the course of the discussion, while we were rehearsing, I said something very mild: "Sooner or later Britain will have to withdraw from Egypt." The discussion stopped, and the producer said, "I think we'd better ask the Foreign Office if you can say that." So much for their boast of their independence. They telephoned the Foreign Office who said, "Yes, Hourani can say it providing somebody slaps him down immediately." I said it in the programme and immediately Sir Frederick White, the discussion chairman, said, "Oh, we can't do that." That was about three years before the withdrawal from Egypt. And somehow, this made me reflect that this was the mood of the time. The implications of the British withdrawal from India had not sunk in.

I've written very few things about politics after that. I wrote something in 1956 after the Suez War[11] and an article in 1967 after the June War.[12] I didn't want to but David Astor of *The Observer* rang me in Beirut and said that the pro-Israeli lobby is getting all the propaganda. Then he said, "Of course we'll have to ask an Israeli scholar to reply to it to be even".

Why didn't I write about politics after that? Partly because it seemed nothing could be done about two issues in the Middle East about which I so strongly cared: the Syrian and Palestinian issues. The French had withdrawn and Syria was independent. It was not doing particularly well, but it was there, a going concern. Britain was not involved; France was not involved. As for the other Palestine issue, from 1948 to the 1960s it did not seem there was anything one could do. Palestine somehow went off the agenda. And by that time there were other people writing about it, there were a lot of people defending the Palestinians. When we'd started, there was almost nobody. There was another reason, which was that I have a very impatient mind. I am not a researcher by temperament. I very much admire people with an obsessive mind who can spend their whole lives studying the same subject. What I really like to do is to impose patterns, to get a lot of material and create patterns. And I knew what I thought and felt about the Palestine Question on a personal level. Nothing that has happened has really changed my mind about the

Palestine Question. I am still as sympathetic as I ever was. Intellectually, it didn't grip me anymore; I began to get bored.

There was something else, too. Being back at Oxford and mixing with people like Gibb and Walzer and the philosophers at Magdalen, my first interest in the history of ideas came back. I decided to write a book to be called *First Views of Europe*, which was going to be about how a few Arab writers in the early nineteenth century went to Europe. Tahtawi and Shidyaq were the ones who came to mind. I became very excited about this, and that was the germ of my book on Arabic thought, *Arabic Thought in the Liberal Age, 1798–1939*.[13] Once I began reading about these Arab writers, I wanted to impose a pattern. People had written about various aspects of this. There were bits of work about the Lebanese literary movement of the nineteenth century, there was some work on Islamic reform by Gibb in his *Modern Trends in Islam*, but nobody had ever tried to put them all together, to create a connected story of the development of Arabic thought. That is why I wanted to do it.

I gave parts of the book in the form of lectures at Oxford over seven years, for small classes. I did a lot of work at AUB, where I got to know about the Lebanese *nahda* (awakening or cultural renaissance) of the 1870s and 1880s. I gave it in another form in Tunis in 1959.

One of the reviewers of the book, I think it was Elie Kedourie, said that it was as if I was driving a kind of road through a lot of material rather like Muhammad Ali driving a road through the old city, with all the dangers. I was quite conscious that I was simplifying it, that I was systematizing it. I was taking articles and turning them into theories. That is how I work and it was a good basis for further work. I think it has turned out to be quite fruitful. Do you remember the article by Donald Reid in which he lists all the detailed works that have come out based upon that book?[14] The book was quite deliberately pointing in a certain direction. I could very easily have tried to write about continuities, about the way these writers think they are breaking new ground but nevertheless are continuing a way which is rooted in their tradition. That did not particularly interest me; I did not really know enough to do it. What interested me was the echoes of European thought that one could catch. I was quite interested in that. I think the other, echoes of Islamic political thought, still needs to be done. It was never really done except in a book by the man who ultimately succeeded me at Oxford, Hamid Enayat, in *Modern Islamic Political Thought*.[15] He was interested in exactly the opposite, but he died very young, before he could complete his work.

Meanwhile, in 1958, something important happened. I was asked to be director of the Middle East Centre at St Antony's College which had been established in 1950–51. And from the beginning they were trying quite consciously to create a centre, on a small scale, like the sixième section of the École Pratique de Hautes Études. They wanted firstly to extend the range of British studies beyond England and the Western world and secondly to encourage historians, sociologists, and economists to study the non-Western world. They were starting a series of centres. The first one was the Russian Centre, the second was the Far Eastern Centre, and the third was Middle East Centre, which started in 1957 with a grant of £7,500 a year for five years. The other centres had to find their own money, but we had a grant.

NEG: Was the grant from the government?
HOURANI: No, from the two oil companies, Shell and British Petroleum. This was arranged by Elizabeth Monroe (a historian of the Middle East at Oxford and former British government official).[16] And so the Centre was founded in 1957. The director on my recommendation was Frank Stoakes, one of Gibb's students who worked for the Iraqi Petroleum Company in Baghdad and wanted to come back to Oxford. When he got there he found he didn't like academic life, he got bored and decided to go back to Baghdad, where the revolution immediately broke out. He finally ended up teaching Middle East politics at Manchester, and I was asked to take over as director of the Centre. What did I take over? A grant of £7,500 pounds a year, which went a long way at that time. The Middle East Centre was an empty house with about 300 books in the library. These were books on the Middle East which happened to be in the college library and were transferred to the Centre. They formed the nucleus of the library. And the Centre had three visiting research fellows at a salary of £800 a year, that was the going rate at that time.

Large numbers of graduate students began coming in the 1960s. Until then people came to Oxford to study with Gibb. Every now and then he'd hand me one or two students, but on the whole he kept them to himself, and there weren't very many. By the end of 1955 Gibb had gone to Harvard without telling anyone until the last moment. We heard about it by rumour. It is the only thing I hold against him. He couldn't tell us.

His successor was A. F. L. Beeston, an extremely nice man whose main interest was in pre-Islamic southern Arabia, with no professional interest in the modern world. One of the nice things about him was that he didn't have the pretensions which some orientalists have. He did not regard what he was doing as a mystery which no one except the orientalist should touch.

I remember the day Fifi [Afaf Lutfi al-Sayyid] wrote to me out of the blue. I wrote back saying, "How are you related to Ahmad Lutfi al-Sayyid, whose articles I've just been reading and writing about in my book?" And she wrote back saying, "He is my uncle." I wrote back to her saying, "Any niece of Ahmad Lutfi al-Sayyid is welcome." So we accepted her, and it was a very close relationship.

In those years, in the sixties, I established two very close working relationships. One was with Elizabeth Monroe. We had a seminar which was great fun. We would pass students backwards and forwards with each other. The other was with Samuel Stern, a professor at Oxford, whom I really got to know at that time. I'd known him since he came to Oxford in 1948. He was very withdrawn, but somehow I got to know him well, and in about 1963 we decided that we would form what we called the Near East History Group. We would meet together every week or two with five or six congenial colleagues and simply read books about Islamic history or discuss subjects. We never dealt with modern subjects. It was an attempt to think about Islamic history. And we decided to have a conference on Islamic cities. We had the conference in Oxford in 1965. It was the first conference I ever arranged, and it was a tremendous success. Bernard Lewis, Claude Cahen, and Ira Lapidus – it was his first appearance, he was a graduate student – were there. Von Grunebaum flew in from Los Angeles, that was a great thing. About twenty people attended. From that conference there came a book which we later called *The Islamic City*, edited by Stern and myself.[17] It still seems to be read.

After that we organized a series of conferences. Samuel, alas, died in 1969 of asthma. His loss meant a great deal to me because we were working very closely together. I was learning a lot from him, but I was also able to help him in various ways. He died with all his work half-done, no books, lots of unpublished articles, about six volumes of which have been published by his students. We went on with the Near East History Group until about 1977. We had about six or seven conferences altogether of which I think about five volumes have been published, and then it gradually died out.

Another very important thing which happened in the 1960s, was that there was another government committee about the future of Slavonic, East European, Asian, and African subjects in England. The committee went to America, and became very interested in the area studies centres, and they decided that there could be no way forward unless the students left the Oriental Departments and were trained by historians and sociologists. Only in that way could they acquire the tools they would need to work on the history and sociology of the Middle East. The committee wrote a report, the Hayter Report, which recommended that the government establish three centres for Middle Eastern studies: at SOAS, Oxford, and Durham. They gave money to Oxford for eight posts. I was responsible for the expansion of Middle Eastern studies at Oxford.[18] Over the next few years we appointed about eight people who were given a period of study in order to prepare themselves to give lectures. I spent most of the 1960s appointing them, supervising their training period, and gradually bringing them into the system. It took a lot of time, there were a lot of students. The 1960s were my busiest period.

Then three things happened. First, my interests changed again. I've had three periods: the first one when I was interested mainly in political history, the second when I was interested in the history of ideas, and the third when I became interested in more general social history. There are reasons for this. One was something about the climate of thought which was changing at the time and the demands of students. By the mid-1960s students who were going to Oxford wanted to do other kinds of subjects, to read other kinds of books. I began to think there are other sorts of history.

Second, I spent two periods at the University of Chicago. In 1962 I was there about six weeks and to my surprise they made me an offer at the end because they had received some money for Middle Eastern studies and asked me to organize them. I said, "Let me think about it, let me come back next year and teach for a longer period," they said "Fine." So I went back the following year and taught for two terms. I worked very closely with three or four of the social scientists and historians, Clifford Geertz, Leonard Binder, Muhsin Mahdi, and Lloyd Fallers, a very brilliant man who had worked on various subjects and was just developing an interest in Turkey. Marshall Hodgson was there, and I got to know him. Jaroslav Stetkevych was there. It was a very exciting group and I was tempted to stay. Had I been unmarried, I would have stayed. At that time my step-children were in their teens, my daughter Susanna was six or so, and we couldn't quite think of how to bring up an English child in Chicago. So we finally turned the offer down, but I remembered it all my life, I'd learned so much. They gave me books to read. I'd always had some interest in social theories. I'd read Max Weber already when I was an undergraduate, I'd read Marx of course. I'd always known Evans-Pritchard, the anthropologist who was an Oxford man. He was a genius, I'd read his books. In Chicago I began reading and thinking seriously about anthropology. I began to think how the concepts of anthropology could be useful to students of history. So gradually I became more interested in social history.

Third, I was caught up in university administration. I was a member of the university Council. I became fascinated by university administration and got to know the whole machinery of the university. The 1960s remain in my mind as a period when I was working very hard, but I was conscious that my mind was being fragmented with too much administration, too much teaching, and trying to write as well.

NEG: You also wrote several articles in the 1960s.

HOURANI: They are basically all the same article, or most of them. There is a paper I gave at a conference, "The Congress for Cultural Freedom", which turned out later to be a CIA front organization. After 1963 I published very little because I got so involved in the administration, in academic politics. My mind was very fragmented. The second was that I was still committed to this book on the Islamic society and the West. I just didn't know how to write it. I tried again and again to write it by drafts, several drafts, but it never got right. The important thing I wrote in this period, the 1960s, was "Islam and the Philosophers of History".[19] This is about how Islam appeared to the European thinkers who tried to work out a system of what happened in history. The other was called "Ottoman reform and the politics of the notables."[20] That I think has had the most impact of any of my writings. It has been used again and again. It has been a seminal article. The other thing, at that time, was the book on the Islamic City, which I edited with Samuel Stern, and my introduction to it.

In 1971 two very important things happened. One was that I decided that the time had come to retire as the Director of the Middle East Centre. I had been doing it for thirteen years, it had taken a lot of my time, and everyone only has a limited number of ideas. I had a feeling that I'd run out of ideas and my younger colleagues had grown into the position. So I said that I was retiring as director, and it was agreed that Derek Hopwood, Roger Owen, and Robert Mabro would take it over in turns. They have done it ever since very well indeed. They were all ready for it by that time. I had established a close working relationship with them, particularly with Roger, through the seminar which we used to have with Elizabeth Monroe. She retired in 1972, so it seemed the logical moment to leave.

The second was that I went to Harvard for a sabbatical leave. From that experience there resulted a personal relationship with Harvard which has been very important to me. I spent the year 1971–72 there. This had two results. First, I acquired a new group of students who have meant a great deal to me. After Gibb retired, Harvard did not have a professor of Middle Eastern history until two years ago when they appointed Roy Mottahedeh, but they went on admitting students of history, and they wanted me to teach them. And so I fell into the position of faculty supervisor. I supervised about eight students at Harvard. Some of them came and worked with me at Oxford, and I would go to Harvard from time to time. They were quite unlike most of the British students. English historians are extremely well-trained on the whole in a very narrow perspective, and there is still a sense in which non-English, non-European history is not taken seriously. It is gradually changing, very, very slowly. In Harvard I found fully trained historians who came to Middle Eastern History with a well-formed historical consciousness. The questions in their minds were the ones historians ask. But I also established close connections with the History Department, and it was very exciting. I still feel that in a way I belong to Harvard. I go back there almost every year. So in the 1970s I got quite a new group of students. And though I had resigned at the Centre I was still a teacher so I still had graduate students at Oxford.

I had hoped that when I retired from the Middle East Centre I'd be able to do more writing, but somehow it didn't happen. The 1970s on the whole were a barren period for me, and that is because I was still committed to this idea of another volume of Gibb and Bowen, and I just couldn't do it. It is from that period that I have the manuscript of the first part which I have never published.

About 1980, again two things happened. First, I decided that I couldn't write the book. I would use all the materials but would use them for other purposes. Second, I decided to retire three or four years early which wasn't because I was at all unhappy with teaching. I liked my students, but I got tired of the endless repetition of teaching. I had become tired of my own voice. I became conscious of the gap that had appeared between myself and my students. I'd never noticed it before. By the late 1970s I was conscious of students wanting something which I couldn't quite give. I was succeeded by Hamid Enayat, which pleased me enormously as he was a great man, and then he died two years later. And with the present financial situation, the post is frozen and perhaps will never come back. It is something which had been built up and brought down.

I was then asked to be the chief academic consultant for a television series, "The Arabs". It was a project of Shaykh Nasir of Kuwait, a cultivated man and a member of the Kuwaiti ruling family, with a wonderful collection of Islamic art, who said he was willing to give $3 million for a television series to explain Arab culture to the outside world. An entrepreneur and artist who had married a Kuwaiti girl was the middleman who arranged the whole thing and found the television company willing to make the programme. But then something went wrong because nobody ever defined what the series was going to be. I was asked to act as the chief academic consultant on the understanding that this would be a series about Arab culture. The people who actually made it, the directors, were not primarily interested in Arab culture. What they wanted to make was a critique of modern Arab society. There was never any meeting of minds, never any understanding among us, and in these situations the advisers are always in a weak position while the directors do what they want. They went into the field, they filmed things, they came back with miles of film, and if I said, "You've done the wrong thing," they would say, "Well, it's too late, we have no time and no money, we must make do with what we have." So it somehow all went wrong. It was never clearly thought out. I was rather disappointed. I had learned that in television there is a professional reluctance to say things with words. Everything was visual images. The words were written at the last moment. They demanded the minimum words, so you would have thirty seconds to explain Islam in twenty-five words. I have a certain contempt for television.

I have just completed a text, *A History of the Arab Peoples*, that in a sense evolved out of that series.[21] It deals with the Arabic-speaking countries of the Middle East. I've tried to be comprehensive. It is organized around three concepts: truth, power, and wealth.

NEG: What do you mean by truth, power, and wealth?
HOURANI: By "truth" I mean what people believe: beliefs and the culture that grows up around them, that is, religion and popular beliefs that were not entirely Islamic. By "power" I mean interactions between organized power and social solidarities. By "wealth" I mean social and economic structures.

In the book I tried to show that there are different rhythms of change. This is something I learned from Jacques Berque's book on Egypt.[22] He shows that there are two cycles of change going on independently of each other and that the rhythms of change that governments and ruling élites try to impose on society are not necessarily the same as the rhythms of change a society generates out of itself. I've tried to make this book as empirical as I can, to follow the course of history as it has developed.

NEG: Have you tried to bring women into the study?
HOURANI: There is quite a lot about women, but not a special section about women. They come in everywhere. They've not come into my previous books because – what can I say – it was not women who produced the Arabic thought of the early twentieth century.

NEG: How can you explain to students what history is, or rather what good history is?
HOURANI: I think history is what we choose to remember of the past and the pattern we impose upon it. There is bound to be the mark of the individual historian and something drawn from the culture of the age. History books written even twenty or thirty years ago read as very old-fashioned. My book, *Arabic Thought in the Liberal Age*, I think, is extremely old-fashioned. Nobody would write like that now, of course, twenty-five years later. So I think history is a combination of a convincing

vision of what happened with respect for the facts in so far as one knows them. I don't think you can do more than that.

I'll tell you what I think is bad history. Bad history is written by the historian who has a passionate interest about what ought to have happened and chooses his materials and quotations by seeing only what he wants to see. History changes from generation to generation. Very few of the works on the Middle East written before the last twenty or thirty years stand up. Of the works on Islamic history, very few except those of Ignaz Goldziher are sound.[23] I think that for good history there must be a basic integrity in the use of the evidence and some kind of pattern which convinces the reader. I think it must be well-written. No more than that. There remains a sense in which history is art. It is not completely scientific, which doesn't mean that I'm opposed to the Annales School's use of quantitative methods. The question is what you do with all that quantification. History is an aid to self-understanding, and that is all. One mustn't think that one can draw obvious lessons from it, but there are other lessons: a lack of historical depth is a serious handicap for an individual, a politician, or a nation. One of the reasons I gave up political history was that it is very difficult not to direct it towards the future, towards your idea of what ought to happen. And that somehow distorts your view of what has happened. I became very disillusioned with policy-oriented history.

NEG: What are your afterthoughts on the issue of orientalism?
HOURANI: I rather regret that Edward Said gave the book that title. Orientalism has now become a dirty word. Nevertheless it should be used for a perfectly respectable discipline. I think it was one of the great seminal disciplines of the nineteenth century, philology in the broad sense, not in the sense in which the word was used in this country, but as it is used in Germany and France. It is the study of the written records of a civilization and of everything one can derive from it. What else can one base oneself on? I think it is a valid discipline. Edward maintained two things, firstly that the orientalists have created their own imaginary world and secondly that they are "essentialists" who think that everything can be explained in terms of Islam. Now, I think one can find quotations of most of the nineteenth-century orientalists which would support that. There was a certain tendency in the nineteenth century to think in terms of national characters. That isn't true only of Westerners writing about Easterners. The English used to write about the French, the French about the English. It was a discourse that did not have a deep reality. Some of them did have a very deep knowledge of the societies. Edward totally ignores the German tradition and philosophy of history which was the central

tradition of the orientalists. Therefore among others he has ignored Goldziher. In his diary, Goldziher describes his visit to the Middle East. He was only able to go there once when the Hungarian government gave him a travel grant. He travelled around, he spent almost a year between Beirut, Damascus, and Cairo. He spent evenings sitting in the cafés with Jamal al-Din al-Afghani. He knew these people as human beings. He shows a deep sympathetic insight into what was happening. He wasn't trying to reduce them to an unchanging essence.[24]

Edward Said was influenced by Michel Foucault, this idea of an intellectual tradition creating its own objects. When Foucault writes about madness, for example, he is saying that we decide what to define as madness. Edward is really applying that saying that we decide who we are and what orientals are like, what they were always like, and what they always will be like. And also there is, of course, a political side to it. Edward was interested in showing a relationship between this system of ideas and imperial power. That is a valid suggestion, but I think he carries it too far when he says that the orientalists delivered the orient bound to the imperial powers.

I think all this talk after Edward's book also has a certain danger. There is a sort of counter-attack of Muslims, who say nobody understands Islam except themselves. I remember, Edward asked this question, "How can one understand the other?" One could answer, "One has to do one's best." We must just do our work as honestly as we can. I think Edward's other books are admirable. The one on the question of Palestine is very good indeed because there he is on firm ground. Still, in *Orientalism* Edward is justified in challenging the idea that only those who come up through the philological disciplines are entitled to write an article on any aspect of Asia. This idea was common in British universities and still is to some extent. It is quite common in universities in this country where the revolution in area studies has never been complete. Most history faculties would not really accept non-Western history. The history faculty of Oxford which has extremely high standards is very narrow. They fully accept English history, Western European history. They will now accept American history. Russian history has come in. Indian history during the British period is accepted, but India recedes into darkness after 1947. Modern Japanese history can be understood within the same framework as Western history so that is all right. But Middle East history is not fully accepted.

NEG: Doesn't the acceptance of a nation's or a region's history come from its political and economic power?
HOURANI: Yes, but there is also I think an academic power, the

power of departments. In England the departments of oriental or near eastern studies are deeply rooted. They are dominated on the whole by Biblical scholars who somehow resent people who haven't gone through the hard philological discipline. When the Middle East Centre at Oxford was announced, a letter of protest came in from one of the people who taught Arabic at Cambridge saying, "These people have no right, what do they know? They haven't studied the languages, they haven't studied the religious systems . . ." And that sentiment is still quite strong.

NEG: Could you describe your most recent work?
HOURANI: In January 1988 I had to give three lectures at Cambridge. They were supposed to be given by Professor Fazlur Rahman, the late Pakistani philosopher and Islamic scholar. He was going to do three lectures on "Islam and the modern world". I was going to arrange a seminar afterwards, but Professor Rahman died and I was pressured to give the lectures, which were an annual series. I said I would not talk about Islam and the modern world but rather the development of European views of Islam in the nineteenth century. I gave three lectures which I have developed in a different form. I try to trace the way in which a certain idea changed into something else in the nineteenth century when the English and French began to write about Islam. At first what European scholars meant by studying Islam was studying the Prophet Muhammad as a historical phenomenon. The kind of questions they asked are: where did his ideas come from, how did the Arab conquest take place, was he a prophet? If he was not a prophet, how could he be explained? What is his role in divine providence in the propagation of government in the world? You find these questions all through the eighteenth and the early nineteenth centuries. But by the end of the nineteenth century there was an idea of Islam as a human culture which had developed over time by human effort. I wanted to find out how this change took place. So I went deeply into Goldziher because our view of Islam and Islamic culture until today is very largely that which Goldziher laid down. I have been reading extensively about Goldziher; his diary is extremely interesting. It is an account of the development of his mind, his travels in the Middle East, his struggles in the Jewish community of Budapest. And his correspondence with T. Noldeke has been published recently with a long introduction.[25] It is clear that Goldziher was influenced by two things, firstly by European Biblical scholars, and particularly German scholars, and in a way he was asking the same question, how do religious systems develop? Whatever you think about the original impulse, whether it came from God or not, it is developed by human beings. Secondly he was influenced by the German philosophers of

the early nineteenth century: Hegel's philosophy of history and behind him Immanuel Kant.

NEG: In his diaries, in his writings, is he self-conscious about his development?
HOURANI: Oh yes, he explained exactly what happened. His great ambition was to write a kind of cultural history of mankind, but he couldn't do it because he had to earn his living by being secretary of one of the Jewish congregations in Budapest. He wasn't given a proper university post until the 1900s so he had no money and all he could do was to write about Islam in his spare time. But the question always was, what was it to be a Jew? He came to the conclusion that Islam was much nearer to the truth than Judaism was. He said, I really am a Muslim. And he meant that. For him, Islam was a rational religion without a sense of being a chosen people, which for him was one of the disadvantages of Judaism. He belonged to the generation of Jews who had been emancipated in the Austrian Empire. He wanted to be a Hungarian of the Jewish faith. He'd broken out of the ghetto.

NEG: Could you give some advice to students who are considering a specialization in Middle East history?
HOURANI: I do not think I have valuable advice to give to students of the new generation, who will inevitably have questions and preoccupations quite different from mine. It would be more useful for them to advise me how I should try to write in a way that will help them.

That said, I might suggest that prospective students, before going seriously into Middle Eastern history, should try to acquire a good knowledge of historical ideas and methods by studying with teachers or reading works in other historical fields which have been cultivated for a longer time and more intensively than the history of the Middle East. At least some of them should learn Ottoman Turkish well and learn also how to use Ottoman documents, since the exploitation of Ottoman archives, located in Istanbul and in smaller cities and towns, is perhaps the most important task of the next generation. Students will probably be mainly interested in social and economic history, but they should not neglect the history of ideas, whether that of individual thinkers or of collective *mentalités*.

Notes

1. Albert Hourani, *Syria and Lebanon* (New York and London: Oxford University Press, 1946).

2. Walter Laqueur and Barry Rubin (eds), *The Israel–Arab Reader: A Documentary History of the Middle East* (New York: Penguin Books, 1984), pp. 94–104.
3. For further information on this report, see Albert Hourani, "Middle Eastern studies today", *British Society for Middle East Studies Bulletin*, 11, 2 (1984), pp. 111–20.
4. H. A. R. Gibb and Harold Bowen, *Islamic Society and the West* (2 vols., New York and London: Oxford University Press, 1950–7).
5. Ibid.; George Antonius, *The Arab Awakening: The Story of the Arab National Movement* (London: H. Hamilton, 1938).
6. Arnold Toynbee, *Survey of International Affairs* (London: Oxford University Press, 1925).
7. ——, *The Western Question in Greece and Turkey: A Study in the Contact of Civilizations* (London: Constable, 1923).
8. ——, "Wednesday afternoons remembered", *Fi sirat Jamal* (Khartoum: University of Khartoum Press, 1988), pp. 127–40, republished in *Islam in European Thought* (New York: Cambridge University Press, 1991), pp. 61–73.
9. Richard Walzer, *Galen on Medical Experience* (New York: Oxford University Press, 1944).
10. Albert Hourani, "The decline of the West in the Middle East", *International Affairs*, 29 (1953), 22ff.
11. ——, "The Middle East and the Crisis of 1956", *St Antony's Papers 4: Middle Eastern Affairs*, 1 (London: Chatto and Windus, 1958), pp. 9–42.
12. ——, "Palestine and Israel", *Observer*, 3 September 1967.
13. ——, *Arabic Thought in the Liberal Age, 1798–1939* (New York and London: Oxford University Press, 1962).
14. Donald M. Reid, "Arabic Thought in the Liberal Age twenty years after", *International Journal of Middle East Studies*, 14 (1982), pp. 541–57.
15. Hamid Enayat, *Modern Islamic Political Thought: The Response of the Shi'i and Sunni Muslims to the Twentieth Century* (Austin: University of Texas Press, 1982).
16. Elizabeth Monroe, *Britain's Moment in the Middle East, 1914–1956* (London: Chatto & Windus, 1963).
17. Albert Hourani and S. M. Stern, *The Islamic City* (Philadelphia: University of Pennsylvania Press, 1970).
18. For further information see Albert Hourani, "Middle Eastern studies today", *British Society for Middle East Studies Bulletin*, 11, 2 (1984), pp. 111–20.
19. ——, "Islam and the philosophers of history", *Middle Eastern Studies*, 3 (1967), pp. 206–68.
20. ——, "Ottoman reform and the politics of the notables", *Beginnings of Modernization in the Middle East: the Nineteenth Century*, W. R. Polk and R. L. Chambers (eds.) (Chicago: University of Chicago Press, 1968), pp. 41–68.
21. Albert Hourani, *A History of the Arab Peoples* (Cambridge: Harvard University Press, 1991).
22. Jacques Berque, *Egypt: Imperialism and Revolution* (New York: Praeger, 1972).
23. Ignaz Goldziher (1850–1921), a Hungarian scholar of Jewish origin, was an Arabist and Islamist who studied at al-Azhar, the Islamic university in Cairo. Goldziher deeply identified with Islam and with Egyptian interests. While in Egypt he spent countless hours at coffee houses talking with ordinary people; he used to rail against the "dominant European plague". He advocated a renaissance of a neo-Muslim indigenous culture. See Raphael Patai, ed. and transl., *Ignaz Goldziher and His Oriental Diary* (Detroit: Wayne State University Press, 1989), p. 27. His *Muslim Studies* are the basis of our understanding of

Islam as a cultural system. See Ignaz Goldziher, *Muhammedanische Studien* (Halle a.S.: M. Niemeyer, 1889–90).

24. See also the review by Albert Hourani of Edward Said's, *Orientalism* (Pantheon Books) in *The New York Review of Books*, 8 March 1979, pp. 27–30.

25. Robert Simon, *Ignaz Goldziher: His Life and Scholarship as Reflected in his Works and Correspondence* (Leiden: E. J. Brill, 1986).

CHAPTER TWO

CHARLES ISSAWI

CHARLES ISSAWI, born in Cairo in 1916, is a specialist in Middle East economic history. Trained as an economist, he served as secretary to the under-secretary of state at the Egyptian ministry of finance, was head of the statistical department of the Central Bank of Egypt and worked at the Secretariat of the United Nations in New York. He taught at the American University of Beirut and at Columbia University, where he was Ragnar Nurkse Professor of Economics and Director of the Near and Middle East Institute. He was Bayard Dodge Professor of Near Eastern Studies at Princeton University from 1975 until his retirement in 1986 and was visiting professor in economics at New York University in 1987–91. He is past president of the Middle East Studies Association of North America, past president of the Middle East Economic Society, and a recipient of the Giorgio Levi Della Vida Award.

Interviewed by Nancy E. Gallagher on 15 and 16 March 1991 at his office at Princeton University.

NEG: Could you begin by describing your family background?
CHARLES ISSAWI: I am a difficult case to sort out. My parents were what I would call "Syrian". In my time, nobody made a distinction between Lebanese, Palestinian, Jordanian, and Syrian. We were all "*Shawam*"; my family was "Christian *Shawam*". It comes from various parts of Syria: my father was born in Jaffa and his father in Nablus. The family came to Palestine in the nineteenth century from Hawran. My father's mother was Damascene; she came from the Sarruf family. In the late nineteenth century an uncle of hers, Fadlallah Sarruf, was a professor at the University of St Petersburg where he taught Arabic. My mother's family is Damascene, with a touch of Greek–Ionian in it; her maternal grandfather, an Ionian possibly of Genoese descent, C. Avierinos, settled on the Lebanese coast and in Acre in the 1840s. I found some records of him in the British and Egyptian archives. So if

you want a blood test, I am much more Damascene than anything else. Culturally I am Lebanese and Egyptian.

My father graduated from the American University in Beirut, came to Egypt, and took a job in the Cairo Office of the Sudan government. My mother's father, Nuʿman Abushaʿr, a Damascene, worked in the Ottoman service and was an Ottoman consul in Liège, Belgium. My mother grew up in Istanbul and in Belgium. My grandfather was one of the founders of the *La-Markaziya* (Decentralization), the Arab nationalist society. When he fell out with the Young Turks and couldn't go back to Syria, he came to Egypt. My parents met in Cairo.

I spent the first eight years of my life in Cairo. I was an only child, but I was not spoiled. My memories of childhood in Egypt are all very pleasant. The curious thing about the Syrians is that we more or less shared a language and culture with the Egyptians, but since there were very few Muslims among us, we were different. Some of us were much more different because in the Syrian community there were many people whose native tongue was French and not Arabic. My mother was one of those.

I grew up in Heliopolis. It was a lovely little place at that time. It had just been founded; that incredible hodgepodge of architecture was just then being built. The desert was all around, it was clean, it was sunny. I can't think of a nicer place to have been a child. Most of my friends were Syrian though very far from exclusively. My closest friends were a Muslim Egyptian family who lived next to my grandmother's. She had practically brought up its four boys, and we were very close. The boys and I played together all the time.

When I was five I was sent to an English kindergarten where I started my love affair with the English language for a very simple reason: boys' literature in English was unique and incomparable; there was nothing like it. I learned French and Arabic before I learned English, but French boys' books were pallid, and Arabic boys' books were non-existent. My love affair with the English language has never ended.

My father was transferred to the Sudan where he was director of the budget, so we spent a few years there. In the Sudan there were no schools. They tried to place me in an Italian school, but it didn't work. I have no memory of it except for the friar who had a very strong index finger. When he hit you with it, it hurt. So I stayed at home where I got my education. My mother taught me French. We got a teacher to teach me classical Arabic. Then I had the biggest luck of my life. Edward Atiyah, the novelist and historian, who had grown up in the Sudan, had just come down from Oxford and had taken a job with the Sudan government.[1] He was a marvellous man. He became one of my two or three best friends. He taught me arithmetic, English, history.

So I continued to have a very pleasant childhood, a bit lonely, because there were not too many boys to play with. I spent much of my time alone in the garden inventing games and imaginary adventures. Then came the question of sending me to boarding school. My parents thought of the Jesuit school in Cairo, though we were Orthodox. My mother had grown up in *Notre Dame de Sion,* a Catholic nuns' school in Constantinople, so she was very familiar with and attuned to Catholic practice, but two things intervened. First of all, I was a rather frail child and my parents thought toughening would help. They judged an English school would be better for that because there were more games and sports. Secondly, my mother always had the horrible thought that if I went to a Jesuit school I might have a religious conversion and become a Jesuit. That thought didn't appeal to her at all. And so they sent me, at the age of eleven, to Victoria College in Alexandria.

Victoria College was a rather peculiar place. I have kept wonderful memories of it. It was run on public school lines in every way. We had blazers, we had prefects, houses, games, all the paraphernalia. It was a lay school, but once a week every community had religious teaching: the Muslims got a shaykh, the Jews a rabbi, the Catholics a padre, the Protestants a pastor. We poor Orthodox were lumped with the Protestants, so we had to do the Bible with the Protestant pastor. On Sundays, we were bused to the Anglican church, a journey I disliked immensely. One day I told the headmaster that I had conscientious objections, but he, not being taken in by my humbug, said, "Nonsense, my boy, I'll beat you until you go." So I went every Sunday which certainly did not do me any harm! Indeed I am glad it familiarized me with the Church of England service, whose prayer book and hymns often come back to me.

The idea behind the school was to train the élite of Egypt and the Middle East. We had people like the Regent of Iraq, one of the sons of King Abdullah of Jordan, Malaysian princes, Iraqi notables, the son of a dissident Kurdish chief. Later a grandson of King Abdullah, now King Husayn of Jordan, came as did Hisham Nazir, the oil minister of Saudi Arabia. We had upper-class Egyptians, Levantines, Greeks, Italians, Armenians, Jews, Syrians. We had the first batch of Ethiopians sent abroad. It was a very mixed place. All the teaching was in English. We had French and Arabic, but those who didn't want to do Arabic could do Latin. I think that we got a good education, more science, geography, history, and literature than Americans get. We also learned to live with other peoples, other races.

The problem with Victoria, though it didn't look so to me at that time, was that they didn't push you very hard. If you were interested in intellectual things, you got a lot out of it. I learned an enormous amount and also, to use that awful word, it socialized me – I'd been an only child, but I learned very easily to get on with others. Many others, without much intellectual curiosity, didn't get very much out of it. There was so much emphasis on games: cricket, football, and swimming were compulsory. If I had put half the work into mathematics that I put into cricket, I would now be at the Institute for Advanced Studies, but I didn't. My proudest moment was when I played for our second eleven, the second cricket team. That was the high point of my life – nothing else since has matched it.

The one subject I didn't do well in was Arabic. It wasn't the school's fault; it was mine. I just wasn't very interested. I coasted along and was very near the bottom of the form. When I was fifteen it suddenly occurred to me that Arabic was a great language and worth studying, and that Arab history was very interesting. So my parents got me a tutor, a former student of the great Ibrahim al-Yaziji, and I began making a serious effort.

After I graduated, my headmaster insisted I go to Oxford. My two favourite subjects had been history and chemistry, but I never thought of taking a degree in either of them. Chemistry was very unpromising in Egypt. Since there were no research facilities, a degree in chemistry would have meant working for Bank Misr fixing dyes or for the sugar company testing sugar. It wasn't very exciting. There were no jobs in history. I did not think I would get a teaching post at the university, because the Egyptians, quite rightly, felt that having had foreigners sitting on them for two thousand years they were going to take the jobs themselves. Finally, I really didn't want to teach. It was very far from my outlook at the time. I wanted to change the world.

NEG: Had you been out of Egypt before you went to Oxford?
ISSAWI: I had been to Lebanon and Syria. Every summer we used to go to Damascus and stay with my grandfather who was great fun. He had travelled widely, he was full of interesting information and always made me look up words in the dictionary. He was a vigorous man. We used to go walking, leaving my mother and father way behind. Damascus struck me as a very gloomy, dull, awful place. I couldn't see anything to it at the time. My grandfather lived in the modern part of the city, but the rest of his family stayed in the old Christian quarter. The beauty of the old houses was completely wasted on me; it was only much later that I discovered how lovely they were.

Lebanon was glorious. We used to go to Suq al-Gharb in the mountains. Things were just beginning – there was no electricity, no running water, and the roads were dusty, though passable. René

Sursock, a member of the leading Orthodox family of Beirut, was just establishing the Grand Hotel. We had wonderful Lebanese food and mezze (Middle Eastern hors d'oeuvres). I have never been able to drink arak (an anise-flavoured liquor), because whenever I was sick I was given castor oil and in order to make me take it they would give me arak. I have never broken the association. We enjoyed the popular poets who would improvise verse and make fun of each other. We walked in the mountains and picnicked. Even as a child I sensed that Lebanon was a much freer place than Damascus. I felt that my parents and their friends, especially the women, were under much less constraint. Altogether Lebanon had the loveliest associations for me.

In 1934 I went as an undergraduate to Oxford. This was my first introduction to England. I went alone, but I was accustomed to travelling alone. The trip from Khartoum to Alexandria took four and a half days so I did not see my parents the year round and sometimes I travelled there on my own. In Oxford, I sat for a scholarship. I didn't know it but Albert Hourani was sitting for the same scholarship, at the same college. We both got history scholarships. I took PPE (Philosophy, Politics and Economics) specializing in economics because I wanted to change the world, and I thought economics was the way to do so. I thought of myself in politics or in government service. I did not think at all of academic life. If I had a hero it wasn't Newton or Einstein, it was Cavour, it was Lenin. So it seemed to me that economics made a lot of sense. I still think it makes sense, though not as much as I did.

I spent three very happy years at Oxford. I took part in a lot of activities: I was a member of the Labour Club and I debated a couple of times at the Oxford Union. I worked rather hard and I did well. I understood immediately the secret of being happy at Oxford. I realized it consisted of little circles of people: the hunting, shooting, and fishing circle, the political circle, the aesthetic circle, the scholarly circle. The main thing was to find your circle, and in mine I was very happy; it was made up of the politically-minded social scientists and historians.

One day a very thin young man with luminous green eyes and a diaphanous complexion walked in and said, "I am Albert Hourani." We started a conversation that has continued for well over fifty years. He and one or two others are the closest friends I have had.

It was the time of the Depression and the one bright spot in the world was Franklin Roosevelt, and he wasn't making such a great success of it either. We lost our enthusiasm for the Soviet Union after the purges and the Hitler–Stalin pact. I remember when one of Chamberlain's cabinet ministers came to dine at Magdalen. We walked up and down the cloisters shouting, "One, two, three, four, what is the National Government for! Huggery, buggery, fascism and war!" We were sure that war was coming. Although we never envisioned the horrors of the gas chambers, we imagined that the Second World War would be even more destructive than it was. We thought London, Paris, and Berlin would be wiped out. The incendiary bomb had taken hold of our imagination, and we thought that whole cities would disappear. It was a grim period, and here was this little island of sanity, light, and beauty in Oxford. We were very conscious of it. Some of my friends said, "We are the last generation; let us enjoy life." On the other hand, I had a good friend who in his second year said, "I am not going to waste my time on this," and he went and joined the Air Force, or rather the equivalent of the ROTC, with the idea that he might as well have a skill when the war came. We got very excited about Spain. As you know, many people went to take part in the Civil War. I felt very strongly about it. I remember that we collected some money for Spain and signed petitions. To us it was black and white: Franco was all black and the Republicans were all white. Now I can see that it was not quite so clear cut.

I received my Bachelor's degree in 1937. I did not stay on for graduate work because graduate work at Oxford meant writing a thesis, nothing else. My professors said, "If you want to write a book, go write a book. Why waste your time and ours hanging around here?" Almost no one stayed on. I never for a moment thought of remaining in England. It was a country I loved and respected, but it was not mine and could never be.

And so in 1937, I returned to Cairo where I lived very comfortably with my parents. I first got a job with the ministry of finance which was by far the biggest and most powerful ministry. The Egyptian government was very centralized. I got a panoramic view of the Egyptian economy and learned a lot about bureaucratic centralization. Then I worked for the National Bank of Egypt. I was given a general training in banking, sent to Upper Egypt to inspect various villages, and finally put in a little research unit. After four and a half years working for the bank, I became rather restless. It was very frustrating with the war going on all around. My impulse was to join the British army, but they wouldn't take me because they had an agreement with Egypt that citizens would not be recruited. I realized that in a sense I was a fifth column, supporting the power which was oppressing Egypt. Many Egyptians were pro-Axis though the government was not.

In 1942, we were very nervous because of the proximity of the Germans. One day, at five in the morning, I jumped when I heard the door bell ring. I opened the door and who was there but Albert Hourani. I said, "Albert, how did you get here?" He said, "I came round the Cape, in the *Queen Elizabeth* with 20,000 men on board." I put him up of course. When I asked him what he had been doing, he said, "I've just written a book on Syria." I said to myself: "Do thou likewise." Albert had written a book, so I was going to write a book. Actually I had been thinking about it. In my work I had learned a lot about the Egyptian economy, since we had good documentation. So I sat down and wrote very fast and produced a book by the following spring. Albert was just about to go to England and I asked him to smuggle the manuscript out. He did so and gave it to Chatham House which agreed to publish it although it took them over four years because of the paper shortage![2]

Just when I'd finished the book, I got a letter offering me a job in Beirut. Cecil Hourani, Albert's brother, had been teaching politics at the American University in Beirut but had decided to serve with the British army and had suggested my name as a replacement. By then I wanted to teach, and I think that I wanted to go to Lebanon. My father had died, and in the summer of 1943, my mother came with me to Beirut, reluctantly because she had been happy in Cairo. In Lebanon, I felt at home in a way that I had not felt before. I had never felt alienated in Egypt, but I now realized that Lebanon was where I belonged. In Oxford, I had always been a foreigner, but in Lebanon I felt at home. I had a marvellous group of colleagues, and it was the best moment to be in Lebanon. It was the beginning of the glorious years.

The country had just been declared independent, and a government was being set up. Very shortly after I arrived, the French arrested the Lebanese president, prime minister, and several deputies. There was a big protest. A group of us professors got together and wrote a very virulent pamphlet against the French. I did the English draft. We printed it clandestinely and carried copies in a push cart, covered with tomatoes, in the dark of the night. We gave copies to the American, British, and Soviet embassies. I still have the pamphlet. We called it, "The Case for Lebanese Independence". Albert Hourani then worked for the Foreign Office at Chatham House and told me they were wondering who the "Committee for Lebanese Independence" was. I was caught up in the excitement of establishing a new country from scratch.

At AUB I taught politics, comparative government and the history of political ideas, as well as introductory economics. We put out a journal, of which I was secretary, and for which I translated articles from English into Arabic and compiled a chronology of current events.[3] The journal went on for a year or so and then our board of directors began to disappear. Charles Malik got appointed as ambassador to Washington, Constantine Zurayk became first secretary of the Syrian embassy in Washington, George Hakim became first secretary to the Lebanese embassy in Washington. When I left, the journal took a slightly different format, but it went on until a few years ago.

I wrote my book on Ibn Khaldun at AUB. I had been interested in Ibn Khaldun ever since an English teacher had told me about him. At the time I was not the least bit interested in Arabic, but later I went to a bookshop in Cairo and bought a copy of Ibn Khaldun's *Muqaddimah*. When I was seventeen or eighteen and working hard on my Arabic, I realized something had to be done to bring his ideas to the attention of a wider audience. This stayed in the back of my mind. At AUB, I brought him into my course on political theory along with Aristotle and Machiavelli. At the time there was a series called, "The Living Thoughts of . . ." and I thought it might be nice to bring out a book called, "The Living Thoughts of Ibn Khaldun". I wrote to Edward Atiyah who was in London at the time, and asked him to see if the publishers of the series might be interested. He wrote back that they might be, so I set about working on it but as it happened, they discontinued the series. Then the UNESCO representative in Beirut said they would be interested but only in the whole *Muqaddimah*. I replied that I wanted to do only the part I was competent to do, that is the social sciences. My study of the social science part was soon published by another London publisher.[4] Franz Rosenthal's monumental translation supersedes it, but was not available until 1958.[5]

I got married while I was at AUB. My wife was one of the two million Poles who were deported to the Soviet Union, many of whom came out through Iran. The Polish government in exile then sent some of the young people, mainly women, to Beirut to study. Some came to AUB and some to Saint Joseph, and one, who became my wife, landed in my class.

In 1946, Musa Alami, the Palestinian leader and philanthropist, approached me and asked if I would go to the Arab Office in Washington, D.C., to work with Cecil Hourani. Albert was in the London office, headed by Edward Atiyah. It was a tightly knit group. I was very excited by this prospect for two reasons. Firstly, I had begun to think that the United States was a very interesting country. Secondly I wanted to do what I could on behalf of Palestine. So we went to Washington. For about six months I lectured, I toured the country, I brought out a little bulletin, the *Arab News Bulletin*. I was very active trying to persuade Americans that their policy would lead to a disaster: "If you set up a Jewish state in Palestine it is going to upset the Middle Eastern apple cart and completely disrupt everything," but nobody was listening. People said, "Oh, yes, they will shout for six months, and then things will quiet down."

It was great fun being in Washington. It was a very small place at that time, but for us coming from Beirut it was a big city. We made friends, visited the art galleries, used the libraries and then the Arab Office ran out of funds. The Arab governments were not supporting it, except for the Iraqi government, but when the Arab–Israeli troubles began, its pipeline to Haifa was closed, drastically reducing its funds. So the question came of getting a job. I had tried to get a leave of absence from AUB, but without success. They had lost half their staff and they did not want to lose anyone else. So I found myself out of a job. I contacted the World Bank, was interviewed, and was told that there were openings but that it was their policy not to employ people to work on their own regions. They feared that if I went out to negotiate a loan in the Middle East, either I would be biased in their favour or, more likely, I would bend over backwards not to be biased and neither was desirable. But if I went to negotiate a loan with Paraguay, for example, I would be neutral.

Meanwhile, a friend who worked at the United Nations called to offer me a post in the Middle East section of the Department of Economic Affairs. I was interviewed and offered the post. I sought out Charles Malik for advice as to which job to take. He looked at me solemnly and said, "My friend, if you work for the World Bank, you are working for American capitalism. If you work for the United Nations you don't know for whom you are working!" My wife and I decided I would work for whoever came first with a contract. The UN came through first, so we came to New York.

The UN was planning to set up an Economic Commission for the Middle East with its headquarters in Beirut. I looked forward to living in Beirut on a United Nations salary with the possibility of travelling all over the region. By then I had got excited by the Middle East. I knew almost nothing about the region, outside of Egypt, Lebanon, Syria, and Palestine. I had done a bit of work with Albert Hourani for the Anglo-American Commission of Inquiry to which I had presented the economic part of the Arab case.[6] But suddenly I was a "Middle East expert" at the United Nations. This came as a bit of a surprise to me, but someone had given me very good advice: "In the United States, if anyone asks if you can design a battleship, you should say, 'Which size?' " I decided if they wanted me to become a Middle East expert I would become one. So I learned Persian; I learned enough Turkish to be able to read economic literature (since then they have changed the language so much I can hardly read it), and I started reading about Middle Eastern economics. The sources were very few.

The Economic Commission was never established because, while we were debating it, Israel became a member of the UN and would have had to be a part of it. The Arab countries said, "No, let us postpone it," and so that project fell through. Although I was disappointed, by then we were enjoying life in New York and I liked my work at the UN so I stayed on. We used to bring out a survey of economic conditions in the Middle East which was unique and very useful. However, I began to feel that I needed more training in economics and decided to get a Ph.D. I had done well not to do graduate studies at Oxford, but where I made a mistake was not to have come to Columbia or Harvard. If I had studied there I would have been a much better economist. I had thought at one time of doing graduate work in Germany, but in 1937 it was not at all attractive. My economics was all right, but it was not the state of the art. So I called and asked for an appointment at Columbia. The Chair of the Department said, "We would like very much to have you, but have you thought of the mechanics of it? You work eight hours a day at the UN, and it would take you two hours to come from Lake Success to downtown and then up to Columbia and back. After six weeks you will be in the hospital." That was the end of my Ph.D.

While I was at the UN I struck up a friendship with Jay [J.C.] Hurewitz, who was working on the Security Affairs Council, in the Secretariat. When he left to go to Columbia we kept in touch. One day, he asked me to have lunch with some of the members of the Economics Department at Columbia, which, at that time, was stupendous. I doubt if there was anything like it anywhere. To my great surprise, the chairman said they were setting up a Middle East programme, would like to introduce a course on Middle East economics, and would I come from the United Nations once a week to give it. I did this for two or three years and then was asked to join the faculty on a permanent basis. I said, "Let me talk to my wife." It took us five minutes to decide to accept, although it meant quite a big cut in salary. The thought of academic life appealed to both of us very much. And so in 1951 I entered the Department of Economics and the Middle East Institute and taught courses on land tenure, oil, and the general economics of the Middle East for the next twenty years.

When I worked for the United Nations, we had asked the Iranian delegation to the UN if they had any graduate students in economics who would like a part time job. We interviewed a few, and I was very taken by a young man, Mohammed Yeganeh, whom we hired. He was a wonderful young man and we became very close friends. He was passionately interested in oil and had accumulated an enormous amount of information. I kept up my contact with Mohammed and in 1960 suggested we write a book on oil.[7] We did this, but I have to say that he did two-thirds of the work. The book could have been written without me; it could not have been written without him.

One day, in 1951, Chatham House contacted me and asked what had happened with my book on Egypt. Two things had happened.

First, it had run out of print almost immediately, and, since we were in the postwar shortage period, it was not reprinted. Second, it had been banned by the Egyptian police as a subversive book, which had delighted me immensely. Now things had changed and I was asked to revise it. The result was *Egypt at Mid-Century*. A few years later they asked me to write another book, because the earlier one had ended just after the Revolution of 1952. I went to Egypt and worked for a few months. It was just after the breakup of the United Arab Republic and the secret police were everywhere. But I had a great piece of luck. I knew a man at the planning institute who allowed me to use its library; I thereby had access to all the unpublished reports and read them eagerly. This was the last of my books on Egypt.[8]

When I started in the field of Middle East economics, in the 1940s, there was hardly anything on the subject, and whatever one contributed was valuable, but by the 1960s a lot was coming out. I eventually came to the conclusion that research on Middle East economics should be done in the region and by institutions like the central banks or the World Bank, which had access to information. And I found myself at an impasse in my own research. I did not know quite what to do.

In 1960, my dean and friend, Schuyler Wallace, said to me, "Have you thought of economic history?" I knew he was right. I had always been historically minded. I liked tracing things back, and there was almost nothing on the Middle East. I started putting together a course on the economic history of the Arab countries. Slowly my interest shifted more and more toward economic history, though not completely.

The result was the series of books on economic history: *The Economic History of the Middle East, 1800–1914*;[9] *The Economic History of Iran, 1800–1914*;[10] *The Economic History of Turkey, 1800–1914*;[11] and *The Fertile Crescent, 1800–1914: A Documentary Economic History*.[12] Each contains a series of essays, previously unpublished archival documents, translated texts from various languages, appendices on weights and measures, and a bibliography. *The Economic History of the Middle East and North Africa* is a synthesis of the more detailed documentary histories.[13]

NEG: What were the sources for your historical studies?
ISSAWI: I started with Western sources. First I read what was published and then I got into the parliamentary papers and consular reports, and went on to the archives, starting with two British archives – the Public Record Office and the India Office – and then the French Foreign Office and the Austrian archives. In 1975 I went to Istanbul to work in the Ottoman archives a bit. It took so long to get

permission that by the time I got it my leave was almost over and I had very little time left to work. I have also worked in the United States archives which contain a certain amount of material. My great regret is not having worked more on local material. This I think is a big weakness, but because of political circumstances in Lebanon and other countries, it was not easy to get there.

NEG: Could you assess your underlying ideas in your scholarly work?
ISSAWI: The dominant note in my thinking has been the sense of underdevelopment of the Middle East compared to Europe and also Japan and some other areas, in the economic, social, and cultural fields. I have tried to apply economic categories whenever I could, simple ones, nothing terribly convoluted, things like rent and marginal productivity and comparative advantage. Until about 1960 I studied this in contemporary terms, focusing on development. After that I thought in more historical terms: the overtaking of the Middle East by Europe in, say, the fourteenth century and the growing gap between the two civilizations.[14] My basic idea already expressed in 1942 in my first book on Egypt was that after 1800 A.D. there was a kind of world economy which came to include the Middle East, but I never tried to work it out in terms of centre and periphery in the way my good friend Immanuel Wallerstein did.[15] My starting point in all my work was that there were economically developed and under-developed countries, and how can we develop the underdeveloped ones.

NEG: Could you comment on your methodological approach to your historical work?
ISSAWI: It should be remembered that, although always very interested in history, I was trained as an economist, not as an historian. During the first half of my working life I thought of myself as a development economist, which means I was concerned with comparison, patterns and trends – indeed my favourite definition of an economist is one who, when asked, "How is your spouse?" replies, "Compared to what?" The comparative method seems to me to make sense for the study of both economic development and economic history. Hence my constant attempt to compare various aspects of the Middle Eastern economies and societies with their counterparts in Western Europe and, to the extent of my knowledge, with Russia, Latin America, the Balkans, Japan, and China. This question, which seems to be of very little interest to professional historians of the Middle East, has been one of my central concerns.

I find the lack of *trends* in the Middle East – that is after the first few, formative, centuries – rather frustrating. In Athenian, Roman, and European – particularly English – political history, one sees a steady development, from one state to its logical successor, "from precedent to precedent". The same is true of European economic history in, say, 1100–1800 A.D. I do not see any such trends in Middle Eastern history, though the fault may lie in my inadequate knowledge. I do not see any progress in Middle Eastern science, philosophy, technology, and economic thought after, say, 1400. Indeed I would go further and say that in the Middle East the period 1400–1800 is one of stagnation. The prevailing pattern seems to be the endless cycles so well analysed by Ibn Khaldun. Of course his model does not apply to the Ottoman Empire, or other "gunpowder empires" to use Marshall Hodgson's term, since they were more able to curb nomad incursions. However, they too seem to have gone round in cycles in which governors, notables, and the urban populace fight and change places with no more result than a replacement of personnel and without bringing about meaningful change. I see no significant trend, no movement from somewhere to somewhere, no progress. Unhistorical as this may seem, I cannot help regarding this aspect of Middle Eastern history as a major deficiency.

I should add that, in its formative centuries, Islamic civilization does show very significant trends. There was the establishment of an imperial state, the elaboration of a religious institution with its law and dogmas and the absorption of a large elements from Greek, Persian, Indian, and other cultures. This is very well brought out in H. A. R. Gibb's essay, "An interpretation of Islamic history".[16]

Of course one may object that it is absurd to expect the Middle East to follow the European or any other pattern. The region should be studied on its own terms, not on those borrowed from another culture. But it is *not* absurd to apply to it questions arising from the study of other cultures, and this is a perfectly legitimate activity for the social scientist. By doing so, a much clearer picture is obtained of the place of any given culture in world history and of the contribution it has made to human progress. In addition, a clearer understanding of the course of Middle Eastern history itself becomes possible.

That said, I should perhaps add that nothing annoys me more than people who spend their time on methodology. I don't believe you should argue about how to do the job; you should do the job. On the other hand I am perfectly aware that what is most prestigious in every science these days is not what you do but the methodological part. This is what gets people excited.

NEG: Why do you suppose this is the case?
ISSAWI: Because people are impressed by high-sounding jargon. People like playing with prestigious ideas. Moreover, methodology

provides an excellent excuse for not getting into the nitty-gritty of history and avoiding the wearisome, but necessary, drudgery over original sources.

I do not like playing with those kind of ideas. If did, I would have stuck to philosophy which deals with worthwhile ideas. I've always been interested in the doing of things rather than how things ought to be done or could be done. I have always avoided fashionable trends and have not joined cliques or "schools", and I've always tried to avoid controversy. If people insist on quarrelling with me, I am willing to pick up a fight, but I am not one who says, "Is this a private fight or may anyone join in?"

I stopped being an activist ages ago. One day I woke up and made a great discovery. I said to myself, "I'm not God, and history is not going to go the way I want it to, but the way it is going to go." History flows. That is my deepest belief. One or two people may have influenced history; Muhammad did, Lenin did, or so I have always believed; I am not quite so sure now. I once wrote an essay that began by asking if Muhammad made any difference and concluded that he did.[17] In this, as in so many respects, I follow my great *shaykh*, Ibn Khaldun. It is quite clear that he does not think that, with very few exceptions, "great men" significantly change the course of history. The course of history is determined mainly by such impersonal factors as *'asabiyya*, demography, etc. – for instance he clearly understood the changes brought about by the Black Death, by which "the whole inhabited earth was transformed".[18]

I am quite uninterested in Foucault or Derrida or Deconstruction – they cannot possibly help me do economics or economic history. I've always wanted to replace Deconstruction by "Reconstruction". This says that a text means what I want it to mean! I am delighted that Deconstruction is passing out of fashion, after it was discovered that its founder, Paul de Man, was a nasty Nazi! In any case, life is short, and I felt that I had another job to do. My job was to get something out in a field in which there was nothing at all. In my historical work, I take from the mainstream school of economics, Adam Smith, Ricardo, Malthus, John Stuart Mill, Alfred Marshall, J. R. Hicks and of course the economic historians, Tawney, Clapham, Henri Sée, and others.

NEG: Were you influenced by the Annales historians?
ISSAWI: I read Lucien Febvre in the early 1940s but discovered Marc Bloch relatively late, well after the war. I read Braudel's *Le Monde méditerranéen* in the late 1950s and got very excited about it. I liked his approach very much. He has his biases, and sometimes goes off at the deep end, but I don't think that detracts from his achievements. For example – it is a trifle – he mentions that the Arabs did not have to

invent a certain kind of sail because they navigated the canal between the Nile and the Red Sea. He doesn't seem to be aware that the canal was blocked in the eighth century and never reopened. Another example: he says that in seventeenth-century Amsterdam the working class was worse off than elsewhere because the cost of living was so high. But the cost of living is always highest in the leading metropolis and he did not ask himself why people flocked to Amsterdam – presumably because wages were still higher. Having said that, I am very impressed by Braudel although he is not very good on the Middle East.

NEG: Did the political events of the era affect your scholarly work?
ISSAWI: The main formative influences in my life were the Depression, the rise of Fascism, and the anticipation of the War. I started with a very favourable view of the Soviet Union, a view which changed radically in the late 1930s. In 1948 I was very concerned about the future of Palestine. I was still at the Arab office, followed the events day by day, and thought the Arabs would do better. In 1956 I was horrified by what the British and French were doing but not surprised by the Israeli participation. In 1967 I was out of commission in hospital. So the war had no immediate impact on me and, although I realized that it would have grave consequences, I felt completely powerless.

At Columbia, however, I was dragged into the fray. I would have been thought of as one of the more liberal members of the faculty. In fact I later told the students, "I am part of the Old Left which you people are rapidly transforming into the New Right!" Fortunately that did not happen; I thoroughly dislike the New Right. When, in 1968, the *jacquerie* came, I was expecting it. I was not in close touch with the students, but my wife was. She was Graduate Student Advisor and they used to talk to her. She was uneasy and tried to talk to the administration – many of whom were close friends – but on this subject they just would not listen.

Although I fully sympathized with the students' concern about Vietnam, and even joined some marches, I was very angry with them for wrecking the universities. I found myself in the company of many professors, each of whom identified it with some prior experience. We had people from Germany and Austria, almost all of whom saw in the students young Nazi thugs. Others identified the police with the Cossacks beating up the unhappy peasants, the students. Still others identified the police with the fascist French. What fascinated me was how each person saw it through his own prism. It was an interesting lesson in historiography, how the eyewitnesses were influenced by their own experiences. If I had been the president I would have called the police the very first day and thrown the students out of the buildings they occupied. I began to understand how revolutions are made by a very small number of people, how the authorities vacillate and fail to act. I think this was one of the most interesting experiences of my life.

NEG: Could you comment on the critiques of "orientalism" of recent years?
ISSAWI: The positive contribution of the critiques of orientalism is that the orientalists took themselves too seriously and needed taking down. Edward Said, however, should have known that everybody is imperfect, everybody is biased, everybody sees only part of the truth, everybody is a child of his age and culture. Why should the orientalists be an exception? Since Europe was the centre of power they saw things through European eyes. What other eyes could they have seen things through? You are either centric (Euro, Sino, Muslim, etc.) or you are eccentric, in the strict sense of the word. To expect the nineteenth-century English and French to look at the Orient as we look at it today is absurd and unrealistic. True, Europe was arrogant and hegemonic. In 1961, and again in 1981, I wrote essays on changes in the Western perception of the Orient.[19] Nor is there anything peculiar in a people considering itself the greatest people in the world: the Chinese thought that, so did the Greeks, so did the Arabs. What is peculiar is that Europe is the only culture in world history which took a serious interest in other cultures and set about to study them. The Greeks took a lot from the Egyptians and the Near East, but they never tried to learn their languages. Nor did the Romans, except for Greek. I have always wondered how the Arabs could look at the ruins at Baalbak and not have the least curiosity about the people who had built them. Even the great Ibn Khaldun failed to realize that the ruins in North Africa were Roman. And yet, in North Africa, in earlier centuries, and in Spain, there were local Christians who knew Latin and could have helped them identify the monuments. Of course the Europeans had their blind spots. What is remarkable is that they were so taken with the Sumerians, Egyptians, Hittites and other buried civilizations, whom the Europeans could hardly wish to colonize! We should be eternally grateful to the orientalists for unearthing these civilizations and deciphering their scripts – who else could have? And also to the Arabists and Iranianists who taught us so much, men like Dane, De Sacy, De Slane, Dozy, Goldziher. So my answer to Said is that of course orientalists were biased, how could they not be? One can be sure that our biases will seem as silly and wicked to future generations as the nineteenth-century biases look to us.

That said, I admit that it is irritating when Europeans and Americans pontificate and say, "We know, and you natives don't know..." My answer, when asked condescending questions, has always been to take the offensive. For instance, when people would find out that I was a Christian they would ask, "Did you get converted or your parents?" I would say, "My ancestors were Christians when yours were eating raw meat," which is strictly true. I remember someone – I think it was Albert Hourani – when asked if he was Syrian or Assyrian replying, "Are you English or Assenglish?"

NEG: Then can we strive for objectivity in history?
ISSAWI: We certainly must try, but I think the Arabs got it right. They took the Greek word for history, *historia,* and made of it *usturah* or "myth", whereas the Arabic word for history is *tarikh.* I often think the Arabs stumbled upon something very important, that history contains a large amount of myth. No sane person would deny that there was a man called Julius Caesar, that Julius Caesar conquered Gaul, that Julius Caesar seized power in Rome, and that Julius Caesar was murdered ... these are objective facts. So history is grounded in facts. But once we leave that kind of fact we are in the middle of conjecture and controversy. I suppose the best you can do is to read the historical materials, try to understand what happened, and form your own opinion, stating with the necessary modesty that this is the best we have so far, with the perfect acceptance of the fact that in less than fifty years' time – or at the rate things are going today in five years' time – someone will say you are all wet.

NEG: How can we incorporate women into the economic history of the Middle East?
ISSAWI: We should as far as we can – after all, they are half the population but they are not included in the labour force. That is one of the biggest jokes ever because women sweat blood. A recent study has shown that, in Southern Sudan, women spend on the average six hours per day carrying water, but they are not included in statistics on the labour force! Obviously we have to revise our whole notion of the labour force, of what constitutes work, to include women. This is easy for the present day, but when you come to past history it is much more difficult. The sources do not tell you very much, but I think if we look very hard we will find something. I tried to keep my eyes open when writing my last books on economic history. Once in a while you come across some indication, but the sources are not very informative. You have to go at it indirectly. You get quite a bit of information on women in the silk reeling industry whether in Turkey or Lebanon because women played a very important part there. You can study the waqfs, as Fifi Marsot [Professor Afaf Lutfi al-Sayyid Marsot] has done, or the *sijills,* as Gabriel Baer has done, and see that women were

important property owners.[20] Another scholar, Ronald Jennings, worked on Kayseri, in Anatolia, and studied its records.[21] He learned quite a lot about moneylending and found that many of the moneylenders were women. Abd al-Karim Rafeq has a similar study on Gaza.[22] So you get snippets here and there. If you go on digging you will get something, and it is very much worth doing.

NEG: What would you consider your main contributions to Middle East studies?
ISSAWI: I think that my main contribution has been the four monstrous books on economic history which I fear are unbearably dull. But there is a lot of information in them and they were the first in a new field. I tried to synthesize my ideas in *An Economic History of the Middle East and North Africa*.[23] It took a tremendous effort bottling up all that information on some twenty countries over two hundred years and putting things together. I did it just in time. I was working on it when Albert Hourani had a heart attack. I maintain that there is a formula: "Issawi Equals Hourani Plus Two". What he does I do two years later. So when he had his heart attack I knew I would have one and prepared for it. I delivered the copy-edited manuscript to the publisher the day before I had my heart attack. I could never have completed the manuscript after that.

I think my best work is *The Economic History of the Middle East and North Africa*, various essays in *The Arab Legacy* and elsewhere, and *Issawi's Laws of Social Motion*.[24] I will insist that you put in a commercial for the latter, as being humorous and wise. It is the most important thing I have written.

NEG: In closing, do you have any advice for students who are considering specializing in Middle East economic history?
ISSAWI: My first advice is that of Bernard Shaw to young men about to get married: "Don't", not because the subject is not worthwhile but because it is difficult. An economic historian must master economics and the main Middle Eastern languages in addition to European languages. You need a grounding in historiography, which generally means studying European history quite closely. You have to have a nodding acquaintance with other cultures – with China and Japan, for example. You should be aware of what archaeology and anthropology can contribute to economic history. When you have sat down and done all that and read your Arabic, Turkish, or Persian sources, time is not in your favour . . . So I'd ask the students very seriously to ask themselves why? My answer would be that without a knowledge of its economic history we are not going to understand Middle Eastern history. And there is so much to be done. But you must be prepared

to sweat blood on, say, Arabic for several years or so and preferably learn another Middle Eastern language – Turkish is very essential for the economic history of the modern Middle East – and in that time you could have learned French, German, and Russian put together. Are you sure you want this? If you say yes, Okay then, let us begin. And welcome to our small, but growing fellowship.

Notes

1. For further information see Edward Atiyah, *An Arab Tells His Story: A Study in Loyalties* (London: John Murray, 1946).
2. Charles Issawi, *Egypt: An Economic and Social Analysis* (New York and London: Oxford University Press, 1947).
3. *Silsilat al-abhath al-ijtimaʿiya,* later *al-Abhath* (Beirut).
4. Charles Issawi, *An Arab Philosophy of History* (London: John Murray, 1950).
5. Ibn Khaldun, *The Muqaddimah: An Introduction to History,* translation by Franz Rosenthal (London: Routledge & Kegan Paul, 1958).
6. Arab Office, *The Future of Palestine* (London: Arab Office, 1947).
7. Charles Issawi and Mohammed Yeganeh, *The Economics of Middle Eastern Oil* (New York: Frederick A. Praeger, 1962).
8. Charles Issawi, *Egypt in Revolution: An Economic Analysis* (London: Oxford University Press, 1963).
9. —— (ed.), *The Economic History of the Middle East, 1800–1914* (Chicago: University of Chicago Press, 1966).
10. —— (ed.), *The Economic History of Iran, 1800–1914* (Chicago: Chicago University Press, 1971).
11. —— (ed.), *The Economic History of Turkey, 1800–1914* (Chicago: Chicago University Press, 1980).
12. —— (ed.), *The Fertile Crescent, 1800–1914: a Documentary History* (New York and London: Oxford University Press, 1988).
13. ——, *An Economic History of the Middle East and North Africa* (New York: Columbia University Press, 1982).
14. See Chapter 8 in Issawi, *The Arab World's Legacy: Essays by Charles Issawi* (Princeton: Darwin Press, 1981); ——, "The Middle East in the world context: a historical view" in Georges Sabagh (ed.), *The Modern Economic and Social History of the Middle East in its World Context* (Cambridge: Cambridge University Press, 1989), pp. 1–28; and ——, "Technology, energy and civilization: some historical observations", *International Journal of Middle Eastern Studies,* 23 (1991), pp. 281–9.
15. Immanuel Wallerstein, *Capitalist Agriculture and the Origins of the European World-Economy in the Sixteenth Century* (New York: Academic Press, 1974); ——, *The Capitalist World-Economy: Essays* (New York: Cambridge University Press, 1979); ——, *Mercantilism and the Consolidation of the European World-Economy, 1600–1750* (New York: Academic Press, 1980).
16. H. A. R. Gibb, "An interpretation of Islamic history", republished in Stanford J. Shaw and William R. Polk (eds.), *Studies on the Civilization of Islam* (Boston: Beacon Press, 1962), pp. 1–33.

17. Charles Issawi, "The historical role of Muhammad", *Muslim World*, 40 (1950), pp. 83–95.

18. Ibn Khaldun, *al-Muqaddima*, edition E. M. Quatremère (Paris: l'Institut impérial de France, 1858), vol. 1, p. 51, vol. 2, p. 264.

19. Charles Issawi, "Reflections on the study of oriental civilization", and "Changing Western perceptions of the Orient", *The Arab World's Legacy*.

20. See below, Marsot personal narrative Chapter 4, and Gabriel Baer, *A History of Landownership in Modern Egypt, 1800–1950* (New York: Oxford University Press, 1962).

21. Ronald Jennings, "Loans and credit in the early seventeenth-century Ottoman judicial records", *Journal of the Economic and Social History of the Orient*, 16 (April, 1973), pp. 168–216, see especially pp. 194–7; see also his "Women in early seventeenth-century Ottoman judicial records: the Sharia court of Anatolian Kayseri", *Journal of the Economic and Social History of the Orient*, 18 (1975), pp. 53–114.

22. Abdul-Karim Rafeq, "Ghazza: dirasa ʿumraniyya wa ijtimaʿiyya wa iqtisadiyya min khilal al-watha'iq al-sharʿiyya, 1273–1277" (Gaza: a socio-economic and urban study, 1857–1861) (Damascus: n.p. 1980).

23. Charles Issawi, *An Economic History of the Middle East and North Africa*.

24. ——, *Issawi's Laws of Social Motion* (New York: Hawthorn Press, 1973); enlarged edition (Princeton: Darwin Press, 1991).

ANDRÉ RAYMOND was born in Montargis, France, in 1925. He studied general history at the Sorbonne, taught high school in Tunis, and prepared a D.Phil. at Oxford and a *Doctorat d'État* in Paris. For nine years he was director of the *Institut Français d'Études Arabes* in Damascus. He was professor of history at the University of Provence, Aix-en-Provence, until his retirement. He was director of the *Centre de Recherches et d'Études sur les Sociétés Mediterranéennes* (CRESM) and vice-president of the *Institut du Monde Arabe de Paris* and helped found and subsequently presided over the *Association Française pour l'Étude du Monde Arabe et Musulman* (AFEMAM). He teaches part of the year at Princeton University. He and his wife live in Aix-en-Provence.

Interviewed in Westwood, near the University of California, Los Angeles on 11 and 14 April 1990, by Nancy Gallagher.

NEG: Shall we begin with your childhood environment?
RAYMOND: Montargis was a small town of 15,000 inhabitants, located to the south of Paris. There was no contact at all with the Arab world. Until my parents, all my family had been peasants. One of my two grandfathers was illiterate and began working for other people at the age of seven years. My father was a very intelligent, very capable person, whose education was stopped at elementary school because my grandparents did not have the means to give him a more advanced education. My father went to war from 1914 to 1918. After that he wanted to have a more stimulating life than that of a peasant. My mother also did not want to be a peasant – she wanted to be a teacher – so my parents came to the town of Montargis after World War I. It is necessary to understand that until 1939 the peasants in France lived as if in the middle of the nineteenth century. It was a harsh life, without many material comforts or great cultural possibilities. It was truly the French peasant world of Zola and Maupassant, nothing like what agriculture has now become. So, my parents moved to town and became workers. My father became an insurance agent and my

mother a milliner. She made hats at a time when women wore hats. So they became petite bourgeoisie, but with a completely rural origin.

I attended a very provincial primary school. Then, from 1941 to 1943 I studied in Paris at a great French *lycée* (high school), Louis le Grand, in the classes which prepared for the *École Normale Supérieur*. But I left the *École Normale* for various reasons. I found it a bit oppressive, and when my family in 1943 was uprooted following difficulties with the Germans, I followed courses at the Sorbonne where I completed a *licence d'histoire* and the *agregation*. The agregation is theoretically a competitive examination to qualify one to teach in a secondary school. In practice, it is a diploma of a very high level which prepares people to go on for advanced studies. During my two years' preparation I studied general history, not at all the history of the Arab world. There was a bit of interest in colonial history, but at the. Sorbonne it did not have much importance. The non-European world, perhaps excepting the Americas, was not an object for study at university. The professors I had at the Sorbonne were all very classical historians in the sense of their formation and their interests. Not one of them had submitted to the influence of the Annales School. They were persons with a very traditional formation. One, Renouvin, was a specialist in diplomatic history and in European history: his interest in the problems of Asia was rather unusual at that time.

In 1945 I did a *diplôme d'études supérieures* on "The terror in the district of Montargis", with Febvre, then the most famous historian of the French Revolution. The *diplôme* was a sort of short dissertation of one to two hundred pages prepared before the *agregation*. It was a very solid preparation.

NEG: What was Febvre like to work with?
RAYMOND: As a "director" he was non-existent. I saw him only two times, the day when he gave me my subject, and the day when I returned to submit it. At that time the professors at the Sorbonne gave the impression of arriving on a little cloud before their students. They descended from their little cloud, and they installed themselves on their podiums. When the class was finished, they arose on their cloud, and one did not see them any more. One never saw professors at that time. For us, professors were situated in a universe very superior to ours.

NEG: When did you decide to become an historian?
RAYMOND: I was always interested in history, and I always wanted to be an historian. I remember that when I was about eleven my parents went on a cruise to Ireland. I asked them to bring me back a book on

the history of the country, and I was very disappointed when they brought me a novel.

NEG: Did you have brothers and sisters?
RAYMOND: Yes, I had a brother four years older than I. He had a brilliant university career; he is a sociologist who taught at the University of Nanterre. He had a career more, let us say, diverse than mine. It was disrupted by the Occupation. My brother was very active in the Resistance. At one time in 1943 he had to disappear in the "maquis", because the Gestapo were after him. When they did not find him they looked for my father, and when they did not find him because he was in hiding, they arrested my mother. But, finally, it turned out well because, happily, she was freed after spending several months in prison in Fresnes. This was fortunate because otherwise she would have been deported to Germany, and God knows what would have happened. My father died before the liberation of France and my brother, who was still underground, was very much affected by his death.

I was also in the Resistance but much less actively and later than my brother. Anyway the war deeply affected my career. I was very influenced by Marxism. Like many in the anti-Nazi resistance, I joined the communist party. It was largely a reaction to the role played by the USSR during the war. I joined the party mainly for intellectual reasons. I had read the classic Marxist works, and I had the impression that Marxism constituted a means of understanding the world and a means of rendering its history intelligible. I remained a communist from the liberation of France in 1944 until about 1951.

From 1944 to 1947 I was a militant in the communist party on the one hand and on the other I was reading at the Bibliothèque Nationale. For the *agregation* one had to be up on what had been written, and on what was being published. I began to be a bit interested in non-European history, in particular the problem which Iran posed between Russia and Great Britain before the war of 1914. But when I passed the *agregation* in 1947 I wanted to work on the Paris Commune. It is very clear in this case that my interests were political. I did not gain my interest in social and economic history through my professors, nor through the Annales School which at that time was coming out of hiding, but from my Marxist leaning and training.

The Annales School had had a great importance before the war, with Bloch, Lucien Febvre, and others. But Bloch was dead, and Braudel had not yet come to the fore. It took a few years after the war for it to revive. I completed my formation at a time when the Annales School was in eclipse.

NEG: Can you explain very briefly the Annales School for the students who are not familiar with it?
RAYMOND: It is a school of history which reacts against what it derisively calls the history of events, of the history of actors, of individuals. It is a history that strives to extricate profound, sometimes underground currents, that have, over a long period of time (*la longue durée*), shaped the evolution of economy and society. It is a school which developed before the war under the influence of Bloch and of Lucien Febvre. In effect, it worked a bit like a lobby, in the good sense of the word, on behalf of equalizing history. The Annales School has had a certain influence on the study of the Arab world, through the work of Braudel, who after the war became a prominent historian, and whose orientation was Mediterranean history. This led to an opening on the Muslim Arab world. Claude Cahen later led scholars to study the economic and social history of the Middle East. Certain books of his do not suggest this; in particular, I think of his thesis on Syria in the time of the Crusades. But Cahen himself was communist at that time. He was very influenced by Marxism and he progressively defined the necessity of a social and economic history applied to the Arab world. The history of the Near East at that time had not yet entered the hands of the specialists. It was often the linguists who were self-improvised historians, and Cahen was one of the first historians by formation who was oriented towards the history of the Arab and Muslim world.

In 1947 my life took a turn linked to two things. First, the aftermath of the Occupation which was a very hard and dark period and a period which generated an extraordinary feeling of claustrophobia for those who had been subjected to it. After the war, I wanted to leave this closed world in which I had lived for five years. Secondly, being communist, I was struck by the events which followed the war and which were linked to the Arab world, struck by the manner in which French politics had led to the catastrophe of the mandates in the Middle East. I was opposed to the bloody repression in North Africa and in Indochina. I was interested to see the Arab world for myself.

On the other hand, I saw the problem of Palestine with much ambiguity. I rather sympathized with the implantation of the Jews in Palestine. It was of course the result of the obsession with anti-Semitism which had been generated by the Occupation and the Holocaust. I had Jewish friends who had been persecuted; certain ones had been deported as were many people in France. I had the sentiment that there was a great historical injustice with regard to the Jews. I understood completely the Jewish point of view regarding the emigration to Palestine and shared the attitudes of the majority of my compatriots. For instance, I remember following the affair of the *Exodus* with a keen sympathy for the Jewish immigrants and not much understanding of the hostile reaction of the Arabs. It was normal at that time and, bizarre as it may appear today, progressive people would at the same time evince anti-colonial feelings in North Africa and sympathy for Zionism in Palestine. It took me a while to put things in order.

And so, in 1947, having passed the *agrégation,* I was ready to teach in a secondary school. As it turned out there were some positions open in North Africa, so I asked to have a post in Tunisia.

NEG: Why did you ask for a post in Tunisia?
RAYMOND: Partly because I had wanted to see other places and this was the chance. Also, I reflected that Tunisia was near to Italy so it would facilitate trips that I wanted to make there. In the event I did not travel to Italy until much later so that did no good. Not so much a direct interest in Tunisia or in the Arab world, more a preoccupation with colonial problems seen from the angle of decolonization. There it was my communist leanings that led me. I did not want to go to Algeria because it was a French territory where the colonization was still very strong. Tunisia was not independent, but it had a much more autonomous status. Having to choose between teaching in a French *lycée* and going to Tunisia, I opted for exoticism. There was no preparation for travel in my familial or local traditions. Tunisia was a Mediterranean country, while Montargis was one of the places farthest from the sea in France. But perhaps my literary education, my readings – Gide and Camus among others – had oriented me towards North Africa. So in October 1947, I left for Tunisia to become an instructor in a secondary school, a *lycée.* It was my initiation into the problems of the Arab world and more generally the colonial world.

I had my first introduction the moment I boarded the train which would take me from Paris to Marseilles where I would embark for Tunisia. At that time one did not take the aeroplane, but went by boat; it was a trip of three days. On the train I met a young woman who lived in Tunisia who gave me a picture of colonial attitudes which profoundly impressed me. In comparing Algeria and Tunisia, she said that she found the natives in Algeria unbearable – probably because she considered Algeria a French land – but that she could tolerate the presence of the natives in Tunisia a little better. I knew bits and pieces of colonial life from my historical and political formation, but I became truly conscious of the depth and violence of French racism in North Africa during this trip. And so I arrived in Tunisia.

It was raining the day I arrived in Tunis and cold, and I found the port of La Goulette very ugly. My first contact was a bit sad. During the first months I lived in the "European city" which I found without interest and completely displeasing, and it was only gradually that I could discover the charm of the *madina,* the old town. Among the elements which helped me to be in contact with the true Tunis was the friendship of the parents of T. Guiga, a student I had known well in Paris. I was introduced to Guiga's father, an extraordinary person. He was a teacher who had worked with the great French Arabist, Georges Marçais, and who had with him made an anthology of Arab texts. I often went to his home in Bab Jazira. This local contact helped me to understand the principles and realities of colonial attitudes and racist prejudices.

I was still a communist at that time, and I continued to be active in the Tunisian communist party, a rather odd organization, which brought a lot of Jewish intellectuals together with a few Arab workers. At that time the official line called for union with the people of France and an alliance among colonial peoples and the French working class which would lead to a harmonious evolution of the colonial countries. It was a view that was completely out of touch with reality as the "incidents" in Algeria in 1945 and the war just beginning in Indochina had already proved. I spent four years in Tunis and I participated in the myopia of the Tunisian communists' attitude towards the Tunisian problem, that of gaining independence; but the communists looked at it in a rather oblique manner. They thought that what was important for the independence of Tunisia was the evolution of France toward a popular democracy. So they had difficult or distant relations with the Tunisian nationalist movement. I found myself in an organization which was supposed to be "popular" but which was truly disconnected from what was happening in Tunisia at that time. If I had not been a member of the communist party, I would have moved closer to the national cause. I would have understood very quickly the importance of the national movement and in particular the Neo-Destour movement which embodied it, with Bourguiba, just back from exile. But the fact that I was active in the Tunisian Communist Party closed my eyes to the Tunisian reality and made me lose long years before I understood colonial problems and Arab problems in general. Anyway it was better to be a militant in such an organization than to follow the general trend of European thought which was in line with the colonial policy.

I learned to understand what a colonial country was, what the French colonials were, who the truly unbearable people were, people who were quite unable to understand the aspirations of the indigenous population. Tunisia, at that time, was just coming out of several years of drought and was in a state of frightful misery. Its social and economic conditions were appalling but it was a very beautiful country all the same.

Since I was in Tunis, I decided to learn the language of the people. So I began to learn Arabic. This caused much hilarity amongst my friends, many of them Tunisian Jews who were totally impregnated with French culture. They found it very funny that a Frenchman – one said "Fransawi" at that time with much derision – disembarked from France with his liberal ideals should set about learning Arabic. As for the French themselves, they were puzzled by the fact that a French teacher was not only a member of the communist party but was also interested in Arab history. As I was *agregé*, that is to say the most elevated level of secondary teachers, I had been appointed to the Lycée Carnot, the grand institution of French instruction in Tunis. There were organized courses in Arabic which were not very popular in the French community where Arabic civilization was judged of rather questionable value, and the Arabic language as useless. And so I began studying classical Arabic at the Lycée Carnot.

I was then thinking of doing what Maxime Rodinson and Montgomery Watt have done: work on the origins of Islam, the period of the Prophet, and try to understand the social and economic factors which led to the emergence of Islam. I suppose that this ambition was the result of the interbreeding of my Marxist convictions and of my interest in the history of the Arabs. I remember that I went to see Claude Cahen on one of my holidays in France. It was at the time when he was still professor at Strasburg, well-known for his works and communist convictions. Cahen was a very open person and he received me kindly. I explained what I wanted to do. He felt that my educational background was too poor to permit me to engage in such a complicated enterprise. So I gave up the idea of working on classical Islam. I was very active at that time. I had my work as a teacher and I was fully engaged in political and labour causes. I was also very interested in the cinema. Cinema had always been my great passion, and remained so until I was obliged to replace it with my passion for history; I could not do the two at the same time. I had purchased a camera – it was very expensive at that time – and made an anti-colonialist film on Tunisia. If I had not been a communist in Tunisia I would have filmed very interesting things; for instance, the national movement at its beginnings. But because I was a communist, I filmed the Congress of the Communist Party and communist demonstrations which were of no interest and were without future. The Tunisian reality was elsewhere.

I spent two years at the Lycée Carnot. My students were French, Europeans, Europeanized Jews, Maltese, and Muslim Tunisians. After a certain time I began to understand the uselessness of professional activity in a French milieu, so I asked to be appointed to the College Sadiqi, the native secondary school. It caused a small scandal because one had never seen a French *agregé* teaching at the Lycée Carnot, the most attractive position that a French teacher could have in Tunis, who asked to go to the College Sadiqi, the breeding-ground of Tunisian nationalists. I was appointed to the College Sadiqi, and I think that it was an important step in my career because I then began to fully understand national problems and to be in contact with Tunisian realities. I was still wrapped in my communist cocoon, with my ears and eyes corked. But gradually I began to have a clearer view of what was going on around me, which also helped me to change my scholarly objectives. The colonial problem was the fundamental problem for Tunisia, but more and more I had the feeling that the colonial era was a sort of a European parenthesis which would come to an end. I thought that it would be important to study what preceded the imperialist period, to study the history of Tunisia, an Arab country, before the installation of colonialism. I thus began to be interested in the history of Tunisia in the nineteenth century. I completely abandoned my first Marxist objective of working on the French Commune of 1871. I abandoned my romantic idea of working on the era before the emergence of Islam. I began to interest myself in the pre-colonial period, to read on this period, which was not an easy task because it was a period about which very little was known at the time, in which few people were interested, and on which very few documents had been published. The great Arabic chronicles on the history of Tunisia before colonization had not been published yet and were largely ignored.

I then decided to enter the French academic world which one did by registering a topic for a doctoral dissertation (*thèse d'état*), the first great moment in the existence of a French "academic", the second being the moment he submits it. Having decided to work on Tunisia in the nineteenth century and having begun to cut out the underbrush of the terrain and to read the literature on these problems, I had now to find a professor to direct my work. There were few people interested in such problems at that time in France, and I quite naturally made my way to Charles-André Julien, the great personage on anti-colonial history, who had been appointed to the Sorbonne following the war.

NEG: Hadn't Charles-André Julien been in the communist party?
RAYMOND: He had been for a short period a long time before. He was a communist in 1920 when he took the side of the Bolsheviks after the split in the Congress of Tours. He played a very important role in the Communist International because he represented North Africa. One or two voyages to the USSR and his personal reflections led him to quit the communist party and to enter the socialist party. When I explained to him what I wished to do he did not encourage me at all. He understood that the study I contemplated would be very difficult

and would pose problems with sources, with language, and with technical difficulties. He recommended that I write a thesis on Paul Cambon and the beginnings of the French protectorate in Tunisia, a clear-cut topic with easily exploitable sources. That did not tempt at all, because what interested me was not French politics, but Tunisia and especially the Tunisians. I wanted to try to comprehend how an indigenous society functioned, and how the evolution of Tunisian history had led to the creation of the protectorate. For me Paul Cambon was completely without interest. Julien was a man who was always alive, with an extremely open spirit. He thought that I had a certain human quality, and he was amused enough to see me as a militant communist, a stage which he had passed a long time before. So he accepted my idea though he certainly found it impractical. With Julien, I never had or rarely had professional discussions on my subject of research. Rather, we discussed at length French politics, communism, Stalinism, colonization, decolonization, the history of contemporary North Africa, and so forth. I should remark here that I never considered that the world turned around my research as if it were of planetary interest, as do some of my colleagues for their own work. It is probably my "English" side; I am not naturally inclined to engage in shop talk. So in 1951 I registered my thesis subject as "Tunisia in the nineteenth century" with Julien as director.

Also in 1951, a fundamental change happened in my thinking. I decided to leave Tunisia. This may seem a bit strange, considering that I had just decided to do a study on Tunisia. On the one hand, I wished to begin to work in the archives of the Affaires Étrangères located in Paris, and to learn Arabic in the École des Langues Orientales to get the necessary training for later research in the Arabic archives in Tunis. On the other hand, I had seen the problems of Tunisia, and I thought that it was not necessary to stay there for ever. So I asked to return to Paris as a teacher. But I was appointed to Bordeaux in the south of France rather than to Paris because of my negative administrative report, a result of my political opinions and my union activities in Tunis. At that time I did not want to go to Bordeaux because my immediate aim was the study of Arabic.

During a conversation, Julien had told me that, if it interested me, he could obtain a scholarship for me to go to Oxford where a new college, St Antony's College, had just been created by a Frenchman (Antonein Besse). At first I found the idea altogether exotic. But with more reflection, and with the threat of an appointment in Bordeaux, I thought the suggestion interesting, knowing that H. A. R. Gibb was at Oxford. So I finally answered that I would like to go. It was a decision of the same order as going to Tunisia in 1947. It was partly accidental, but it had an utmost importance in my formation as an historian and in my final specialization. Until that moment, I had more or less educated myself. At that time in Oxford there was a remarkable team: H. A. R. Gibb, Richard Walzer, Joseph Schacht, Geoffrey Lewis, and from 1951 on A. H. Hourani. They were very remarkable people.

NEG: Was Oxford as exotic as Tunis?
RAYMOND: Yes, it was very exotic for me. In 1951 England had just come out of the war; there were still ration cards for food. England had withstood the blitz in 1940, had stood alone and had led the fight against the Nazis with heroism, and had largely contributed to our liberation. I had much admiration for the British, and it was an exciting idea to be there. Of course I found the system at Oxford completely different from all that I had known. Also, I had not yet completely terminated my career as a communist. From this point of view England and Oxford contributed to my isolation from the ideological and political milieu in which I had long lived. I gradually distanced myself from the communist party (very "exotic" in England), though not completely from Marxism. Until now I think that a certain number of fundamental ideas of Marxism are valuable and that in the domain of history, for instance, historical materialism is an important tool.

When I left Oxford I had ceased to be a communist altogether. It was the time of the so-called "White Shirts plot" in the USSR, an anti-Semitic affair which unfolded in the last days of Stalin. I had probably come under the influence of Julien who waged war against my political prejudices. He reminded me of the Moscow Trials before the war, of the repression and terror of the Stalinist era. The arguments were particularly strong coming from a man who had had such long and impressive political experiences. He was truly someone who had lived the socialist movement from the beginning of the century until decolonization. The combined influences of Julien and of Oxford helped me to abandon communism towards 1953 without the personal crises many of my contemporaries, such as the well-known historian Emmanuel Leroi Ladurie, experienced and described.

Also, I came under the influence of Albert Hourani, who had just arrived in Oxford and who accepted me as his first student there. First, he helped me to separate the problems of the Arab world from the problems of international communism. The Arab world became a region with specific problems which had nothing to do with what I had hitherto considered essential, that is to say the international workers' movement. Second, thanks to him and to a lecture he gave – I remember as if it were today, in a small sunny room in Magdalen College – I began to understand the Palestine problem.

At that time, in 1951, the war in Palestine had ended only two years before, but Hourani already had formed a synthetic view of the origins of the problem and of the unfolding of events and perspectives that was truly remarkable. Understanding at last the Palestine question was, of course, a decisive step. It was Hourani who made me understand the Ottoman Empire in the framework of which my own research was later to develop. All my career as an historian of the modern Arab world is a result of his teaching and example. As a general historian I was formed in France, but my formation as an historian of the Arab world I owe largely to Albert Hourani and to Oxford where I studied Arabic in a rational way.

Since I was a historian I decided to write a D.Phil. in history. I chose a Tunisian subject which I could study in England and which would not require too many Arabic sources, which were for me still inaccessible. I wrote my D.Phil. on "British politics in Tunisia from 1830 to 1881" mainly from the archives of the Foreign Office in Chancery Lane. It would have been better for my later research if I had concentrated on the study of Arabic and Turkish.

In 1953 Julien, who was my mentor, had me enter the Centre National de la Recherche Scientifique (CNRS). There I finished the writing up of my thesis, largely rewritten by Albert Hourani with admirable patience, which I submitted in 1954. Then, I began to work in the archives of the Quai d'Orsay, still on Tunisia in the nineteenth century, which was to be the subject of my future French doctorate. Again thanks to Julien I obtained a scholarship at the French Institute in Damascus. The purpose of this was to improve my Arabic and to get to know the Near East. Thus in 1954 I went to the French Institute in Damascus where I spent a year. Most of those who are professionally active in France in our field have spent some time at the Institute. It gives an exceptionally formative experience because one finally finds oneself in an Arab milieu, with a remarkable library and the possibility of local contacts. I was very interested in contemporary problems, and for a year I sent articles on the situation in Syria to a French journal, *La Tribune des Nations*.

Syria was at that time a thrilling country, for in 1954 the dictator-ship of Shishakli had collapsed, and it knew one of the rare periods of democratic and parliamentary life it has experienced since its independence from France in 1945. It was bursting with politics, abounding with quantities of journals and political parties. At the University of Damascus, where I was taking courses in history and Arabic, the great forces were the communists and the Muslim Brothers who were more active and influential at the time than the Baath Party which was later to seize power.

So I spent a year in the Middle East learning Arabic, working on Arab history, and travelling around in Syria, Lebanon, Palestine, and

Egypt. I went to Jerusalem and to Cairo, and so I began a bit to orient myself to the eastern Arab world. The following year, in 1955, I was appointed to a slightly more elevated status, the position of "pensionnaire" at the French Institute in Cairo. It was also a more stable situation.

Before leaving for Egypt I had contacted Gaston Wiet, the specialist on Egypt. At that time in France one had to write two theses for the *doctorat d'état*, a principal and a secondary thesis. I went to see Wiet for advice, and we agreed that I would do my principal thesis on nineteenth-century Tunisia and my secondary thesis on the guilds of Egypt basing it on the book of Jabarti, the great historian of eighteenth- and nineteenth-century Egypt. So I went to Cairo where I studied Arabic and worked on Jabarti and on the history of Egypt. Normally, I should have stayed in Egypt at least three to five years, but I spent only a year because the Suez Crisis cut my stay short.

NEG: What did you think of French policy at that moment?
RAYMOND: I resolutely opposed French policy. Now, many people let it be believed that they took positions they did not take. At that time many specialists said that the Franco-British blockade would affect Egypt, and that Egypt would collapse. I was convinced of the contrary, from the experience I had of the situation in Egypt. I tried to make my position known through a letter I wrote to *Le Monde* on the Suez Crisis in response to an article it had published that was hostile to Nasser. Although my letter was, in my opinion, quite judicious (as the following events proved) it was never published by *Le Monde*. *Le Monde* is very selective in publishing letters from readers, and I have a small stock of "*lettres au Monde*" about various topics (Egypt, Tunisia, Palestine) which were never published. The French had a poor understanding of the Suez affair and Egyptian policy. I remember Byzantine discussions in Paris, where one admitted that the bottom of the canal was Egyptian, but considered that since the water was international, French intervention was justified. France was generally delirious on the subject but took up the Suez affair as a means of controlling events in Algeria, where the national war of liberation had begun two years earlier.

So I returned to France where I continued my work on Egypt in the Parisian archives and libraries. In 1957 I was appointed to the University of Tunis. I spent two years in Tunisia because the possibility of returning to Egypt was very minimal at that time. Tunisia had just won its independence from France, and I spent a very interesting time there. The war in Algeria was the main issue and I was very active in opposing French colonial policy by writing letters, petitions and participating in a study group about the Algerian problem. One issue of the newsletter we published was posted in Algiers with threatening comments for all the authors, which of course made us very happy at that time. Then I was appointed to the University of Bordeaux where I was to direct the small Department of Arab Studies. I spent seven years in Bordeaux, from 1959 to 1966. While I was there, I decided to reverse the order of my research, to do my principal thesis on Egypt and my secondary thesis on Tunisia. I no longer worked on a limited subject such as Wiet had proposed, but on the larger subject of the social and economic history of Egypt in the seventeenth and eighteenth centuries. It depended largely on the availability of information and documentation to do a study such as I envisaged, that is a work of social history.

At that moment [1962] the publication of Stanford Shaw's book *Administrative and Financial Organization of Ottoman Egypt* was a decisive factor in my orientation. Shaw showed that it was possible to use the Ottoman archives which until then had been very little studied.[1] The Turkish historical 'school following Barkan's studies had much used these archival documents, but more from the perspective of institutional, demographic, or financial history than from the perspective of a global social history.[2] That was what I wished to do. So for that I had to have access to the archives. Following diverse vicissitudes, I was able to spend a year going through the documents of the religious tribunals (*mahkama*) in Cairo. My objective was to treat the archives not only from the demographic, administrative, or financial angle but as a source for the reconstruction of the Egyptian society, just as Western researchers had used notary documents, which were the equivalent of the documents which I was finding. I had to establish my own method because this type of research did not exist in our field, my aim being to make a quantitative study out of the very detailed documents of inheritance I found in the *mahkama* archives.

NEG: What led you to establish this new method?
RAYMOND: I was influenced by the general ambience of this period which put the accent on the importance of social and economic research. The influence of Claude Cahen who had become my thesis director for my Egyptian research was fundamental. And like more or less all the historians of my generation I felt the influence of the French Annales school of history. I was oriented very strongly towards studies of *la longue durée* and towards research on society and economy. I do not believe I was directly influenced by the teaching of the main leaders of the Annales school, but the Annales ideas had become dominant ideas in the field of historical research.

I tried to apply to the study of early modern Egypt a method used by Jean Sauvaget in medieval Syria. This method was based on the liaison between archival work and the study of urban archaeology. I think that the study of the city, the study of monuments, the study of urban structures, supplement the information given by written sources for the knowledge of social structure, and that one ought to make the two parallel. When I was in Cairo, I devoted, let us say, half my time to the archives of the religious tribunals, and the other half to visits in the old city so that I could make a very detailed survey of Ottoman Cairo. Such research was not without risks. It was the Nasser era, and with the "spymania" then prevailing many people wondered what I was doing in the old city photographing or studying the monuments which were in general without interest. It was not the "touristic" grand Mamluk monuments which interested me, but the little monuments, often in bad condition or not even monuments at all. Sometimes people threw stones at me, and it often happened that I ended my visits in the local police station where I would explain myself. It always worked out very well, generally ending with a cup of coffee, and everyone was content. Sometimes the curiosity of Cairene people about my activities brought very interesting exchanges of information which helped me in my work and may have convinced the inhabitants of those poor neighbourhoods of the importance of an historical legacy which was being neglected in the pursuit of modernization.

I returned to Bordeaux, and after a year I was appointed director of the Institut Français de Damas. I left for Damascus in 1966. I spent nine years as director of the Institute, from 1966 to 1975. For many years I was also directing an archaeological mission on the Euphrates. It was very interesting work, organizing research. All researchers, all professors, should from time to time participate in a task of collective interest of this type.

This sojourn in Damascus slowed the completion of my work on Cairo because I was very busy, but finally I finished my work on *Artisans et commerçants au Caire au XVIIIième siècle.*[3]

NEG: What did you attempt to demonstrate in Artisans et Commerçants?
RAYMOND: The book is in fact more than the title suggests. It is an essay on the economic and social history of Egypt during the second part of the Ottoman period which began in 1517 and which ended in 1798. I was impressed by the fact that a large number of researchers had written on the Muslim economy, always describing it as an economy in continual decline since the Ottoman conquest that by the eighteenth century had reached a state of quasi-total exhaustion. This is the thesis developed by Sauvaget in his very admirable book on

Aleppo. I was also struck by the fact that the researchers had written of a "disarticulated" society, one that was dominated by a "ruling caste" of foreign origin, which replicated itself, and by a total disharmony. My intellectual formation led me to be very vigilant with regard to what could be considered the product of an ideological attitude, originating in the framework of the colonial political system, with regard to Muslim society. This "Syrian school" is in this case a remnant of a school which was developed in the very colonial ambience of French Algeria.

Thus I studied the mechanisms of the economy, by using the local sources which were very rich, rather than the external sources – consular reports, travellers' accounts – which are inevitably biased. The study of the tribunal archives, in particular those dealing with inheritances, reveals an economic activity which was in no way about to expire. Its new activities, for example, the coffee trade, were, in fact, animating a commerce of international importance.

The local sources helped correct the Eurocentrism of the classic studies. They showed that the Ottoman empire very much constituted a dynamic "world-economy". The role of Europeans in this economy was only marginal, and it was only towards 1750 that the first effects of Western economic domination appeared, causing the decline of traditional activities such as the manufacture of cloth and the production of sugar. And it was only in the nineteenth century that the decadence became definitive, because of the overwhelming European competition.

My sources described a society that was not at all egalitarian despite the tenets of "Islamic uniformity" that have sometimes been described. It was very inegalitarian, and this inequality expressed a certain internal dynamism. The society was dominated by a class of great merchants (*tujjar*) who were able to replace spices, in decline since the beginning of the sixteenth century, with a new product, coffee. The contours of the popular strata of this strongly hierarchical society are not always easy to define, but we well know of its existence and of its often violent reactions to political oppression and to sometimes intolerable material difficulties. I believe that the emergence of the "political" life of this popular Cairene society toward the end of the eighteenth century and the beginning of the nineteenth (with its participation in the rise of Muhammad Ali) constitutes a major phenomenon which has scarcely been realized up to now.

The material study of the indigenous population and of the ruling class also led me to contest the description of a society uniquely characterized by the opposition of the subjects and the foreign ruling institution. They were thought to be separate and antagonistic. In fact, the existence of contact points, through the "professionalization" of the military and their "protection" of the subjects, led to a more nuanced description of a social organization in which corrective elements existed. There was a certain homogeneity that was more coherent than had been believed.

I think finally that the serious attention turned to these three centuries of Egyptian history and the effort to throw light on the structure and actions of the Egyptian masses who were not uniquely passive but who played an active role, revealed a period that was not merely "colonial" and which is crucial in understanding Egyptian history. From this point of view, a long road has been travelled since the 1970s, when interest in the Ottoman period was considered extravagant, up to the end of the 1980s when the Arab historians themselves took this rediscovery in hand, and when a more "balanced" view of this period could be defended.

Soon after the book appeared, my sojourn in Damascus came to an end. The nearly ten years I spent in Damascus were, in retrospect, among the happiest of my life. I returned to France, to Aix-en-Provence, where I had been appointed to a university with an important department of Arab studies, incontestably one of the best in France. Thanks to the presence of Robert Mantran, it had become a centre of research on the Ottoman world.[4] It also had a research centre, the Groupe de Recherche sur l'Économie et Politique de l'Orient (GREPO) which specialized in Egypt and on the problems of traditional housing. This centre was an additional attraction for me. I centred myself in this double sphere, university teaching and collective work at GREPO, until I decided to take early retirement, five years ahead of time, in 1988.

NEG: Why did you take early retirement?
RAYMOND: I should say frankly that my university work did not seem sufficiently gratifying to justify continuing it. This decision had nothing to do with the Department of Arab Studies or with the research team to which I belonged. Both were composed of specialists of very great merit who have remained friends and with whom I still actively collaborate. Rather, it was the result of a crisis in confidence of the incapacity of the French university to find its way (because of institutional bureaucracy and its mode of functioning) to organize the development of its studies, to define the priorities that would permit, for example at Aix, to focus on what should have been a priority: the Mediterranean and Arab studies. A reform of the university is ongoing. I hope that it has more success than the three or four attempts at reform during the past twenty-five years.

We have tried to do things that I think are important and which should have enjoyed the active support of the university. We received but a small, miserly-calculated assistance. It was not even possible to arrange, in a satisfactory manner, the replacement of Robert Mantran and myself, despite the risk of compromising the specialization of Aix in Ottoman studies which had been patiently built. I add that a system in which individual and collective effort is scarcely taken into consideration because this effort overturns the egalitarian ideal of the academic world does not justify that one totally invest oneself in it. Let us not speak of the disastrous state of the libraries. I thus took without regret a liberty which permitted me to come to Princeton and to continue my own research in a more favourable setting.

The past few years have, however, been positive. From 1980 to 1989, I was associated with the formation and development of the Institute of the Arab World in Paris, an institution whose statutory and financial problems have not prevented it from becoming an active centre for the understanding of the Arab world in France and in Europe.

In 1984 CNRS asked me to organize a research centre for Mediterranean studies of which the activity and equipment contrasted favourably with the dilapidation of the university. I endeavored to make this centre, which was attached to CNRS and to the universities of Aix, an institute specializing in the Arab world. When I passed it to my successor in 1989 it was the most important French centre, and without doubt the most important European centre in this field, with library and documentation facilities and research personnel (a hundred persons in total) of which the quality stood out remarkably in comparison with the customary support services in this field. CNRS, I believe, appreciated my efforts.

I also contributed to the founding and development of an association of professionals concerned with the study of the Middle East, AFEMAM (Association Française pour l'Étude du Monde Arabe et Musulman), conceived basically on the model of the American Middle East Studies Association (MESA) or the British Society for Middle East Studies (BRISMES). It always seemed to me that in addition to the lack of financial and institutional support the researchers and instructors in France suffered from an excessive dispersal and an insufficient knowledge of the local research. AFEMAM, during the four years in which I was director (1987–90), helped solve these two problems through its annual publications, annual meetings, and its patient work with the academic and administrative authorities. The publication, at the beginning of 1991, of a general statement of our studies ("Studies on the Arab and Muslim world in France") demonstrates the utility of this project.[5]

NEG: Could you describe the orientation of your work during this period?
RAYMOND: The work I have undertaken on the Arab cities is, to a

large extent, an extension of my research on Cairo. While studying the structure of the city and its evolution, I had inevitably outlined comparative research dealing with the other great Arab cities of the Ottoman period. One of the main difficulties I encountered while working on the economic and social history of Cairo was that there were no similar studies to compare my results with. On the cities, however, there was a large corpus of studies which had been developed and refined. The general tendency of these studies was to be very critical of the "anarchical" character of the Arab cities and very negative about the Ottoman period in this respect. This seemed to call for a thorough reappraisal. Moreover, certain of these studies, beginning with the most magisterial of all, that of Sauvaget on Aleppo, seemed to me marked by contradictions between a global thesis and a decline accentuated in the Ottoman period, and the results of their own research which demonstrates that Aleppo flourished under the Ottomans. My library research, in particular at Harvard in 1981, was complemented by visits to the cities I wished to study – Damascus and Aleppo, of course, but also Fez, Algiers, Tunis, Mosul, and Baghdad – and resulted in the publication of two books, *Great Arab Cities*, which is an introduction to the topic, and above all, *Grandes villes arabes*.[6] These studies, preceded and followed by numerous detailed studies on these cities, or on aspects of urbanism during this period, permitted me to proceed with a re-examination of the orientalist thesis (above all French in origin) on Muslim and Arab cities.

My critique of the perfectly absurd notion of the "urban anarchy" of the Arab cities (for an "anarchic" city would be inevitably destined to disappear) led me to research the specific principles of the organization of the Arab city which are *not* those of the ancient city nor of the medieval city. By describing certain specific institutions of various types (the *sharīʿa* courts, religious foundations, *waqfs*, professional communities, quarters and neighbourhoods – religious or ethnic) one could comprehend how the city "functioned".

First, I found that it functioned not by following "spontaneous" mechanisms, as I had written in 1969, but by following types of original regulation, with the intervention from time to time of the central power. Previous scholars had envisioned the central power during the Ottoman domination as repressive, or at best, inert, but I found it to be very active. The study of the "imperial orders" is on this point very edifying.

Second, I learned that the structure of the Arab city obeyed a strong internal logic. The characteristics of this city, including its division into quarters and the irregularity of the urban network, were factors which converged in its organization and in its coherence. Envisioned from above, the global structure of the city, with its powerful centre, unfolded in successive circles. It was very precise and explains its vitality.

Third, I was able to demonstrate that the existence of exclusive social groupings and of marked socio-economic inequities were factors of tension which contributed to the organization of the city and constituted one of its fundamental characteristics.

Fourth, the Ottoman empire, by its very existence, through the creation of an enormous economic unit, permitted, at least during two centuries, an urban expansion. Sauvaget had demonstrated this for Damascus and Aleppo without, however, extracting from his own work conlusions which contradicted his *a priori* ideas.

These are, I believe, the results of my research of the past fifteen years. They are not totally new, but together they permit us to embark upon useful reflections on the urban achievement of the modern Arab world.[7]

NEG: Have your contacts with students played a role in your research?
RAYMOND: My situation as emeritus professor permits me to continue to direct a certain number of research projects that are already under way. The French doctoral thesis is a long affair, even with the disappearance of the *thèse d'état* which has humanized it a bit. I have worked with a certain number of researchers of great promise, some of whom are now engaged in university teaching or research. The direction of the thesis is an absorbing work. It is very difficult but finally very fruitful. If one wishes to apply oneself well, it is preferable not to have too many to direct. It ought to be a collective work, in which one can learn much if the researcher has talent. I would like to continue to carry out this work, with as much attention and care as was spent on me. When certain of my students take a bit more time than I wish to give them on account of other pressing tasks, I think of the indefatigable generosity of Charles-André Julien, Gaston Wiet, Régis Blachère, Claude Cahen and Albert Hourani. The teaching which I have done at Princeton has on the other hand permitted me to keep contact with the discipline of teaching which is very stimulating for professors, especially when the class is composed of dynamic and intelligent people. The students do not know the extent to which they render us service by forcing us to clarify our own ideas, to organize them, and sometimes to re-examine them. The course which I gave this year at Princeton on the history of the Arab city has been, from this point of view, very useful.

NEG: Does your historical method allow us to learn more about the roles of women in Middle East history?
RAYMOND: My research has never focused particularly on the role of

women. This is probably a mistake, for I have had the occasion to state in my work on the society and economy of Cairo how the role of women was more important than one generally supposes. Though they were socially protected and isolated, women were very active economic agents. One sees this very clearly in the documents of the *waqf* and the *mahkama*. Women also constituted an element of stability in society: one needs only to see how often the wife of the emir was married to his successor (a phenomenon which appeared in the Mamluk period) to appreciate the central importance of women in the dominant society. On women's "public role," two citations of Mamluk historians are relevant. In 1436 Ibn Taghri Birdi noted the death of the princess Jalban, wife of the sultan Barsbay [r. 1422–38], remarking, "She was beautiful, wise and had executive ability. If she had lived until her son came to power (Yusuf, who reigned briefly in 1438) she would have conducted his government excellently."[8] And Ibn Iyas who, with regard to princess Zaynab [d. 1479], widow of the Sultan Aynal [r. 1453–61], noted the authority which she enjoyed under the reign of her spouse: "She administered the affairs of the state, making appointments and dismissals. Her influence was immense and she commanded respect."[9] This role diminished perhaps during the Ottoman period because Ottoman society was more bureaucratic, but we know in the eighteenth century some cases of women having had great political influence. Even in private life the structure of habitations reveals that women were probably less strictly segregated than had been supposed.

That said, the Muslim ideological atmosphere was not favourable to women. The innumerable attempts to separate them from public places, from markets, especially, and to restrict their right to ornaments demonstrate that. Still, the very fact that the attempts had to be frequently renewed indicates that no religious or political edict could prevent altogether women's participation in public life.

NEG: Can you comment on the "orientalist debate"?
RAYMOND: The debate over orientalism and orientalists is a debate that seems to be permanent in many publications of the Arab world. In Edward Said's publication, the confusion between the orientalism of writers, artists, and travellers, and the orientalism of scholars did not help clarify things. The many "obsessions" of orientalists which are malignly raised cannot be explained in this manner. On the other hand, the "orientalists" have demonstrated, on occasion, a certain lack of sense of humour.

What does the debate amount to after all? To state that the orientalists belonged to a society that was determined by, and shared more or less, the colonial ideology and its appetites, ought not to upset anyone. The works of the "orientalists" inevitably reflected the prejudices of their times. The result is sometimes dismaying: I think for example of what was written by certain French historians of the Algerian school on the "Arabs" or on "the Turks". But such studies represent one per cent of a production which was in general important and which remains the basis of what we know of these countries. The history of Algeria by Grammont, for example, has not been surpassed after thirty years of independence.[10] In certain cases, there has been cooperation, casually or organized, with the adminis-tration which managed the colonial enterprise. One could say – but it would be a bad joke – that it would have been useful if the colonial administration had been more informed by the specialists' warnings so that they would have extracted the logical consequences of its actions. This was not ordinarily the case. If the colonial advisers had expressed their views honestly and sincerely, there would be a dossier that would be more useful to study and to analyse than hurling abuse at the bad conduct of the scholar.

We can read the reports which Louis Massignon wrote for the Affaires Étrangères in the 1920s, and we can understand his views on the Arab world and of French policies towards it. The same Massignon, forty years later, was picked up more than once by the police on the streets of Paris while he demonstrated for Palestine and against the torture in Algeria.

In sum, that which counts and which ought to be retained in our analyses, is the positive work which orientalism has produced. It has been considerable, and the "orientals" themselves recognize this because they study, in translation, the major works of this orientalism as an important source of knowledge about the orient. The "orientals" are certainly irritated to see themselves described or judged in an incomplete, erroneous, or even stereotyped manner. Lane was, wrongly by the way, taken as an example of this bad representation of the orient by the occidentals, but I will be pleased when one can cite for me an oriental work of the same quality on the same subject.[11] While Ahmad Amin wrote his *Qamus* on the customs of the Egyptians, published in 1953, he did not hesitate to borrow largely from the *Description de l'Egypte* and from Lane's *Manners and Customs* first published in 1836.[12]

In France there is similar sentiment against French history written by "foreigners", not to mention the manner in which American cinema describes France, for that would be anecdotal. Should this sense of irritation turn into a sense of violation? If so, it is necessary to evoke the psychoanalytic background of Said's work, the sense of political injustice.

In any case, the orientalism which existed in the nineteenth century when it flourished, is now dead. It ended with the publication of *Islam and the West* by Gibb and Bowen. This was the last orientalist work, which was factually very remarkable but also a significant failure.[13] Since then, we have had specialists of literature, of religion, and of history devoted to the Arab (or Muslim) world. I myself am an historian dedicated to the modern history of the Arab world and to the history of Arab cities. I could have just as well dedicated myself to the history of the United States. I am much less concerned by a debate which I find *démodé* than by the fact that my government has never consulted me on the policies it ought to adopt in the Arab world, policies that I have resolutely opposed during the greater part of my active life, and against which I have publicly demonstrated on many occasions.

A more serious problem remains. Are contemporary societies ready to accept that a critical evaluation be made of them without the accusation of violation, or of malevolent intention? The progress of intolerance in this domain leads us to make a somewhat pessimistic response to this question. The solution is without doubt in closer cooperation between researchers of the "observer" nationality and of the "observed" nationality. This would reduce risks of mutual misunderstanding and fearsome accusations. The perfect qualifications of our Arab colleagues, who combine an intimate knowledge of language and milieu, render this cooperation possible and guarantee that it will be fruitful. If an "orientalist" method is to be abandoned, it is that of relying on the local informant, the furnisher of raw data, like raw materials for the industries of Europe. The terms of intellectual commerce, like the terms of international trade and commerce, ought to be balanced.

NEG: Finally, have you advice for students who are just beginning their studies?
RAYMOND: What I wish American students to consider is that although the United States is an island, the exterior world exists. I have always been a bit shocked by the limited interest of American students in it. I have a great admiration for the American university system and for its libraries. One of the great problems in France is the extraordinary poverty, the misery, of our libraries. But there is a tendency to find that the English bibliography is altogether satisfactory, and that it is not necessary to go farther. I hope that American students of Middle Eastern history should not be affected by a certain myopia that affects many students of the Near East who do not know foreign languages and who are incapable of carrying out research done outside their country.

Notes

1. Stanford J. Shaw, *The Financial and Administrative Organization and Development of Ottoman Egypt, 1517–1798* (Princeton: Princeton University Press, 1962).
2. Ömer Lûtfi Barkan, *Türk toprak hukuku tarihinde Tanzimat ve 1274 (1858) tarihli Arazi Kanunnamesi (The Tanzimat and the Land Law of 1271 (1858) in the History of Turkish Land Law)* (Istanbul: Maarif Matbassi, 1940).
3. André Raymond, *Artisans et commerçants du Caire au XVIIIième siècle* (Damascus: Institut français de Damas, 1973–4).
4. Robert Mantran, *L'empire ottoman du XVIème au XVIIIième siècle: administration, économie, société* (London: Variorum Reprints, 1984).
5. AFEMAM, "Les études sur le monde arabe et musulman en France: Contribution a un état des lieux – propositions" (Aix-en-Provence: Association Française pour l'Etude du Monde Arabe et Musulman, 1990).
6. André Raymond, *The Great Arab Cities in the Sixteenth–Eighteenth Centuries: An Introduction* (New York: New York University Press, 1984) and *Grandes villes arabes a l'époque ottomane* (Paris: Sindbad, 1985).
7. See, for example, André Raymond, *Le Caire* (Paris: Fayard, 1993).
8. Ibn Taghribirdi, Abu al-Mahasin Yusuf, *History of Egypt, 1382–1469*, translation by William Popper (Berkeley: University of California Press, 1954–60), IV, p. 207.
9. Gaston Wiet, *L'Egypt arabe de la conquête arabe à la conquête ottomane, 642–1517*, vol. IV in series entitled *Histoire de la nation égyptienne*, ed. Gabriel Hanotaux (Paris: Société de l'Histoire National, 1938), p. 173.
10. Henri Grammont, *Relations entre la France et la régence d'Alger au XVIIième siècle* (Algiers: Adolphe Jourdain, 1879–1888).
11. Edward Lane, *An Account of the Manners and Customs of the Modern Egyptians* (London: C. Knight & Co., 1836).
12. *Description de l'Egypte, ou, Receuil de observations et des recherches qui ont été faites en Egypte pendant l'expédition de l'armeé française* (Paris: Imprimerie impériale, 1809–1828); Lane, *Manners and Customs*.
13. H. A. R. Gibb and Harold Bowen, *Islamic Society and the West: A Study of the Impact of Western Civilization on Moslem Culture in the Near East* (2 vols. New York and London: Oxford University Press, 1950 and 1957).

CHAPTER FOUR

AFAF LUTFI
AL-SAYYID MARSOT

AFAF LUTFI AL-SAYYID MARSOT, born in Cairo in 1933, specializes in the history of modern Egypt. She studied at Cairo University, the American University in Cairo, Stanford University, and Oxford University where she was the first Egyptian woman to receive the D.Phil. She is currently professor of history at the University of California, Los Angeles. She was voted "Woman of the Year" by the Arab–American Press Guild and has been president of the Middle East Studies Association and the American Research Center in Egypt. She lives in Los Angeles with her husband, Alain.

Interviewed at her home in Los Angeles on 8 December 1989 by Farzaneh Milani and on 30 March 1990 by Nancy Gallagher.

FM: Could you tell us about your family background?
AFAF MARSOT: I come from a mixed background in that my father was Egyptian and my mother was Turco-Circassian. My father, Saʿid Lutfi al-Sayyid, was the son of an Egyptian landowner and an ʿumda or village mayor. So my background was a mixture of the traditional Egyptian and the traditional Turco-Circassian cultures. The family was very wealthy, and we were materially spoiled, but my mother was a strict disciplinarian so we had discipline and indulgence hand-in-hand. My father was educated at Oxford. He was in the government; he was governor of Giza. Before I was born, King Fuad (King of Egypt, r. 1917–36) pensioned him off at the age of forty to get at my uncle, Ahmad Lutfi al-Sayyid, who was called the 'teacher of the generation' because he was the rector of Cairo University. My uncle was a philosopher, a journalist, and a reformer who helped transform the archaic Arabic language into modern standard Arabic. He also helped found two of Egypt's most important political parties, both of which potentially undermined the power of the monarchy: the Wafd and the Liberal Constitutionalist Party. My father then worked for Marconi, a private radio station that became the Egyptian State Broadcasting Corporation. He was director of the Arabic Section for twenty years.

When Faruq came to the throne he took a liking to my father who had a great sense of humour, and to compensate him for what his father had done, Faruq made him under-secretary of state for social affairs, at which he remained until he retired. My mother attended the Mère de Dieu, a school run by French nuns. I have two elder brothers, but I was always the apple of my father's eye. I was the one who was always with him. On Sundays, for example, it was my father who took me out, not my mother. Every summer for ten years my father and I would go to England or Austria and spend two months there. He would meet his friends, a mixed crowd of Egyptians, Syrians, Iraqis, Lebanese and discuss the political issues of the day. I would often ask questions and I absorbed by osmosis the politics of the Arab world.

I did not have very much primary schooling because I was a bit of a sickly child, and my parents preferred to keep me at home as long as they could. So I had an English governess who taught me at home. I later went to an English school which I attended for nine years. Then I entered the Faculty of Medicine to do premedicine at Cairo University.

FM: Do you remember how many women were in the medical school with you?
MARSOT: I think there were altogether 100 women and about 900 men. The women sat on one side of the classroom and the men on the other. When any of the men would come and sit with us because they were our friends, the other women would look askance at us and wonder why we were sitting with these men.

My father and I had to play a game because my mother did not want me to study medicine. She thought I would never get married if I studied medicine because I would be over twenty when I finished and would therefore be too old to find a husband. So we lied to her and told her I was in the faculty of sciences which lasted only four years, rather than the six required by medical school. This worked for a while, but at that time, the late-1940s, there were riots all over the country. Egypt was in a political uproar, and to enter the university campus you had to have a permit. At the gate they would ask you what faculty you were going to and you would tell them. One day my mother was giving me a lift to the university, and I made the mistake of saying "medical" and she looked at me and said, "OK, this is the last year you will be in medical school." She wasn't wrong because the year after that she forced me out.

After leaving premedical school I decided to enter the American University in Cairo. At that time one majored in economics or sociology. I did not like economics so I majored in sociology. I spent three years at AUC and graduated with a Bachelor of Arts degree in sociology. Then my mother said, "Right, now you will sit at home and wait to get married". In that year I took German and Italian lessons and studied to become a tourist guide. This was the first batch of professional tourist guides that the government was turning out. For a couple of months I worked as a tourist guide and got fearfully bored.

Eventually a friend of mine and I managed to enter a new graduate programme that Cairo University had created in political science. We were admitted, but in a sense it was illegal because women were not supposed to be allowed into the programme. I passed the first year with honours. Meanwhile, the administrators had learned that they could not give degrees in political science to women so they flunked the two women in the programme. That is how they got rid of us. So then I said I was going to go and study political science in America.

FM: Why America?
MARSOT: I wanted to see what it was like. I'd never been because we'd always gone to Europe. When I told my father I wanted to do a Master's Degree in political science in America, he agreed and helped me arrange it. Two weeks before I was due to leave we broke the news to my mother. She said, "Absolutely not", but I wheedled and wheedled until she agreed. I went off to America and did a Master's in political science at Stanford University.

Stanford was very sexist at that time. Graduate women in political science were treated like second-class citizens and not allowed to take certain seminars such as in international law. Otherwise it was fun being there.

Upon completion of the Master's Degree in 1956, I returned to Egypt. That year the Suez War broke out, and I became a volunteer nurse working in a psychiatric ward in Cairo caring for shellshocked troops. When the foreign troops evacuated Port Said, Sanaʾ Barakat, a close friend of mine, and I went to Port Said where we took over the children's ward in the Mabarra hospital. We were in charge of the children who had been wounded in the war. I lived with these people for months. Next I volunteered at the United Nations' office in Ismailiyya. The UN was coordinating the clearing of the Suez Canal. One day a friend told me that an English language teacher was needed at the American University in Cairo. I said that I did not know anything about teaching, but he assured me that there was nothing to it. So I began teaching at AUC.

FM: All this must have been very unusual for someone of your generation. Did you ever feel different from other children when growing up?
MARSOT: I was brought up like a little princess. I was always being surrounded by governesses instead of being surrounded by other

children. So I accepted the fact that being different was normal. If I wanted to go to the university and everybody said, "Oh, Fifi is entering the university, how shocking"! I enjoyed that. My father's sister was very offended that I chose the university over marrying her son. A friend of my parents said, "My daughters do not want to go to the university. What are we, greengrocers to send our daughters to the university"? I don't know why greengrocers and not butchers or bakers. When upon graduation I wanted to work *everybody* except my father opposed me. My mother, my brother, they all said, "What do you want a job for, you are taking a job from some poor person who needs the money". So I said, "OK, if I can't have a job I will volunteer and become a tourist guide". We were paid almost nothing and would give whatever tips were inflicted on us to the drivers. Later when I decided to work at the American University, I found that it was great fun to earn my own money, and that work is dismissed as irrelevant unless it is remunerated.

FM: It seems your father always supported your goals. Could you explain that?
MARSOT: He may have been much more far-sighted than the rest of the family. He used to say, "Get an education; you never know what is going to happen". My mother would say, "Why? What is going to happen, we are rich people". When the revolution came and our land was expropriated, I told my father, "You gave me a capital worth more than all our land put together". He did not anticipate the revolution, but he thought his daughter should have a profession in case she was unable to manage our land or needed for any reason to be independent.

While I was teaching at AUC my adviser from Stanford came on a visit to Egypt. She said to the president of the university that I should be teaching political science and not English. So I began teaching political science and English. After I had taught three years the university administration announced that they were going to fire everybody who did not have a Ph.D. I said, "This is my chance"! One of the American professors at AUC got me a fellowship to study English literature at the University of Utah. I loved literature; I used to teach it as well as English language and political science. So I told my mother I was again going off to America to study and she said, "Where in America?" I explained where Utah was, and she said, "This is too far; why don't you go to England where we can visit you every year?" I decided to go to Oxford because my father had gone there, so I consulted Magdi Wahba, a scholar at Cairo University and an acquaintance. He said, "You want Albert Hourani". So I read something by Albert called, "The decline of the West in the Middle East".[1] In the article he discussed the situation of power on one side and powerlessness on the other which characterized the colonial period, and I decided that this was the man I wanted to work with. I wrote him a letter and said, "Can I come to Oxford and work with you?" Magdi had recommended me to him, and Albert said, "Yes, of course".

When I entered St Anne's College in 1960 he told me, "We don't do graduate or doctoral degrees in politics at Oxford; we do history". I decided to read history with him, and that is how I used my training in political science. During the first quarter he said, "I would like you to write me a couple of papers on assigned topics". I wrote a few papers for him, and at the beginning of the second quarter he said, "Now start writing your dissertation".

I had wanted to work on my uncle, Ahmad Lutfi al-Sayyid, because he had played such an important role in the political life of the country and he seemed to be regarded by Egyptians with great respect – even by Nasser and the army who had asked him to become president of Egypt after they had ousted Naguib – an offer he had declined pleading age. When I proposed my topic to him he said, "Write about something that really matters, I'm only one man". So I decided to write about the most controversial era in modern Egyptian history, that is the Anglo-Egyptian era. I think I was one of the first to use Egyptian materials to write a history that was generally written sitting in England in the Foreign Office. I used the Mustafa Kamil papers, which were in the national archives, the published works of the Egyptian historians, and above all knowledge gained from my father, my uncle, and family friends. The result was my dissertation which was published under the title *Egypt and Cromer*.[2]

FM: How did Mr Hourani influence you?
MARSOT: Mr Hourani is the man who taught me how to think. Before that time I was a clever parrot who got everything right and did her work without thinking much about it. I had sailed through university acquiring ideas and regurgitating them. Albert taught me, for example, to ask why we admire Shaykh Muhammad Abduh, to ask "What did he do, how is he connected to historical change?" Mr Hourani is the one who taught me how to think historically. I owe him a tremendous debt and whatever is positive in my way of teaching I owe to him because he treated the students like his own children. He would worry about us; he would invite us to his house to meet other academics; whenever anybody was visiting we were always invited to meet him or her. He really looked after us, and he taught me that this was the way you treat students, that they should matter to you. He is one of the very few historians who has created a school: we call ourselves "Awlad Albert" (Albert's children). Mr Hourani, my father, my uncle, and Bahi al-Din Barakat were the four people who formed

my mind. Before the 1952 Free Officers revolution Bahi al-Din Barakat was the chief state auditor and after the revolution one of the three regents. He was one of my father's closest friends and like a second father to me. I later had a very close intellectual relationship with him.

Being at Oxford was a formative experience in itself. When I was growing up in Egypt, I was in a special kind of cultural milieu. I was surrounded by Westernized Egyptians who went to foreign schools, read foreign books, listened to foreign broadcasting, to classical music and who felt more at home discussing European literature rather than Arabic literature. They were missing out on the cultural heritage of their country. The more I studied history, the more I had to teach myself culture all over again. The pre-1952 era was a golden age for the 10,000 Egyptians with money. It was a wonderful period for us growing up, but it was a very unreal period. The greatest satisfaction was finding my cultural roots again, realizing what I was missing out on. At Oxford I began to learn my history and my culture.

I even began to learn my religion, because I had gone to a missionary school where I got the Bible every day of my life. I read the Quran for the first time at Oxford. I grew up in a household which observed Ramadan religiously. My father was always reading the Quran, but we were not religious in the deep sense. My mother became very religious when my elder brother joined the Foreign Legion, and she went on the Haj several times. When she was in her seventies she joined a mystical order and started praying. She had been a very fashionable, elegant woman, but at the end of her life she was wearing the *hijab* (Islamic head covering). She became a very devout religious person. My father knew a lot about religion, but he was neither devout nor religious. He was a believer, but he wore his religion very lightly. During Ramadan he was the only one in our house who never fasted. He never prayed, but he would give the *zakat* (Islamic tithe). He built a mosque in his village and would distribute clothes every year to all the peasants. I grew up in two religions. At home we were Muslims while at school Christianity was dished out. In a sense it made me very much of a cynic because everybody was telling me where the right path was. How could you have two right paths? Either they are both wrong or they are both right. I learned about Islam when I became a scholar of the Middle East, and then I became interested in Sufism, and I read a great deal about it. I have learnt a great deal about Islam, about Muslim civilization, and about my own roots through my studies, but I am not a devout person.

The odd thing about being in Oxford was that it made me more aware of my Egyptianness and my Arabic culture than I had ever been. This was because at Oxford one studied both the good and the bad in history. The English missionary school fed us a negative version of Egyptian history while the nationalist movement gave us the idealized version. In a sense in Oxford, one was trying to discover reality from amongst the myths. And therefore it made me realize both the grandeur and decadence of my own culture and history. And of course having the uncle I did and having the father I did, I was very conscious of the nationalist movement from the point of view of the Egyptian. So in a sense I discovered my Egyptianness abroad because in Egypt it was taken for granted. For instance the first time an Englishman said to me, "When you stole the Suez Canal from us . . ." I nearly fell out of my chair. I thought, "But it was our canal, how did we steal it from you? All you did was buy shares in the damn thing." And so because I was under pressure I had to learn more to justify, to understand, to explain. It kept on pushing me to learn more about Egyptian history. I set out for myself the goal of covering 200 years of modern Egyptian history from beginning to end. This is what I am doing in my work. My first book, *Egypt and Cromer*, covered the era from 1882 to 1907. My second book, *Egypt's Liberal Experiment*, covered the era from 1919–1936.[3] Then I wanted to go back in time, because I wanted to learn what had shaped the later years. So in my book, *Egypt in the Reign of Muhammad Ali*, I studied the Muhammad Ali era and nineteenth-century Egypt, and now I am going back into the eighteenth century.[4]

The five years that I spent in Oxford were the happiest years of my life. I thought I would remain in Oxford for the rest of my life. I was the first Egyptian woman to get the D.Phil. from Oxford. I was the first woman to give a speech in the Oxford Union. I was the first female junior fellow at St Antony's to live at college. It was perfectly lovely living in college. I met my husband, Alain, at St Antony's.

FM: How did you announce it to your parents?
MARSOT: I married him first. Then I went home and told my mother I wanted to marry a foreigner. The roof fell in over my head. We had scenes, absolute scenes, she was going to commit suicide, I was going to commit suicide. Neither of us had any intention of committing suicide. My father was ill and not really conscious of what was going on so I could not bring him over to my side. Then I went to our closest friend. He said, "Go back to England and write to say that you are married." So that is what I did. I wrote to my mother that I was married, and that if she wanted to see me again she had to be nice to my husband. Otherwise, I said, I wouldn't come back to Egypt. The next week I got a telegram from my mother saying, "All is forgiven, come back home, we will welcome your husband." My husband and I went back to Egypt during what were perhaps the worst years of the

Nasser period, from 1965 to 1968. A great number of my childhood friends were not allowed to visit with us because their husbands were bureaucrats, high government officials, or military people who were not allowed to consort with foreigners. It was a very difficult period. In 1968 I was invited to spend a year at the University of California, Los Angeles. We came for a year and have been here ever since.

FM: How do you think being a woman has affected your life?
MARSOT: It has affected me in that there were certain things that were closed to me. I wanted to enter the Egyptian foreign ministry to become a diplomat, and Nasser gave orders to flunk the women. It was only about ten years later that women diplomats were allowed, but by then I was in Oxford. I wanted to get a degree in political science, but I couldn't do it in Egypt because I was a woman. I had to go to America to get my degree. Certain professions such as medicine were discouraged simply because I was a woman.

FM: So it was always a disadvantage?
MARSOT: But at the same time, once I got my degree ... no, to be quite honest, it was a disadvantage. There were a lot of obstacles. I had to leave my country to make a name for myself as an historian of my own country.

NEG: Why did you call your first book Egypt and Cromer *and not* Cromer and Egypt?
MARSOT: Because Egypt was the most important element. A year later John Marlowe, a British historian, produced a book on the same topic but from the British point of view.[5] I was writing as an Egyptian. Everyone of my books has Egypt in the title. That is very deliberate.

NEG: Would you describe it as empirical narrative history?
MARSOT: Absolutely. It is a narrative because that was the kind of history that was written at the time. You settled at the Public Record Office and wrote military or diplomatic history. You went to the Quai d'Orsay to read the French diplomatic archives, you went to Egypt, to Abdin Palace, to read the waqaʾi al-misriyya (Egyptian Official Gazette), and you pieced the narrative together based entirely on the empirical material. The notion that you could use economics, that you could use social history appeared much later, and it was a completely different approach. In the 1960s that is not what you wrote.

NEG: Social history began in France in the 1930s with people like Marc Bloch and Lucien Febvre.
MARSOT: Yes, but it didn't get to England.

NEG: Nobody ever asked, "What is your theoretical framework?"
MARSOT: Nobody thought of theoretical framework. That would have been regarded as a bias, as beginning with preconceived notions. The idea was that you wrote history as though it was a *tabula rasa*. You let the material speak for itself. Nobody at that time thought you only get answers to the questions you ask. This is something Albert told me about five or six years later. We were talking about somebody who had received a large grant to go and study and had come back with nothing. Albert told him, "You only get answers to the questions you ask." This man obviously did not ask the proper questions. That is when it occurred to me that you have to ask questions of the material before you even look at it. I suppose that in the back of my mind I had certain questions already. I was an Egyptian who was brought up in a more cosmopolitan milieu than normally, who had been brought up in two cultures. I had a lot of subconscious questions: "Why do the British who are so wonderful at home, behave elsewhere like perfect beasts? Why do people who claim they have the most perfect democratic government behave in the most undemocratic fashion in Egypt?" I think this was what moved me to write on Britain in Egypt.

NEG: Then did you ask the reverse, why the Egyptians behaved as they did?
MARSOT: That in a sense comes in the second book, *Egypt's Liberal Experiment*, because I asked, "Why did all these brilliant people, my father's friends and relations, whom I had such admiration for, make such a mess of Egyptian politics from 1919 to 1952?" What triggered the question was the Nasser revolution. I wanted to understand what made the most talented people fail and why. That was why I wrote the second book. Now I would like to rewrite it because I disregarded the economic component. I have come to realize that economics were directing the political relationships. I still haven't come to terms with the Nasser revolution because it is too recent.

Egypt and Cromer shows how the Egyptian élites, who were partly of fellah (peasant) and partly of Turco-Circassian origin, collaborated with the British to maintain their privileges. The British dominated Egypt with the most callous indifference and were extremely unfair and unjust to the Egyptians because it suited their imperial interests. But the Egyptian élites and the Egyptian monarchy accepted to be dominated by the British because it suited their vested interests. They accommodated the colonial system. It was others, mostly outside the élite circles, who resisted it.

Meanwhile, I became interested in mystical orders, especially the two that were paramount in Egypt, the Bakriyya and the Wafaʾiyya. That led me to my interest in the ulama. The articles on the ulama were the beginning of my interest in socio-economic history.[6] The first article was rather tentative, and then I realized that money and power were one and the same thing so the succeeding ones demonstrated the power of the high ulama as the unwritten leaders of Muslim society and the influence they wielded based on how much money they had and how much property they possessed.

After coming to the United States, to UCLA, I decided to continue my study of the British in Egypt. I had written a history of that era to 1908, so went on to the later era which I knew best. That study became my second book. Bahi al-Din Barakat, whom I mentioned before, gave me his father's memoirs – his father was Zaghlul's (1854–1927) nephew – which he had never given to anybody else. I spent a whole summer going to sit with him every morning, asking him questions about Egyptian political life. I found that the colonial patterns I had written about in my first book continued, but the economic component became more clear to me. The élites who accommodated the colonial existence, especially those of fellah origin, made their money selling cotton to the British. How far could you push the British then? In a sense it showed me that the divisions in Egyptian society were economic but were influenced by personal squabbles, with each man wanting to be number one. Amongst the top contenders, I'd put Saʿd Zaghlul, founder of the Wafd Party and the nationalist leader of the pre- and post-World War I era, who had an enormous ego. The ruling élites all believed that the British were not going to let go, so they used them. At the same time the British used the Egyptians and played them carefully against one other, and above all they used the monarch whom they kept on the throne. And therefore the king played their game. There was, of course, on some level a nationalist ideology, there was a definite attempt to bring a liberal form of government to Egypt.

I then became fascinated by Muhammad Ali. At that time Elizabeth Monroe, the senior fellow at St Antony's, was writing a biography of St John Philby, and I thought of writing a biography of Muhammad Ali. I was also interested in the notion of biography and psychohistory so I considered writing a psychohistory of Muhammad Ali. Then I decided to write a more general history of this period because in that way I could continue my original intention to "fill in the blanks" of Egyptian history. I felt that Egyptian history had been very badly served, that much of what had been written was based entirely on non-Egyptian sources. I reflected that a study of the Muhammad Ali era, along with my studies of Cromer and the liberal age, would cover nearly two hundred years of Egyptian history. The result was *Egypt in the Reign of Muhammad Ali.*

The Muhammad Ali book was no longer narrative. It was more topical. Wallerstein's book had a great effect on me.[7] I began to read more on dependency theory. I read Eric Hobsbawm, E. P. Thompson, Guillermo O'Donnell, André Gunder Frank.[8] I would pick an idea from here, reject an idea from there. I definitely rejected the Weberian idea of oriental despotism. I wanted to write about Muhammad Ali from an Egyptian outlook. Who was Muhammad Ali important to? He was important to Egypt. When people say I should have used the Ottoman archives, I say, "Yes, I should have, but I was writing the Egyptian version of Muhammad Ali, not the Ottoman version and certainly not the European version." When people query my interpretations I am not terribly interested because I am writing from a certain personal viewpoint. I am interested if a reviewer tells me that I am wrong about events or that my factual evidence was not sufficient to prove what I wanted to say. If a reviewer tells me that my interpretation was wrong, I reflect that my interpretation is as valid as theirs, perhaps even more valid, because I have at least gone into the Egyptian archives and drawn out all the material on Muhammad Ali which nobody else has done. One reviewer commented that I wrote as an Egyptian patriot – why should an Egyptian patriot not write the history of her country? Would an American patriot be discredited for writing a history of the Civil War or of the Revolution? Eurocentrism is still alive and well!

My interpretation comes from reading original sources, from what Muhammad Ali himself said. I read with questions in mind about Muhammad Ali and then allowed him to answer those questions. One question was, "Why did you embark on wars of expansion?" The answer was supplied in his own material and is very clear: "I need to expand to support my industrial projects". Why did you embark on industrialization? "Because Egypt can grow and develop only if it is industrialized". That led me to the idea that this man was a mercantilist, that he was simply following European mercantilist thought, and to check that I investigated economic source materials.

NEG: Where did you find these materials?
MARSOT: In the Egyptian archives.

NEG: No one had used them?
MARSOT: A few French officials had used them to write panegyrics on Muhammad Ali, and some had been edited and published in Arabic but with no analysis or interpretation.[9] Nobody had used them as extensively as I did.

NEG: Do the Arabic or Egyptian sources paint a more positive picture than the European sources?
MARSOT: Yes, but there is no such thing as an objective piece of

material. When the consuls reported to their governments about Muhammad Ali, they were trying to advance their own opinions. When Muhammad Ali wrote to his son Ibrahim, he was trying to advance his own opinions. You have to use the sources very critically. "Why is he saying this? Why did he do what he did?" These are the questions you have to ask. "Why does one consul say this about Muhammad Ali and another consul say exactly the opposite? Why does a man who met Muhammad Ali for half an hour write a whole book on the man, destroying Muhammad Ali and his work in Egypt?"

NEG: How can you find out a person's motivations?
MARSOT: You have to look back at the person and see why he wrote this about Muhammad Ali. Why did he say that Muhammad Ali had very shifty eyes, why did Palmerston begin by praising Muhammad Ali and end by calling him a waiter in a coffee shop? Then you look at Palmerston's policy, what he was out to get in the Middle East, what events happened in the Middle East to change his opinion. Then you have to do the same thing for Muhammad Ali.

When I was done with the Muhammad Ali book the editors of Cambridge University Press asked me to write a short history of Egypt for the general reader who does not want a single footnote.[10] They said to write it so that first year university students can understand it. It was great fun to write; I enjoyed it thoroughly. I put in my ideas on Egypt and on the development of Egyptian society, so it is not merely a book of facts. It has also got my own interpretations of history.

NEG: Did the major political crises of that era affect your formation as a historian?
MARSOT: The Palestine War of 1948 was a very anxious period because my mother was away from home. She was a volunteer nurse, a major in the army nursing corps. I was always horrified when there was an emergency because my mother would be away from home for weeks at a time. I was in high school then, and I had a number of Palestinian friends. The war was something very real because they were refugees from their country. It became something very living not only because of the sirens going off and having to go to bomb shelters, but because I saw the result of people being displaced from their country. At the same time I had cousins who were military men who were out there fighting, and the war became very immediate, part of our family life. Between 1948 and 1952 I was more occupied with the upheavals that were going on within Egypt – the Muslim brothers, bombs going off, the assassination of the prime minister. We were more conscious of the internal situation and thought very little of the

outside except that there was a new state called Israel that was our enemy.

The 1952 Revolution was the first major upheaval in my family because it directly affected each one of us. It was most traumatic. It brought into existence something that we had been talking about: change, overthrowing the monarchy, the corrupt ruling élite. In the beginning all of the younger generation identified with Nasser and his crowd. Then there was a *khaybat amal* (disillusionment) with their corruption, their greed, their nepotism, and their incompetence. There was a *prise de conscience* as well, "Why are we doing this to each other?" I remember my father once meeting Shaykh al-Baquri, the minister of waqfs, and saying, "You are the only one of the revolutionary crowd that I like because you don't set up half of Egypt against the other half. You enjoin us to come together." That struck me as one of the most profound things he ever said. Instead of divide and rule *à la Britannique*, the government was dividing and ruling in a new style, setting up the new élite against the rest.

The 1956 Suez Crisis had a personal effect on me because, as I mentioned, volunteering in Port Said and Ismailiyya, I saw the war at first hand. In Port Said you had to close your nose because of the smell from the corpses all around you. You heard all the stories, it made war a very real thing to me.

In spring of 1967 we were sitting behind the Pyramids, at the Tent City, having dinner with the French ambassador and the French press attaché who was a family relation of Alain. We were watching the lights of Cairo and all of a sudden the lights went out. It was a blackout. We were all saying that war was imminent. A few weeks later the press attaché called and said, "My wife and children are leaving for France." My husband and infant daughter were French citizens and for all I knew France would be involved again as in 1956, and Alain would be interned. We left for Paris and the next day we went out for a walk and returned to learn that Egypt had just been bombed. What was not expected was the utter defeat of Egypt. One had excuses to make in 1956 but none for 1967. The 1967 war probably revived my interest in politics, in power politics, which I do not write about directly but which is always in the back of my mind. I was asking, "What alternatives do the man or woman in the street have to autocracy?" "What happens to ordinary people under autocratic regimes like those of Nasser and Sadat?" The newspapers were censored ... That brought me to the idea of thinking what happens to people when you have a dictatorship. I started writing about alternative movements and women's organizations, and that led me to a very old-fashioned idea that maybe certain things are passed on from one generation to the other. A world ethos is passed on from one generation to the other.

How do you learn what the philosophy of the person in the street is? Written philosophy is élite philosophy and is not something that the person in the street absorbs. Sixty per cent of the people are illiterate, yet they are thinking people. How do they communicate? I have always been fascinated by the joke not only because it makes you laugh, but because it tells you a great deal about people, their attitudes toward rulers. Jokes and proverbs are a way people communicate their attitudes toward authority and political power. I wrote articles on jokes and proverbs, on alternative activist groups, and of course a series of articles on the ulama, Egypt's traditional community leaders who were outside the formal political establishment.[11]

While researching the economic status of the ulama I had continually come across references to women proprietors, and I decided to write a book on women in eighteenth-century Egypt. I started out intending to do a quantitative history to describe the kind of property that women owned in the eighteenth century. Once I began to research the topic, I decided to do a social history of the period. You can't write about women if you don't write about men, though the opposite is done often enough. So I changed the focus. Instead of making it simply an analysis of the urban property owned by women I expanded it. Now it is a social history of the period with women as my pivot. I need to say more about these women than simply to give an account of how much property they owned. What does the fact that they owned property tell me about their society? I talked about four different strata in society bringing in property that women owned. The central thesis was that in the latter half of the eighteenth century, a period of turmoil and change, women acquired much more wealth, much more property, and much greater involvement in the market-place than they had had in the seventeenth, early eighteenth, or the nineteenth century. My reason for that is that in a time of political turmoil the men were preoccupied with public affairs so the women took over management of their own private property and did a very good job. It is no great invention. Eighteenth-century Egyptian women were entrepreneurs. They bought and sold and were respected by society. On the other hand, the nineteenth century had a negative impact on women. The centralized state, the integration into world commerce, the adoption of Western economic institutions, the inflow of European businessmen, all militated against the involvement of women in the marketplace. Thus women are only now recovering the ground lost in the nineteenth century.

I went to Egypt and gave this in a lecture at the American University, and I got tremendous feedback from the audience. A young woman who is doing land tenure at Princeton called Maha

Ghalwash pointed out that in the nineteenth century when women inherited property and land they turned it over to the men. This never happened in the eighteenth century when in every *waqfiyya* (deed of religious endowment) the woman says that she is using her own money (*maliha*), that her husband is only her representative (*wakil*), and that she is endowing such and such an amount for the specified charitable purpose. There was a very clear separation between the woman's property and her male guardian's property that becomes blurred in the nineteenth century. This begs the question, "Why?" The answer is found in the fact that Muhammad Ali introduced the state system, Westernization, modernization, and technology. This peripheralized women because the institutions he introduced were European institutions that did not recognize the legal existence of women. The state system eliminated private enterprise so élites were turned into bureaucrats and women entrepreneurs were removed from the picture. Bridget Hill has shown how women in the eighteenth century became marginalized by the introduction of advanced technology.[12] She shows that in the early part of the eighteenth century, women were blacksmiths and builders, but by the end of the period there were no women blacksmiths, no women builders. In the early eighteenth century there was little distinction between women's and men's work, but this changed with the advent of capitalism and industrialism.

NEG: How did you become interested in writing about women?
MARSOT: If you read all the history of the world up to the nineteenth century there were no women in the world: there were only prominent men. In Ottoman history you do read about the *valide sultan* (the sultan's mother), but she is never named. I myself had scarcely mentioned women except perhaps in one article on the Mabarra (hospital) women.[13] Yet I had always been interested in writing about Arab women. So the discovery of the unexpectedly rich source materials on eighteenth-century women and my long-standing interest in Arab women led to this project.

NEG: Has the Annales school influenced your approach to history?
MARSOT: The Annales school said history is a history of peoples and not of rulers. In the first book, *Egypt and Cromer*, I said that in Egypt personalities count more than anything else. Now I believe that while personalities are very important, one must take into account the social and economic structure. That came from the Annales school.

NEG: As of 1990 what has the "orientalist debate" come up with?
MARSOT: The sad thing is that we are still producing orientalists.

Many of the new generation who claimed that they were doing new work are doing the same kind of work and are not even asking the questions that need to be asked. They are still looking at the Middle East as an exotic, different culture. Edward Said tried to change that in his book, *Orientalism*, with an abrasive but necessary critique of the field, but clearly there are still those who prefer the "old" approach rather than to look at the Middle East from within, to try to understand what makes it tick, to concentrate on raising new questions to which they would provide new answers. I am rather disappointed because I thought the new generation would come up with a new and exciting school of thought.

Feminist theory is the most interesting thing that has come out of the 1970s and 1980s. Some of it has gone overboard, but that is understandable when women's roles in history have been ignored for so long. Feminist historians are coming up with new ideas, asking new questions, using a new vocabulary.

NEG: Do you have any advice for students considering specializing in Middle Eastern history?
MARSOT: Prospective students should know that one cannot do bits and pieces of history, that one cannot understand the nineteenth century without understanding the earlier periods. My advice is to begin with general history and then choose a period or subject. It doesn't have to be the contemporary period. The student has to learn Arabic and Turkish or Arabic and Persian. Arabic is indispensable for the religious or religio-cultural component because the Quran is written in it. It has to be an Arabic that is sound enough to read the archives. The student has to go to the Middle East, to become acquainted with the people, to feel the heat of summer, to feel the cold of winter, to taste the food, to smell the odour of the place to understand how a people thinks. One can sit in a library and edit manuscripts but will learn nothing about the culture. One needs to see the light on the Nile, the desert at sunset to understand Egypt.

Notes

1. Albert Hourani, "The decline of the West in the Middle East", *International Affairs*, 29 (1953), 22ff.
2. Afaf Lutfi al-Sayyid Marsot, *Egypt and Cromer: A Study in Anglo-Egyptian Relations* (London: Murray, 1968).
3. ———, *Egypt's Liberal Experiment* (Berkeley and Los Angeles: University of California Press, 1977).

4. ——, *Egypt in the Reign of Muhammad Ali* (New York and Cambridge: Cambridge University Press, 1984).

5. John Marlowe, *A History of Modern Egypt and Anglo-Egyptian Relations, 1800–1953* (New York: Praeger, 1954).

6. Afaf Lutfi al-Sayyid Marsot, "The ulama of Cairo in the eighteenth and nineteenth centuries", in Nikki R. Keddie (ed.), *Scholars, Saints, and Sufis: Muslim Religious Institutions in the Middle East since 1500* (Berkeley and Los Angeles: University of California Press, 1972), pp. 149–65.

7. Immanuel Wallerstein, *Capitalist Agriculture and the Origins of the European World-Economy in the Sixteenth Century* (New York: Academic Press, 1974).

8. Eric Hobsbawm, *The Age of Capital, 1848–1875* (New York: Scribner, 1975); E. P. Thompson, *The Making of the English Working Class* (London: V. Gollancz, 1963); Guillermo A. O'Donnell, *Modernization and Bureaucratic Authoritarianism: Studies in South American Politics* (Berkeley: Institute of International Studies, 1973); André Gunder Frank, *On Capitalist Underdevelopment* (New York: Oxford University Press, 1975).

9. Asad Rustum, *A Calendar of State Papers from the Royal Archives of Egypt relating to the Affairs of Syria, 1940–1943* (Beirut: American University Press, 1940–3).

10. Afaf Lutfi al-Sayyid Marsot, *A Short History of Modern Egypt* (New York and Cambridge: Cambridge University Press, 1985).

11. See, for example, Afaf Lutfi al-Sayyid Marsot, "The beginnings of modernization among the rectors of al-Azhar, 1798–1879", in William R. Polk and Richard L. Chambers (eds), *Beginning of Modernization in the Middle East* (Chicago: University of Chicago Press, 1968), pp. 267–80; ——, "The wealth of the ulama in late eighteenth-century Cairo", in Thomas Naff and Roger Owen (eds.), *Studies in Eighteenth-Century Islamic History* (Carbondale: Southern Illinois University Press, 1977), pp. 205–16; ——, "Revolutionaries, fundamentalists, and housewives: alternative groups in the Arab world", *Journal of Arab Affairs*, 6, 2 (Fall 1987), pp. 178–97; ——, "Popular attitudes towards authority in Egypt", *Journal of Arab Affairs*, 7, 2 (Fall 1988), pp. 174–98.

12. Bridget Hill, *Women, Work, and Sexual Politics in Eighteenth-Century England* (Oxford: C. Blackwell, 1989).

13. Afaf Lutfi al-Sayyid Marsot, "The revolutionary gentlewomen in Egypt", in Lois Beck and Nikki Keddie (eds), *Women in the Muslim World* (Cambridge, Mass.: Harvard, 1978), pp. 261–94.

MAXIME RODINSON, born in Paris in 1915, is a specialist in oriental studies. He studied Old Ethiopic and Old South Arabian languages and Near Eastern anthropology at the *École des Langues Orientales* (School of Oriental Languages). In World War II he was stationed in Beirut and subsequently worked in the antiquities service in Lebanon and Syria. After working as a librarian in the Bibliothèque Nationale, he succeeded his professor, Marcel Cohen, at the *École Pratique des Hautes Études* (Practical School of Higher Studies). Trained as an orientalist, he considers himself a "*sociologue*", a term with a rather different sense than the English "sociologist". The term "social historian" would more commonly be used in the English-speaking world. In 1981 he became a corresponding fellow of the British Academy and in 1985 a Chevalier of the Legion of Honour in France. He lives in Paris.

Interviewed at his home in Paris by Nancy Gallagher on 19, 20, and 21 August 1988.

NEG: Can we begin with your family background?
MAXIME RODINSON: I was raised in Paris in a communist milieu. My father and my mother were Russian Jews raised in the Russian Empire. In 1885 my father emigrated to Paris, where he later met my mother. He had attended a high school in Smolensk, Russia, where he was in the milieu of those who struggled for social reform. In Paris, he was a founder of a trade union in which there were only Jewish workers. My mother was twenty years younger than he. She was a worker like him. In another context he would have been an intellectual, and she perhaps. My father was an anarchist around 1890, then a socialist up until 1920. My parents became communists in 1920 following the *Congrès de Tours*, where the majority of the *Parti Socialiste Français* voted to join the Third International.

NEG: Your mother was also communist?
RODINSON: Yes and more ardent, at least at the time I became aware

of these things. Much later I was very astonished to learn that when she arrived in Paris in 1902 she was still saying her prayers, but when I knew her, that is to say more than twenty years later, she had, like my father, detached herself from Judaism. My father was more intellectual, my mother more fanatic. She became more devoutly Stalinist than he was. In short, both were Russian Stalinists.

NEG: What work did she do?
RODINSON: She and my father did the same work. That is how they met. They made waterproof garments by coating material with gum diluted in kerosene. I used to go fetch cans of kerosene from a garage. The solution smelled very bad and caused occupational diseases. We lived in a series of houses, one of which still exists. On the ground floor, the workroom consisted of two rooms on the street, and we lived in two other rooms in back. I learned to read by myself, in *l'Humanité*, the party's journal, which I used to fetch each morning.

NEG: Do you have brothers and sisters?
RODINSON: I had one sister who died recently at the age of 80. She did not wish to continue her higher education. She had the same mother but not the same father. She worked in radio but was anti-intellectual. Once she said to me not long before her death, "Mama used to take us to the meetings, which bored me terribly: I understood nothing, while you enjoyed them." I was at all the demonstrations from the age of three or four when my mother would take me. I recalled the other day, when I was in America, that I had been taken to a demonstration for Sacco and Vanzetti.

So my father was one of the Russian emigrants. At first he was involved with the purely Jewish trade unions made up of Yiddish-speaking workers. Later he mixed with all kinds of Russians, especially trade unionists and socialists. He helped preserve the library where Lenin used to look for books. The library had Russian socialist and anarchist literature. I have some books on anarchism which certainly came from there. And I have *Capital*, by Karl Marx, the old French translation of 1872, which Marx revised, a volume that belonged to this library. The library was next to where I was born, in the thirteenth arondissement, on the Avenue des Gobelins. Unfortunately, the library and the house itself were torn down two years ago. I was very unhappy about it. Marx lived in Paris from 1843 to 1845. He lodged in this street on which I now live, rue Vaneau, first in the very house where we are now, for some months, then across the street. Several months ago I purchased a studio across the street at one of the places where he stayed. He also had an office there where he edited a review.

In the English translation of my book, *La fascination de l'Islam*, you will see the dedication to Moise Twersky, a very interesting man and a friend of my family.[1] I was always torn between my parents' ideas and his. My parents were communists, he was liberal. We had one of those "salons" of poor Jews in Paris. He came every Monday, and we would drink tea from a samovar. He was the son of an Hasidic rabbi who made miracles in the Ukraine, and he was very Voltairian, very critical and sarcastic. He was anti-Stalinist while my parents were Stalinists. They argued all the time, and they liked each other very much. I always hesitated between these two tendencies: the communist and the liberal. This was reinforced by the French primary schools I attended. I hesitated very much: should I adhere to the party or no? I remember saying to Twersky, "You have an image of the world that is false. You believe that this world is an assembly of people, like an academy where each one rises in his turn to deliver his own speech, one opposing the other. But in reality the world is made of forces in battle." He was very shocked and said to me, "What an image of the world for such a young man." It was the time of Hitler: there was only one force strong enough to oppose Hitler, and that was the Soviet Union represented in France by the communist party. Moise Twersky committed suicide in 1940 after France was invaded. The Vichy government made a census of the Jews. He understood immediately what that meant and he committed suicide. Now I often think of him. He was about fifty or sixty years old in 1940. Moise Twersky was anti-Zionist: everybody around us was anti-Zionist. My parents, my friends, we were all internationalists, and we had no interest in Jewish nationalism.

At the age of ten or eleven, I began to read books on the culture and history of non-European countries. I read about Islam, and it fascinated me. There was a French collection, in a library where I studied, which appeared in the 1840s called "l'Univers pittoresque". It had a book called *Arabie* by Noel Duverger that fascinated me. I have other memories that show my interest in Islam. One was when I was at primary school, certainly before the age of twelve, we had a curious library system. When lots of borrowed books had been returned, one of the pupils would climb on to the platform and ask, "Who wants this book or that book?" My hand went up when he read out the title *The War of Mahomet* [Fr. for Muhammad]. Everybody laughed at my sulky expression when I got the book which was entitled the *War of Dahomey*. But I read the book all the same. It was about the French conquest of Dahomey (today Benin). I still have some memories of it, but it was not the war of Muhammad. When I was fifteen I knew by heart the genealogy of Adam to Muhammad.

At that time you had to pay for secondary school, and my parents did not have much money. I had taken an exam and had won a scholarship, but it was still not enough to complete my baccalaureat for there were many other fees.

At that time I had very fearful ideas about the bourgeois world. I thought one had to pay attention to not be caught up in its hostile snares. So what to do? I had read the brochure of the *École des Langues Orientales*, now the *Institut National des Langues et Civilisations Orientales*, which announced that it prepared its students to be interpreters in the consulates and embassies of France. This appealed to me. In addition, the school was free, and one could enter it without the *baccalauréat*. It only required an entrance exam and the knowledge of two foreign languages. I had learned a little English in the last years of primary school, but I did not know another language. So I took up Spanish and learnt from a book called *Spanish in Thirty Lessons*. Then I sat for the entrance exam.

During the exam, they quizzed me on literature, history, Spanish, and English. I was questioned on history by a professor of modern Greek. I was terrified, because I thought one had to beware of the bourgeoisie. I did not know that the professor was a communist. When he said, "Tell me about socialism in the nineteenth century", I said to myself, "Oh la la. This is a trap." I began with Saint-Simon. He waited a moment and said, "Good, that is enough for Saint-Simon. Who was there after that?" I replied, "There was Fourier", and spoke extensively about Fourier. He said, "Good, and who after? You speak only of the French, but there were others who were foreign." I spoke of one or two others. Then he said, "But wasn't there another who was more important than these men?" I replied, "No, I do not see." "A German, who lived in London, who had a great beard?" I did not see. Then he said, "Have you heard of Karl Marx?" "Very little", I said. So he asked, "By comparison, the socialism of Saint-Simon and Fourier, is called utopian, while that of Marx is what?" I had to say, "Scientific socialism", but I feared that he would answer: "Not scientific at all". It seems that afterwards he gave me a good mark. I heard that he remarked to his friends, "You see the bourgeois education, they know all about Saint-Simon, Fourier, etc., but you have to extract the name of Marx."

And so I entered the school. To become a diplomatic interpreter, one could choose to specialize either in the Far East or the Near East. For the Far East only one language was required, Chinese or Japanese, as these languages were considered very difficult. If one chose the Near East, one had to learn three languages as Near Eastern languages were considered less difficult. I chose the Near East. Arabic and Turkish were required, and you could choose Persian or Amharic for the third language. I would have liked to study Persian, but I thought that Marcel Cohen, the only communist professor there, could protect me against bourgeois manoeuvres so I chose Amharic. The school was not properly speaking a part of the university system.

It depended directly on the ministry of education and was on the same organizational level as the university. While studying Arabic, I continued to read about the origins of Islam, and it interested me more and more. In addition, I studied anthropology and sociology. I entered the school in 1932, and I completed all my diplomas including my *baccalauréat* in 1935/6.

The year 1937 was the beginning of my serious life. First, thanks to Marcel Cohen, the one who was communist, I was accepted by the *Caisse Nationale de la Recherche Scientifique* (National Fund for Scientific Research) which later became the *Centre National de la Recherche Scientifique* (National Centre for Scientific Research) (CNRS). I did not have any chance of becoming a diplomat because I was still very proletarian. The centre had been established by the socialist government in 1936, which planned to develop France in all domains, cultural, scientific, etc. The centre had been part of this optimistic plan. I was one of the first grant holders. Second, I joined the communist party. Third, I was married. Fourth, I was temporarily liberated from military service. Every year I had had to come up before a medical board, to see if I could be drafted into the army. But I was very thin, weighing 50 or 52 kg. Finally the military found that I was not suitable. I then began a thesis on comparative Semitic linguistics.

NEG: Were your parents happy with your academic pursuits?
RODINSON: They did not quite understand, but were content all the same because it represented a social promotion and hope. They themselves continued to make their waterproof garments. My father was very old, he was born in 1865. He was 72 in 1937. But they were dismayed when they saw me learning Hebrew. For them, Hebrew was the language of the rabbis and when they saw that I was copying Hebrew letters they said, "Look how he has tumbled into such foolishness." They did not understand that one could study Hebrew, other Semitic languages, or the history of the Jewish or Islamic religions in an objective way.

When war broke out in 1939, I was drafted into the army after all because they needed men. The military commission was accepting everyone. They put me in what was called "auxiliary service", second class units that did not have to carry arms. More specifically, I was put in the quartermaster corps, the support services that supplied the food, uniforms, etc. I was forced to attend a military school to become an officer in the commissariat services. I said to the colonel, "I do not have the aptitude; it is useless." He said, "Do what I say: sign." I attended the school for four months. It was in the middle of the war so we were moved to Issoudun, Berry, Bordeaux, and finally Brittany. I failed the exam and became a soldier, second class, in the commissariat services. I was then stationed in Tours.

In May 1940, as the Germans were occupying Somme, near Amiens, the French military bureaucrats suddenly discovered that it was necessary to comply with a treaty between France and "Free Poland". Some Poles had escaped and had formed a Free Poland government which had brigades in Britain, France, and Syria. The Free Poland government had signed a treaty with the French government which had agreed to furnish commissary supplies to the Polish brigades in French or French-controlled territory. So the French military arranged for soldiers and officers to travel by boat to Syria to supply the Poles. It had made up a list of three officers and ten soldiers, but none of the soldiers wished to leave Tours. Since the beginning of the war, I had been trying to find a way to practise my Arabic. I had even asked Louis Massignon, my former professor who was in the ministry of war, to put me in a corps in which there were Arabic-speaking soldiers, but he said he could not arrange things like that. So I asked the captain to cross out a name and put mine in its place. This was done with the stroke of a pen. The one I replaced was very happy for he, like most of our comrades, was convinced that Beirut had lions in the streets. I had a small radio I was going to take to listen to the news. He said, "But you will not find electricity over there."

We arrived in Beirut, I believe the third of June 1940, and went to look for the Poles who were based in Homs. When we arrived they were very astonished and asked us, "What are you doing here?" We told them, "According to the treaty, we have to give you your supplies." They replied, "We have been here for six months so you would think that we have found a means of obtaining supplies for ourselves." We said, "That is true. What to do?" Our officers then departed for Beirut to ask the *état-major* (general staff) what to do, and we were left with the Poles. The officers were told that it was not the moment for such problems with France being invaded. We were to check their papers, their accounts, anything, but none of us knew Polish. Meanwhile, France had capitulated, and the Poles left for British Palestine to continue the war. We did not know whether to continue the fight under de Gaulle or to rally behind Pétain. We did not know quite what was going on in France. Nobody knew who de Gaulle was. It seemed he was a kind of royalist. Finally, we decided to stay there and wait, but if things went badly we would go to Palestine.

I was demobilized in December 1940 and decided to remain in the Near East. I was aided by a Frenchman, a professor whom I had known in France, an anti-colonialist who had made a good study of the Lebanese dialects. He was in touch with the Arab nationalists in Syria and Lebanon. He recommended me to a college in Sidon, and I succeeded in getting a contract.

I had no money when I was demobilized, but my sister-in-law, who was a teacher in the south of France, succeeded in sending me a bit of money. I had to return my clothes to the army. I managed to keep the shirts, but I had to return the rest. So I went to the *suq* (market) to buy a vest and trousers. Wearing this curious suit, I arrived in Sidon where I spent the school year. I taught French and French literature in the higher level at a Muslim secondary school.

In 1941, Syria and Lebanon were invaded by the British. The French Vichyist troops had withdrawn to the north. I was in Sidon at the time the British entered. We were bombarded by the British flotilla which hit everything, in the north, the south, the suburbs. The British troops were mostly Australians, but there were also some French Gaullists and Palestinian Jews among them. After some hesitation, I formally joined with the Gaullist forces. After the British–Gaullist victory, I was able to bring my wife and my son, who was then three, to Beirut.

Meanwhile, an archaeologist I had met in Sidon had become Director of the Antiquities Service of Free France in Beirut. Though it had been defeated, France still had power over many things in Syria. I found a place with the antiquities service. Since it was wartime, we worked to protect the works of art. We made efforts to replace a column that had fallen and the Lebanese or Syrian police prepared summons in Arabic against offenders who stole stones or damaged columns, and so forth. The police then made the summons over to us to take the necessary steps. I translated the summons into French.

I spent many years in Beirut. I had two more children there. It was the first time that I had been outside France. Beirut was a very nice town, it was very agreeable. I had learned Arabic in France, but this was my first experience speaking Arabic with people. I was very enthusiastic, exultant. After I was demobilized, I made trips here and there in the Middle East, and at the end of 1941 and beginning of 1942 made contact with the Lebanese and Syrian communist parties. Before that I had begun to detach myself a bit from politics, but because of the war I was again caught up in the communist–Stalinist frame of mind. I was very friendly with Syrian and Lebanese communists. I would help them to obtain printing paper for the communist newspaper, for example. Later, I was appointed to the staff of the French Institute in Damascus. And so we spent the war like that.[2]

During the war I wrote some articles in the newspapers and in the communist journals. They were not exactly my first publications, for before the war I had made a contribution to a bibliography of Muslim art.[3]

In 1947 I returned to France. The French government practically expelled me from Lebanon and Syria, because I had been active with the Lebanese and Syrian communists. I had made speeches on the radio. I had taught courses on Marxism in Beirut. Recently a friend at the French Institute in Damascus found a report about me which was unflattering. Anyway, perhaps I would have done the same thing had I been in the government.

In March 1944 de Gaulle had decreed that government officials in Syria and Lebanon who had joined Free France would be given government positions. After the victory, we were required to fill out papers asking us what posts we wanted. I asked to be appointed in one of three fields: the diplomatic corps, libraries and, I think, museums. I was first appointed to the diplomatic corps for the Near East, but I decided that I would prefer the library service instead since I wanted to write scholarly works. The next day a telegram arrived from the Quai d'Orsay in Paris saying that my appointment was an error, and that they did not want me in the diplomatic corps after all. To be sure, they had read in my dossier that I was a communist. I was furious. I thought of counter-attacking, for the communists were represented in the government. Then I said to myself that this was crazy, for the day before I had freely chosen the libraries. So I was appointed librarian at the Bibliothèque Nationale, in the department of printed oriental works. I stayed there from 1948 to 1955. That was the era when I was very active in the French communist party. The party had much developed by the time I returned to France.

NEG: What became of the Lebanese communist party?
RODINSON: It was undermined by Stalin, who supported the partition of Palestine and the creation of a Jewish state. From May to June 1947, I lived that dilemma from one day to the next. On the last day that I was in Lebanon, I passed by the party office to donate a bit of money and to say goodbye to my friends. The secretary-general, Nicolas Chaoui said, "Wait a moment, a telegram has arrived from New York. You must translate it for us." The telegram was about Gromyko's speech at the United Nations supporting the partition of Palestine, implying the creation of the state of Israel. For them it was a shock, a catastrophe, because the day before, the Soviets and therefore the Lebanese communists themselves, had been against partition and for a united Palestine. For them, it was like the Hitler–Stalin Pact of 1939 had been for us. As one used to say, it was the death of the soul. They decided to support the Soviet Union all the same, but in so doing lost much of their following.

Back in Paris, I began to write articles for the communist party publications. I began to prepare a large manual of Marxism that has never appeared. It was thanks to the party that I began to write on general subjects. I wrote a polemic against Levi-Strauss, among others, and in 1953 I wrote my first article against Zionism, "Zionism or socialism", which was not so bad, though unhappily it had some unfortunate sentences dictated by my Stalinist ideas of that era.[4]

NEG: Your first major study was Magie, médecine, et possession à Gondar?[5]

RODINSON: Yes. I had begun the study before the war for my *diplôme*. I had wanted to choose a subject in sociology, ethnography, or anthropology, but I could not do field research in Ethiopia, so I worked on a text. In 1931–3 there had been a French anthropological mission from Dakar to Djibouti which had brought back some 200 manuscripts. Marcel Griaule, an ethnographer who directed the anthropological mission, gave me permission to use one of the manuscripts. The manuscript was a register of people who performed magic or medical cures in the town of Gondar. While I was working at the Bibliothèque Nationale, I translated, edited, and commented on the manuscript. I received the *diplôme* in 1955. The study was not published until 1967, 12 years later. It was a very specialized book, which could not appeal to a large public.

In the preface, I said that I intended to study parallel phenomena like magical medicine in Arab culture, such as the exorcising of those who were thought to be possessed by demons, and I studied these practices in Cairo. I continued this interest for some years. I have many documents on the *zar* rituals of exorcism in Cairo that have never been published. In Cairo I made contact with sorcerers, especially a female sorcerer. I found her again some years later, in 1970, and I believe in 1974. She is dead now. I later went to see her husband.

In 1955, I was elected to succeed Marcel Cohen, my former professor, who was professor of Old Ethiopic at the *École Pratique des Hautes Études* (Practical School of Higher Studies), 4th section, in the Sorbonne. It was a good moment for me to be elected as his successor. I was not too favoured for other posts because of my communism. Marcel Cohen was communist himself, the only one there, and he favoured me. The others said, "One communist goes, another comes; we are used to it." So I was elected to succeed him. It was probably the only place of higher education that I could have worked in at that time. Despite the obvious advantage, I hesitated because I had just been accepted at the Centre of Scientific Research. But in the end I chose higher education. I do not know if I was right. I only had to teach two hours each week, but there were the preparations, the theses, etc. It was not so bad: there were three, four, ten students, maximum.

It is a curious thing about French education. The *École Pratique des*

I am tempted to declare myself a positivist. Current studies by philosophically minded and literary minded people spurn any study resorting to the categories of reality, time, circumstances. Now and then I dream of one of these people being accused of having committed a crime in Bordeaux when on that day when he was in Paris. If the judge were to say to him, "You say that you were in Paris, but the category of place is not important and there is no such thing as a sure fact", the accused would protest and suddenly become very positivist.

NEG: Was Mohammed *well-received in the Islamic world?*
RODINSON: Yes and no. Until now it has been translated into Turkish but not into Arabic. It circulates under the table, discreetly: it is sold under the counter. You find it in Muslim countries, in some libraries, or in bookstores in out of the way places. It is read widely on the sly. But there are editions in English, Italian, Spanish, Dutch, and other languages.

NEG: Could you explain the origins of your book, Islam and Capitalism*?*[8]
RODINSON: A professor of Arabic literature had organized a symposium called something like "Has Islam aided or hindered the spread of capitalism?" There were four or five speeches. I made mine very short and critical. I had not had enough time to prepare it, but the topic excited me. Later in the book, I presented a more developed version of my ideas. I said that the question asked in the symposium was badly put because Islam is neither hostile nor favourable to capitalism. It is another thing. Capitalism developed as a result of factors outside the sphere of religion or anti-religion. This is the point I developed in this book. Max Weber wrote a book which is taken as saying that Protestantism favoured the development of industrial capitalism. Since his language is very difficult, that is what is generally understood. But if you read his work closely you will find that his ideas are not far from what I argued in *Islam and Capitalism*. My book was translated into Arabic, badly translated, and into many other languages, not always well understood, but until now it still sells in France and other countries.

NEG: Could you comment on the origins of Israel: A Settler-Colonial State*?*
RODINSON: In 1967, before the Six-Day War, Jean-Paul Sartre had decided to devote a special issue of his review, *Les Temps Modernes*, to the Arab–Israeli conflict. He was urged to by the general state of mind at that time and especially by Claude Lanzmann, who later became famous for his film "Shoah" (Hebrew for "disaster", currently used to signify the Holocaust). Lanzmann had been in the resistance and had

done very good work during the Algerian war, but he was preoccupied with the Holocaust. Sartre asked Lanzmann to organize this issue, with half Arab and half Jewish articles. I was asked to contribute, but I energetically refused to be in either the Arab or the Jewish part. I said that I was neither Arab nor Jewish, religiously speaking. Sartre and Lanzmann gave me a bad time, but finally they put me outside the two sections. My article, "Israel, fait colonial?" ("Israel, a colonial fact?") was a revision of what I had written in 1953 in my Stalinist article I mentioned before, but I deepened the analysis.[9] This article was later translated into English by the Trotskyists in New York and published as a little book with a new title *Israel: A Colonial-Settler State?* and a curious introduction.[10] It too was immediately translated into Arabic. There were two or three translations in Arabic. The book was even circulated in Syria by the ministry of culture. The ministry used it for propaganda, but it was honest because at the end of the book there were statements that were not so flattering to the Arabs at this time, but the ministry included them all the same.

NEG: How did you come to write Israel and the Arabs?[11]

RODINSON: The subject of the Arab–Israeli conflict became popular following the 1967 war. Penguin Books, a British publisher, asked me to write it. I did not want to spend too much time on that because there were other projects that interested me more. I thought it would take two months. In reality it took five or six months and it appeared at the beginning of 1968. The goal was to extend my earlier analysis a bit farther. I had always been a pedagogue. I had always been exasperated when I heard false ideas, so I said to myself that these false ideas must be corrected.

Meanwhile, I continued to give lectures in the sixth section, *Sciences économiques et sociales*, of the Sorbonne. One lecture was on the historical sociology of the Middle East. I drew my salary from my position as a professor of Ethiopic in the fourth section, *Sciences philologiques et historiques*, but taught and did the administration in the sixth section. From 1959 to 1971, I was in the *Sciences économiques et sociales* delivering lectures in addition to my paid teaching of Ethiopic. I wanted to drop Ethiopic altogether and work solely in the sixth section, but I wanted to do this in stages, to retain the position in Ethiopic so that someone after me could take it. But Fernand Braudel, who was then president of the sixth section, did not agree to my plan. Finally, in 1971, I said to myself, "Either they nominate me professor in the *Sciences économiques et sociales* with a salary while retaining the chair of Ethiopic or I go." So I went. Later, I realized that I would have had fifty or sixty students instead of the ten in Ethiopic. I would have had to supervise their theses and studies, and would have had no time for writing books. So I remained professor of Ethiopic until I retired in 1984. I still teach Ethiopic for free.

NEG: About this time you published your collection entitled Marxism and the Muslim World. *Do you believe that Marxism and leftist ideas are finished in the Arab world?*[12]

RODINSON: I believe that classical Marxist ideology is finished for the moment, but that it exists in a subterranean way and under special forms. Leftist ideas are in no way finished. All the world is influenced by the ideas of the left, even very conservative people. Among the Khomeinists one can find Marxist influences. My general theory is that dissension, protest, and ideas of revolt always exist, but that they need theories to shape them, to give birth to militant organizations and actions. So when Stalinist or Marxist ideas were in circulation, they were influential in Islamic countries as elsewhere. Now, there are all sorts of reasons why they no longer seem feasible, so people find other theories. Now, Islamic theories are shaping dissent.

In 1970 Lutfi Kholi and my other friends in Cairo asked me to deliver a lecture on Marxism and Islam. I said that "Marxism" did not exist in itself. I said that there was Marx who had ideas on various subjects, and then the Marxists after him who declared themselves his disciples. Marx had said that he was "Marx but not a Marxist" in about 1880 when Lafarque, his son-in-law, had told him that people were declaring themselves Marxists or anti-Marxists. Nevertheless, there was a big unfolding of Marxist movements of all kinds. It is the same thing in many fields. For example, the Christians. The Roman Catholic Pope said that Luther was not a Christian. Luther said that the Pope was not a Christian. There are philosophical ideas supported by Marx or by some Marxists that contradict other Marxist ideas. One system was declared by Engels, Lenin and others to be the only true Marxist philosophy. Marx himself might have had other philosophical ideas. I have a book here, the best manual on philosophical Marxism, written by a Catholic priest who was very sophisticated in philosophy, a Pole by origin.[13] He shows that there were many common points between the Marxist and Thomist philosophies. Among the ideas that are more or less derived from some of Marx's ideas, are ideas on society. Here I am more or less in agreement with the general lines. I call this sociology. I have explained some of these ideas in an article entitled "Marxist sociology and Marxist ideology", which appeared in the review of UNESCO.[14] Of course, there is no *one* Marxism. Nothing in that sense exists; it is scholasticist to believe that the things exist because there are words implying that. It is the scholasticism of the Middle Ages. I am positivist in one sense, and not in another. I am Marxist in one sense, and not in another. I am orientalist in one sense, not in another. The meanings of words change over time. It is like the great dispute of the Middle Ages between realists and nominalists. I think that pure Marxism does not exist in itself, but that there are varying degrees of Marxian ideas.

NEG: How did you come to write The Arabs *?*[15]
RODINSON: A publisher asked me to write a short book for the series of popular books, "Que sais-je?", about the essentials which everybody must know about the Arabs. For this little work I used some articles I had previously written for encyclopaedias. But I did not succeed in condensing the matter into the very limited number of pages wanted by the publisher, so they published it separately.

The best known of my books is *Mohammed*, I believe. And it is the dearest to my heart.

I have always continued to write scholarly articles along with my polemics. I have written articles on Semitic linguistics and on the history, culture, and material life of various Islamic countries and Ethiopia. I have written articles for the *Encyclopaedia of Islam* and elsewhere on the liver, on vehicles, on the moon, on the influence of Islamic countries on the West in the Middle Ages, and even on cookery in Muslim countries.

NEG: In your books, you seldom mention women.
RODINSON: This is because it is very difficult to write accurately about women. Women on the left, socialists, and even academics, have occasionally asked me to speak on women in Islam or sometimes on Algerian women. I have refused because it is very difficult to generalize. For fourteen centuries Islam has been or is dominant in countries from the Philippines to Morocco. I have signed petitions for this or that group of women, but to write something around this topic needs a very careful study. Women have been very oppressed, yes, it is true, but on the other hand certain women were powerful. So I hesitate when I am asked to give an exposé of one hour about women in Islamic countries. Some feminist women once said to me, "You said that a woman's lot was not so bad, but in reality it was terrible". Others said to me, "You said there was oppression, but there was no oppression." Politically, women as such were not so important. The women who had political power derived it from their associations with men. What interests me is the sociology of history, the determinants of history. In general, in history, it is one people against another, a class against another, men and women together, the women subordinate. The struggle of the sexes passes on a terrain that is neither political nor historical. There have been revolutions of races, of peoples, of classes, but there have not been revolutions of sexes. When one

studies the Middle East, one is preoccupied with colonization, decolonization, with the Islamic resurgence, and so forth. The role of women is not different from the role of men in all that. In Algeria, during the War of Independence, much importance was given to women like Jamila Boupacha, but after independence women lost their political prominence.[16] It is true that the status of women in Islamic countries is an important indicator of modernization and democratization. Many males support some kind of Islamic fundamentalism because they want to rely on classical Islamic law to safeguard their male privileges.

NEG: Could you comment on the orientalist debate?
RODINSON: Edward Said wrote a polemic against orientalism in a style that was a bit Stalinist, but I do not understand why his book had such success in the United States. The average American is not interested in orientalism. Said deals only with the English and the French orientalists who lived in colonial empires. He ignored others entirely, especially the Germans, who were in fact the great masters of European and American orientalism. But orientalism was begun much earlier, by scholars who were not part of a colonial empire.

NEG: Could you comment on Michel Foucault's interest in the Middle East?[17]
RODINSON: Like many philosophers, would-be philosophers, or people who studied some philosophy, Michel Foucault was not afraid of giving peremptory opinions on matters of which he was very ignorant. Once I had a little dispute with him. In 1978, on the eve of the Iranian revolution, he left for Iran where he met with intellectuals of the left and with Bani Sadr. Foucault was much taken with them and returned and wrote what was in my opinion a completely idiotic article. He wrote that in Iran there existed a spiritual politics, a model for all the world. I wrote an article against this in *Le Nouvel Observateur*, and he replied without saying much. Finally, he thought that no one had understood what he had written, and he abandoned the subject, which was better. Then he died.

NEG: What are your current projects?
RODINSON: I jump from one project to another. I began to write my memoirs. It took me 200 pages to get to the age of ten so I broke it off. I had wanted to do something more quickly. I then compiled a collection of my articles on Islam and politics. The editor is from Brussels, he is a friend who wishes to publish it in two years' time. The articles are finished, but, unfortunately, I have to write an introduction. In the meantime I launched into a study of the relations between ideological and political power across the centuries. It is always the

same story with me. I interrupted that study to write an introduction to my nephew's book. He is professor of Arabic in Madrid. He wrote an enormous thesis in Spanish on the inspector of the *suq* (market) in Muslim Spain and in the world of Islam in general. In the introduction I discussed the markets of all the peoples of the world, the Aztecs, for example, and in the end I wrote about pre-Islamic markets. I still have not had time to write up my material on the *zar*.

In the introduction to my collection of articles, I am asking, "What is Islam in comparison to analogous movements? What are the resemblances and the differences?" Much has been written from the point of view of comparative religion, i.e., the comparison of religious ideas, but I am writing from the point of view of the structure of religious (and ideological) organizations and movements. This, to my mind, is more important than doctrine. It is my materialist grounding: in all the religious movements – Manicheism, Taoism, Judaism, Catholicism, Protestantism – what is important from the viewpoint of historical and social dynamics is the structure of organizations and movements.

NEG: It seems that topics such as Marxism, Zionism, and capitalism are more important to you than the zar.
RODINSON: Yes, they *are* more important and their history is more interesting to me. About the *zar*, there have been many books that have appeared since I studied it. Other scholars have written on ecstatic religion, mixing problems of psychology and psychoanalysis. It is very complicated now. I had wanted to do something simple on what I studied in Cairo, but I did not find the time. In my Introduction to *Le Cuisinier et le philosophe*, I said that I never made battle but for God.[18] I meant, of course, that I battled for what were, in my opinion, good causes. I took the title from a Hebrew book of the Middle Ages, *The Wars of God*. In truth, that was always an underlying polemic in my studies, and, in this, I was following the Stalinist path. I always wrote books in one direction against another, or nearly always.

NEG: After a long life of political and scholarly activity, would you consider yourself optimistic?
RODINSON: In the beginning, I was a communist and optimistic. But now I see that those who have worked out the plans of a better society have in no way succeeded, and when one reads history it is always the same thing. Plato tried to influence history: he made a trip to Sicily, to Syracuse, to the tyrant Dionysius, but he returned because there was nothing to be done. I have given up "general" optimism, but one can

achieve some things in very limited areas. I have written that the outcome of revolutions is not so much in the general improvement of things, but in fresh demands. Before the eighteenth century nobody demanded that governments govern according to the wishes of the people. There has been progress, but with many failures and much falling-back on the way.

Notes

1. Maxime Rodinson, *La fascination de l'Islam* (Paris: Librairie François Maspero, 1980) translated into English as *Europe and the Mystique of Islam* (Seattle and London: University of Washington Press, 1987).
2. Professor Rodinson's parents were arrested in Paris and killed at Auschwitz in 1943.
3. Maxime Rodinson's contribution may be found in L. A. Mayer (ed.), *Annual Bibliography of Islamic Art and Archeology* (Jerusalem, 1938); ibid., vol. 3, 1939.
4. ——, "Sionisme et socialisme", *La Nouvelle Critique*, no. 43, February, 1953, pp. 18–49.
5. ——, *Magie, médecine, et possession à Gondar* (Paris: La Haye: Mouton, 1967).
6. ——, *Mahomet*, 2nd edn (Paris: Club Français du livre, 1961); translated as *Mohammed* (London: Allen Lane, The Penguin Press 1971).
7. ——, "Problèmatique de l'étude des rapports entre Islam et communisme", *Colloque sur la sociologie musulmane*, 11–14 (September, 1961), pp. 119–49, translated as "Relations between Islam and Communism", *Marxism and the Muslim World* (New York: Monthly Review Press, 1981), pp. 75–112.
8. ——, *Islam et capitalisme* (Paris: Edition du Seuil, 1966); translated as *Islam and Capitalism* (New York: Pantheon Books, 1974).
9. ——, "Israel, fait colonial?", *Les Temps Modernes*, vol. 22, no. 253 *bis* (1967), pp. 17–88.
10. ——, *Israel: A Colonial-Settler State?* (New York: Pathfinder, 1973).
11. ——, *Israel and the Arabs* (New York: Pantheon Books, 1968); *Israel et le refus arabe. 75 ans d'histoire* (Paris: Editions du Seuil, 1968).
12. ——, *Marxisme et monde musulman* (Paris: Editions du Seuil, 1972); translated as *Marxism and the Muslim World* (London: Zed Press, 1979).
13. I. M. Bochenski, *Soviet Russian Dialectical Materialism (Diamat)* (Dordrecht, Holland: D. Riedel, 1963).
14. Maxime Rodinson, "Marxist sociology and Marxist ideology", *Diogenes*, 64 (Winter, 1968), pp. 57–90.
15. ——, *Les Arabes* (Paris: Press universitaires de France, 1979); translated as *The Arabs* (Chicago: University of Chicago Press, 1981, and London: Croom Helm, 1981).
16. For information on Jamila Boupacha see Alistair Horne, *A Savage War of Peace: Algeria, 1954–1962* (New York: Penguin Books, 1979); for women in the Algerian revolution, see Marie Aimée Helie-Lucas, "Women, nationalism, and religion in the Algerian liberation struggle", *Opening the Gates: A Century of Arab Feminist Writing*, Margot Badran and Miriam Cooke (eds.) (Bloomington: Indiana University Press, 1990), pp. 105–14.
17. For an introduction to Michel Foucault, see Colin Gordon (ed.), *Power/*

Knowledge: Selected Interviews and Other Writings, 1972–1977 (New York: Pantheon Books, 1980).

18. J.-P. Digard (ed.), *Le Cuisinier et le philosophe: hommage à Maxime Rodinson* (Paris: Maisonneuve et Larose, 1982).

NIKKI KEDDIE, born in Brooklyn in 1930, specializes in the history of modern Iran. She studied history and literature at Radcliffe University and received her Master of Arts Degree at Stanford University and her doctorate at the University of California, Berkeley. She taught European history at the University of Arizona, Tucson, Western civilization at Scripps College in Claremont, and modern Middle Eastern history at the University of California, Los Angeles, where she is professor of history. She has received a Rockefeller Foundation Fellowship, a John Simon Guggenheim Fellowship, and has been president of the Middle East Studies Association and a guest scholar at the Woodrow Wilson Center for International Scholars. She currently lives in Santa Monica, California.

Interviewed at her home in Santa Monica on 7 January 1990 by Farzaneh Milani and on 22 April 1990 by Nancy Gallagher.

FM: Can you tell us about your early years?
NIKKI KEDDIE: My parents named me Anita [Ragozin], but I grew up being called Nikki. When I was three, my family – I have a brother two years older than I – moved to a small town in upstate New York where my father was the manager of a textile plant. We stayed there until I was six, when we moved back to Brooklyn where I went to public school and then a private school, City and Country School. I now learn that it is the oldest remaining private, progressive school. It had its seventy-fifth anniversary this year. It was a very good school; it had the idea of learning by doing. We did all sorts of projects: there was a theme each year such as the Middle Ages with manuscript production, or the Renaissance with printing. It was the best school I've ever attended, and a lot of people who went there ended up having fairly important positions. I guess the most important is a friend in the Chinese foreign service, now ambassador to Great Britain. When I was about ten we moved to Manhattan. Before that I used to commute on

the subway from Brooklyn to this school. I went to a very good high school, Horace Mann-Lincoln, also quite a well-known progressive school. It belonged to Teachers' College of. Columbia University, which closed it down a couple of years after I was there. I was interested in history even then.

My parents were very interested in intellectual things although they were not professionally intellectuals. My mother had wanted to be an engineer. When she was twenty, she came to the United States from Russia. She had had to stay home in Bessarabia (Moldavia) during World War I, although her family had gone ahead, because they didn't have enough money to guarantee her immigration. She went to the University of Wisconsin and wanted to become an engineer, but they told her that women couldn't be engineers in the U.S. (although they could even in pre-revolutionary Russia), so she majored in mathematics, although she did not do it professionally. From time to time she worked, mainly as a translator from Russian into English. She translated the first edition of Vasiliev's important history of the Byzantine Empire. My father read a lot. We always had books at home, and we saw a lot of theatre when I was a child. My parents were very permissive. I remember mainly eating hot fudge sundaes, reading comic books, and listening to the radio a lot. My parents really didn't bother me about it which maybe is an indication that you really don't have to push your kids if you have a general environment that encourages education.

I didn't start reading fiction and poetry until I was a junior in high school, and then I got very interested in Russian literature. But already when I was eleven I said that I wanted to do a report about some other part of the world, not Europe, so I did one on the Mongols, which I remember as being taken from one book, because the school's sources were limited. But I did get interested in the idea of looking beyond the West. We made up and put on plays at City and Country – I don't for the life of me know how it was done, because there was no script. It was some sort of cooperative project. These plays were usually historical, and often quite distant in time or place. There was one on the fourteenth-century English peasants' revolt in which I was King Richard II – on the wrong side. My brother was in one on India in which he was Nehru. This was before Indian independence. My class did one on China in World War II, so whoever was guiding us was guiding us not only toward history and politics, but also to areas other than Europe.

In 1947, I went to Radcliffe. At that time all the classes were coeducational, except for sections of elementary classes, but Radcliffe still had a separate identity [from Harvard] and gave separate degrees. I majored in history and literature, which was a combined honours major. You picked either a period or a country and the major would cover anything cultural in that period, including art and philosophy. It was a very good major. I picked nineteenth-century European history and literature. Their nineteenth century went from 1789 to 1939 – a very long century. At that time I was interested in Italian history and did my B.A. thesis on the Italian socialist party.

Even before Radcliffe, I was very involved in left-wing politics. I grew up in the far left. I was influenced by my parents who were leftists, especially my mother, so I wasn't revolting. If grade school was ice cream sundaes and radio programmes, then college was definitely political activity. It is interesting that people in the far left were pioneering in subjects that did not become part of the national agenda until the 1960s. We worked for special efforts to admit more blacks to universities and to get them better jobs, and we fought for women's rights. Most people stress all the negative things about the far left, its very naive acceptance of things that were going on elsewhere, but what we actually did wasn't, in the great majority of cases, to support the Soviet Union, but rather to work for peace and for issues like civil rights and women's rights. We helped set up the first NAACP chapter in Harvard and Radcliffe. I was involved in a temporarily unsuccessful but ultimately successful struggle to open the undergraduate library in Harvard, the Lamont Library, to women.

They had done an incredible thing. They built a new Harvard library, and although the old library, the big Widner Library, was then open to women, the new undergraduate library, where they put practically all the books that were of interest to undergraduates, was not open to women. This was particularly hard because at Radcliffe at that time we lived further away from campus than the Harvard people did, but most of our classes were on the Harvard campus and you had to walk over there. You might have an hour between classes, and exactly what you wanted to do was to go to the library and read books for your courses in that hour. There was only one little crummy place where you could go with your own books. It was a really discriminatory thing. And when we approached them they said the exclusion of women was in Thomas Lamont's will. It actually wasn't in Thomas Lamont's will; he didn't say to bar women. All he said was that it was to be a library for the use of Harvard undergraduates. If they were going to bar Radcliffe people they should have barred Harvard graduate students or faculty members and anyone who was not a Harvard undergraduate. And they said, "Women and men in the stacks together make noise or they do terrible things." They judged that partly on the basis of summer school when women were allowed. They said it had been noisier then, but that was because the Lamont Library was the only air-conditioned place on campus so people came there to cool off. We didn't succeed when I was there, but within a few years the policy changed.

I might add that while I was at Radcliffe a couple of Harvard friends who had decided to go on to graduate school changed from the European field to the Far East, and that may have given me some of the idea to study non-Western history. Already by the time I left I thought I might want to switch to what we might now call (or what we would have called a few years ago) the Third World. I had the feeling that the Third World was less studied and hence a more interesting area.

Then I came to Stanford, where I got my M.A. in one year. I went there because my husband had a job at Stanford as an instructor of Western civilization. I had got married when I was nineteen. I was an undergraduate in history and literature and he was a graduate student in history. We were in the same kinds of political activities. At Stanford I did an M.A. thesis on "The philosophy of history of Giambattista Vico". I really didn't like Stanford very much then. It is much better academically now. At that time the historians and the fellowship office treated me as second class, as some kind of beginner who couldn't take graduate seminars yet, and they said they couldn't give me a fellowship or even tuition because my husband was teaching there (at $3,200 a year!). So I switched to Berkeley. It was the only other possibility because my husband was teaching Western civilization at Stanford, and I couldn't leave the area.

Berkeley is a good school, and I loved going there, even though they didn't have anyone who taught Middle Eastern history. The only places that had Middle East programmes were Princeton and Michigan, and Princeton didn't admit women at that time.

FM: So you commuted to Berkeley?

KEDDIE: For two hours each way because I didn't want to drive. I took a car from home to the train, then a bus, and finally a trolley. My former husband had only a three-year contract at a time when jobs were very hard to get, and I think that it was a lot of strain on him, especially when he approached the end of his contract. He had favoured my going to Berkeley and not Stanford, but it was a strain. The first year I commuted two hours each way three days a week. The second year I wanted to take seminars, which were in the late afternoon or evening, so I stayed in Berkeley three days a week, and I think that made it more strained. I think there were other causes that helped break up the marriage.

Then I moved up to Berkeley and became involved almost immediately with the person who became my second husband. That was a rebound thing. You often lose judgement when you are young. I know practically nobody who confirms the view of youth as being the greatest time in your life. I think the younger years are years in which you often feel youself kind of pushed around by emotions and hormones and things you cannot control.

FM: How long did you stay in Berkeley?
KEDDIE: I stayed in Berkeley until 1957. I got my degree very young, when I was 24, in 1955. I wouldn't take that date too utterly seriously because I had had only a year of Persian and two of Arabic at that point, and didn't really know Persian yet. I did a thesis that didn't involve Persian language material. If I had waited until I had learned Persian better, it would have taken me longer. However, they scarcely taught Persian at Berkeley then, so I had to wait until I could take it elsewhere.

FM: So at Berkeley you decided to study Iran?
KEDDIE: Yes. I didn't have any ties to Iran, which everybody seems to think is very peculiar. At the time, Iran was in the Mossadeq period, which was especially interesting. Iran also appealed to me as a country with a very long cultural tradition, like Italy. It had an ancient history with a lot of artistic and literary achievements and was politically interesting. So I chose it.

FM: Were you working with someone at that time?
KEDDIE: There wasn't anybody at Berkeley. That was also peculiar because most people seem to think they have to work with somebody who knows something about their field. I worked mostly with the late Joseph R. Levenson in Chinese history. He was a very brilliant and fascinating historian who tends to be downgraded now. This is for reasons that don't have to do with his originality or early impact on the field. There is a tension between those who say good things about the cultures of non-European regions and those who say critical things. He did critical intellectual history. He was a real genius. Most unfortunately, he died at the age of 48.

I knew people mostly in Japanese and Chinese history, but I had the feeling that because there were so many good smart people in Japanese and Chinese history it would have been harder to get a job in those fields, especially as a woman. Also, I wasn't convinced I could master Chinese: it is hard to remember characters and also to look up things in the dictionary when there is no alphabet.

FM: How did you choose your dissertation topic?
KEDDIE: I didn't have the possibility of doing a monograph, partly

because even if I had known enough Persian at that time there was extremely little Persian language material in this country. R. K. Ramazani remembers that I wrote him a letter asking to borrow his copy of Kasravi's classic history of the Iranian constitutional revolution, *Tarikh-i mashruta-yi Iran* (History of The Constitution of Iran).[1] I couldn't go abroad, because, for political reasons, I couldn't get a passport. So I chose a very general topic, the "Impact of the West on modern Iranian social history". I am sure it would embarrass me if I reread it, but some people still comment on it. I kind of knew that it wouldn't work as a general book, although interestingly enough, in the back of my mind I had the idea that twenty-five years later I could use a lot of the material in a general book and indeed I did. That is one reason I was able to get *Roots of Revolution* out so quickly.[2] That is a completely different book, but on the earlier period the dissertation research was helpful.

FM: You had started learning Persian?
KEDDIE: Yes, they had Professor Walter Fischel at Berkeley who mainly taught Arabic, but who knew some Persian. I had taken Arabic, two years, especially with William Brinner, who was a fine teacher, and I took more later. Actually I think by now I've had more Arabic than any other language, which doesn't mean I know it terribly well. In addition to what Persian I took at Berkeley, I also worked with a tutor. I took an intensive summer course at Harvard, and later I worked on it with a tutor when I went to Iran in 1960.

FM: After you graduated from Berkeley, what happened?
KEDDIE: I didn't have a teaching job right away. I had a one year research job in Berkeley concerning India and Pakistan. My second husband had a job in Oakland, and we thought we might stay in Berkeley, so I got a secondary credential. Actually, I never got the credential because I never wrote away for it, but I could have. I did all the course work, and did my practice teaching in high school, in world history and world literature. I was even a secretary in a real estate office for a month. We were also cook-managers one summer in a Yosemite high camp. I used to be a very good cook. Then my husband's situation changed. He had a job that involved physical labour, and he injured his back so he couldn't continue. At that point he was willing to leave Berkeley. For a few months we went to Tucson, Arizona, so he could help his father with a vitamin business. I thought I could spend most of my time doing research. When we arrived in Tucson, his father said he could pay him only $200 a month, which wasn't as bad as it sounds now, but you couldn't live on it so I had to

get a job. As there was nothing appropriate, I took a half-time job as secretary to the dean of the Graduate Division of the University of Arizona.

My academic teaching career started when a professor in the history department there died from a heart attack, and they needed somebody to take over his courses immediately – in European history, twelve hours a week. He didn't have to teach twelve hours a week, but they gave me twelve. So I took over all these courses in history and political science. That was a great break for me because I was writing around for jobs, and I certainly improved my chances after I started teaching. I ended up with four job possibilities. This was a period before jobs were advertised, and you were not supposed to write around. Your professor was supposed to recommend you for jobs he had heard about. I wasn't on particularly good terms with the professor who chaired my dissertation committee, and he wasn't in my field anyway. So I wrote about seventy-five letters to places in general. As three out of the four jobs that came through were from people I knew, I am still not sure it was useful to write around broadside to people I did not know. I got an offer from Scripps College in Claremont to teach what was essentially the third year of Western civilization, though it had a Third World component. My then husband wanted to go back for his Ph.D. in economics, which he could get in Claremont so we went there in the Fall of 1957. Then there was another chance – I am sure lots of people have chancy histories, but women probably more – because in my fourth year at Scripps, Professor Gustave von Grunebaum came out and gave a talk there. I talked to him and later gave papers at a couple of conferences in the Los Angeles area, one at UCLA which he attended. He was also an editor of *Comparative Studies for Society and History* and had read an article I had submitted to the journal and which was published there.[3] He was a remarkable man in many ways and, unlike most of his peers, didn't care what credentials you had. I would have had a very hard time getting a job at most major universities in the Middle East field, because I didn't have people in the field to recommend me, but he didn't care about things like that. He was very good at spotting people and didn't worry about the proper lineages. He also didn't discriminate on the basis of colour, nationality, or gender.

I was at Scripps for four years, one of which I spent in Iran. The first two I was teaching in a Western civilization programme, and then I did Asian history. We had two historians: the other did America and I did the rest of the world. I began publishing. I wrote one article based on my research job in Berkeley called "Labor Problems in Pakistan", published in 1957, and not very relevant to anything anymore. I have another article, which I don't think anybody reads, but it is really one of my best articles. It was published in 1959 in *Diogenes*, the international journal of UNESCO, and is a general analysis of Asian intellectual history. It discusses and compares major intellectual trends in different Asian countries, based especially on their different relationships to imperialism.[4]

Meanwhile, it had become possible to get passports because there was a Supreme Court ruling in 1958 which said that the government couldn't deny passports. So my husband and I decided to try to go to Iran. He was willing to do his economics thesis on Iran. So we applied for grants and went to Iran for 1959–60. During that year we found no other American scholars doing research in Iran, though there might have been some archaeologists. It is really amazing to remember when one thinks of the 1970s, when American scholars seemed to be everywhere in Iran.

My topic was the Constitutional Revolution of 1905–11. A number of people who have subsequently decided on this topic have come to the same conclusion as I did, that it is a topic which has a huge amount of material in Persian and English, and you really can't master it all unless you are willing to devote very many years to it. But at the time nobody knew that, so I ended up going to Iran with this topic in mind. Indeed I have a lot of research notes on it, concentrating on the pre-revolutionary period, especially the Tobacco Movement of 1890–1, which started out as an article and then became a book. As of 1990 no Western scholar had covered the Constitutional Revolution. Recently Mangol Bayat, my former student, and Janet Afary have done more general works on this revolution.[5]

It was very interesting to be in Iran, and quite adventurous at that time. We were part of a small group which somebody had dubbed "AWOPs" or "Americans without privileges". Practically every American in Iran had either duty-free entry of goods – groceries were sent in from Europe – and/or commissary privileges, which even Fulbright fellows got. We had very little money and it was hard to live with American habits on the Persian market. In 1960 there were very few Iranian canned or processed foods, and meat was not always safe, even when cooked.

I wouldn't say it was harder being a young American woman in Iran than it was in America. It was hard to be taken seriously in both places. When I had my business cards made in Iran, I said I was an assistant professor, and they made it sound like I was an assistant to a professor, which was the European system. I should have just put *ustadh* (university teacher), but I didn't, and people kept asking me what professor I was assistant to. It took me months and months to get the late Sayyid Hasan Taqizadeh to see me, but when he did I got a lot of good interviews. It was he who first told me that many intellectuals who pretended to be religious Muslims really were not, and gave details regarding men he had known during the Constitutional Revolution.

It was kind of rough, but in America it wasn't much better. For example, in summer of 1958 when I was at Harvard, people said I should see a certain scholar a few years older than I – still around and who shall remain nameless – who had spent some time in Iran. I had had my degree for a few years, I had published a few things, and I told him I was going to apply for an SSRC fellowship to go to Iran the following year. He said, "Oh, those only go to really important people in the field." It turned out that he had had one. He almost scared me out of applying. Often the really big people – not only von Grunebaum at UCLA and H. A. R. Gibb at Harvard but also Vladimir Minorsky, Maxime Rodinson, Claude Cahen, Albert Hourani, and Bernard Lewis with whom I began friendships between 1959 and 1963 – took me seriously.[6] Those who didn't tended to be those just a couple of years older than I was, or older academics insecure about their own scholarship.

In Iran there were a number of people, such as Taqizadeh, who at first didn't take me seriously, but in the end I was able to get through to many of them. I certainly didn't have a bad time with anybody, except one old man who told me I was dressed wrong. It was very hard to adjust to the fact that there were very different mores among different Iranians. When we came to Tehran in September of 1959, there were all these women walking around with skirts above their knees which wasn't what I expected. In fact, it was the first time I had ever seen it. I thought it was some kind of a local thing, but it turned out that a major Paris designer had just come out with skirts above the knee. He was the most famous designer, and people used to say, "he comes out with something in Paris and the next week it is in Iran", even though it wasn't yet accepted in Europe. You had women with beehive hairdos, wearing mini-skirts and very high-heeled shoes with very pointed toes. Taqizadeh had given me a whole list of people to try to talk to, but somehow it hadn't registered that there was some kind of religious connection for the man who objected to my sleeveless dress, which was common summer attire in Tehran. It was quite interesting in retrospect: I went in a dress with a full skirt well below the knees, and he went on and on about how I should not dress like that, it excited men too much.

I started out not liking Iran much, but I ended up really liking it, partly because it was strange and hence interesting to me.

Then I had one more year at Claremont during which there was an academic crisis in my life. Luckily it turned out fine. I had just learned I was to be terminated at Scripps (because the other historian found me uppity), and the next morning the phone rang. It was von Grunebaum offering me a year's position at UCLA. This kind of juxtaposition doesn't happen very often, but you sometimes make up for your bad luck with good luck. There had been a woman, Marie Boas Hall, before me in the UCLA history department, but there were some real anti-woman people in the department, some very openly and others not openly.

There was a group called the History Guild, which I hadn't known anything about. It is made up of historians of all the different schools of Southern California. Women were not allowed to become members until Marie Boas applied, and, after arguments, it changed its membership policy and admitted her. I was still at Claremont when I began receiving invitations to the Guild. I attended a meeting which was held at Claremont. A member of the UCLA history department, when I said I was coming to UCLA, commented, "You know what I think about women and academia . . ." I said, "No, I don't." And he said, "I don't think they belong there, but it's all right for them to come to parties." He added, "I quit this organization when they let in their first woman, and I'm just now coming back." I hadn't realized he had quit over the admission of his own colleague.

When there aren't a lot of women at a school, it is rather isolating. On the other hand, I knew quite a few historians, mainly because I go to international conferences. People noticed me more because I was a woman.

When I was at Scripps I was divorced from my second husband. That marriage had been a mistake from the beginning.

NEG: As you mentioned, research carried out on your first trip to Iran resulted in the book entitled Religion and Rebellion in Iran: The Tobacco Protest of 1891–1892.[7] *Would you consider the book to be a narrative history?*
KEDDIE: I think the Tobacco book is pretty much narrative history though I try to bring in social, economic, and religious trends. The first book on Jamal al-Din al-Afghani is mostly an intellectual analysis, rather than a narrative.[8] The second book on Afghani, the long biography, is mostly narrative, but I don't think of myself as a narrative historian.[9] My articles are not narratives, and in many ways I have always been most interested in the kinds of problems and analyses I stress in my articles.

I also wrote some early analytical articles: "Western rule vs Western values", "Religion and irreligion in early Iranian nationalism", and "Symbol and sincerity in Islam".[10] The books are also concerned with answering problems, but you often have to have more narrative in a history book. In the articles, I was dealing with new approaches to intellectual history problems and with the relations between Islam and politics. I was, strangely enough, one of the first to ask, "Why did the Iranian religious class, the ulama, uniquely in world history put themselves on the side which was opposed to the rulers, to the shahs (I am not talking about the current situation, but rather the pre-1914 era) and actively participate in an anti-government revolution"? It was a unique phenomenon. In "The roots of the ulama's power in modern Iran", I suggested reasons for the unique position of the Iranian ulama.[11]

In trying to explain a figure like Jamal al-Din Afghani, a topic that I got into from these questions about the Iranian religious classes, I discovered that a whole series of people considered to be Islamic religious figures involved in these radical movements were not very religious at all. Afghani is not the only one. A couple of participants in the radical wing of the Babi movement probably were freethinkers identifying themselves with the religious opposition. Afghani himself is a very complicated figure. He was certainly not in a traditional religious mould at all. If anything, he was something like an Islamic deist. Aristotelian-based or Platonic-Aristotelian-based philosophy was important in Iran much later than in other parts of the Middle East. Afghani had grown up in this tradition and in the tradition of some of the radical religious movements of Iran. These movements would come out with a new synthesis which tied religion to more rationalist ideas as well as to a political activism of a new kind. I would say that Afghani and that kind of person whom we see again in a new guise today, such as Ali Shariati, come out of this tradition. At the same time I tried not to get away from economic and social forces working on these people, and on political events, although that was not my main focus. My approach to Afghani was earlier suggested in Albert Hourani's *Arabic Thought in the Liberal Age* and Elie Kedourie's and Homa Pakdaman's work, but mine was more extensive and had some new ideas.[12]

I try not to simply summarize what various intellectuals have said nor to analyse the influence of some past people on the person I was studying. I have tried rather to put the person in the political context in which he was living. At the time, this approach to intellectual history was reasonably new in Western and Chinese intellectual history. It is not so special now. If you want to reduce it to a single sentence, it is bringing these newer methods of social and intellectual history into Iranian history and breaking with older philological or simply straight narrative traditions. But it is also important to know what questions are important, like the ones about the relations of the Iranian ulama to politics.

I worked on the Afghani book for a long time, from 1963 to 1971. It was published in 1972. After that I worked for a time on articles and edited books. I think editing books is important, by the way. From early 1971 there were a few years when I was in a really deep depression and didn't do much of anything. I had the idea of doing a general book on modern Iran, but I thought I would wait until the shah fell or died. I did write an article called "Is there a Middle East?" in which I tried to say that the concept of the Middle East shouldn't be reified.[13] In some ways, it is part of the Muslim world, in some ways part of the Mediterranean world. I said that the term does make sense as a kind of a series of concentric circles. The areas closest to the Mediterranean which have more trade and agriculture tended to develop more than the semi-arid and the very arid areas. The three areas have interdependent economies. The very arid areas form a kind of border, not only in Africa, but Arabia and Afghanistan, delimiting the Middle Eastern cultures, so in some sense there is a Middle East as a cultural unit. The presence of, and frequent conquest by, nomadic tribes from the more arid areas is also an important characteristic of the Middle East.

My next project was *Roots of Revolution* which came out in 1981.[14] I called the book an "interpretive history" though today the word "interpretive" like the word "discourse" has been ruined by people who mean something post-modern and relativistic. I meant that I was trying to get at history in a way that brings in interpretations and not just narrative history. It is deliberately doing something that people tend to do anyhow, which may be part of the reason it has been successful: it emphasized those factors that looked important in the 1980s, such as religion and politics. I was conscious of doing that. It is possible that they won't look as important in the 1990s.

NEG: Has the current interest in social history and the Annales school influenced you?
KEDDIE: I suppose that the people who do social history have influenced me to try to look at what identifiable groups of people do, instead of looking entirely at individual intellectuals, or individual powerful people. To me social history is the kind of history that deals with such groups as workers, peasants, nomads, ulama, women, or ethnic groups, and I think I have done that in my writing to a considerable degree. I have studied the nomadic way of life and the interaction of nomads with other groups. I think it is one of the distinctive things about Middle Eastern history which many historians now don't like to write about because they don't like to make Middle Eastern history look somehow inferior to or different from Western history. So they don't talk much about nomads. I think, to the contrary, that the heavy presence of nomadic tribes since particularly the eleventh century with the Turkish invasions was of major historical

importance. I think there was even before the eleventh century a decline in productivity in the soil with erosion, desiccation, and salination. This is one reason why settled agriculture declined and the area was open to conquerors and dynasties.

I don't think that the big questions of why there wasn't economic development and why there was economic regression can be discussed without the nomads and the underlying geographical and ecological phenomena such as the declining fertility of the soil. I have written an article suggesting that geography and technology are neglected fields of Middle East history.[15] I think that for the world in general, but particularly for the Middle East, historians tend to deal with the kinds of things they are familiar with in their own lives, like intellectuals and politics. People have gone into new areas recently, but these are partly based on interest groups such as ethnic groups or women. Technology really hasn't been stressed. Yet I think technology, ecology, and geography and their interaction with human beings are extremely important. They help explain why the Middle East was the earliest developing area. The Mesopotamian and Egyptian civilizations developed because of the great river valleys and the relative ease of irrigated agriculture. At a later stage when the Northern Europeans mastered the heavy plough and knocked down the forests with iron tools, those areas became much more productive. I am greatly oversimplifying the argument, but you can read a thousand history books without learning about the influence of geography and technology. I think it is terribly important, even though it is not an area of primary research for me, and I want to encourage people to work on it.

I am interested in economic history, though not so much of a quantitative type. I go to a lot of international economic history conferences, so I have some idea of what economic historians are doing, and I guess it is the less quantitative, more social history-oriented kind of economic history that I appreciate more. I am not conscious of having been influenced by the Annales intellectuals. I have read some Braudel and Marc Bloch. I think the Annales work is very good. It gets into new areas of history, but in general I would say that Marxism has had a much greater influence on me than the Annales school.

NEG: Could you assess how Marxist thinking has influenced your writings?
KEDDIE: Marxism, which of course is interpreted differently by different people, provides an analysis that combines both structural and historical features and emphasizes explanations for change – all matters of interest to historians. It is also, in principle, universal and not racist or sexist, even though Marx himself and many of his

followers were often both. In principle, however, it stresses the importance of circumstances, and not innate superiorities and inferiorities, in determining the lives of people and peoples, and says that some nations advanced more quickly basically for economic reasons, and not because their people were superior. This approach long made it attractive to Third World intellectuals also. Marxists in fact tend to underrate the differences among societies and cultures, and this is one reason many intellectuals turned to more nuanced and culturally-oriented views. Others were disillusioned by the political failures or even the crimes of self-styled Marxist regimes, especially after they took power. But the basic idea, based on fundamental interactions of groups of people with their environment and with developing and changing technologies and ideologies, remains important for understanding history.

Part of my own formation comes from the fact that I have learned a great deal from living in other countries. In addition to a total of three years in Iran and many months in other Muslim countries (mostly for my work on Afghani and for current work on Islam and politics), I have spent a great deal of time in Europe. I spend most summers there, primarily in London, which I find an excellent place to work. Also as a result of an invitation from Claude Cahen, professor of Islamic history, and Gilbert Lazard, professor of Persian, I was visiting professor for two years (1976–8) at the Sorbonne, at the University of Paris III, which has a Middle East programme. Luckily I had an excellent French teacher in high school who was French and who insisted we speak only French in class – a radical idea at the time. I have also attended a number of international conferences. Hence I am in touch with the excellent group of French social scientists who work on Iran: Bernard Hourcade, Yann Richard, Jean-Pierre Digard, Paul Vieille, and others. I also know many scholars who concentrate on the Arab world in France, England, and Italy, as well as many persons from the Middle East and Pakistan. However, I identify more as a historian, influenced by anthropology and sociology, than as an area specialist. In fact, the majority of my friends are non-Middle East specialists, particularly historians and social scientists.

I have found it useful and interesting to spend time abroad. In Pakistan, for example, I met many brilliant, courageous, and strong women, including Asma Jilani, a leader of the Women's Action Forum and of Human Rights groups, and Abida Husain, now Pakistan's ambassador to the United States. Many of the friends I made in Iran are now in the US, so I think of them now as American friends.

Among my activities have been photography, sometimes professionally, and videotaping interviews. I have taped interviews with activist women and with a number of interesting Muslim personalities worldwide. I have even given courses on photography, audiotaping, and videotaping for historians, because I think these are increasingly important, especially in fields like women's history, where written documentation is limited.

NEG: How would you assess current trends in historical writing?
KEDDIE: Economic history has been strong for a number of years and continues to be. I think it is important to grasp that economic history can shed light on social structures. In Europe the congresses of economic historians are always interesting. Their participants continue to break new ground, as in ecological history and world economic history. The main current trend, which I think is trendier in the United States than in Europe, is deconstructionist discourse. I'm mildly sympathetic to some of the elements of deconstruction. To take a thing apart, to see how it sits within society and to identify the forces that lead people to state certain things intellectually is valuable. The trouble is that so many of the people going into it get carried away until that is all they talk about and they seem not to believe in reality any more. They believe in texts and in deconstructing texts. Even though a lot of the people who do it are on the left, I think it is essentially reactionary, non-communicative, and élitist. It gets some intellectuals into a little élite group who communicate only with each other. It gets them away from thinking that the world and its problems are real. I think Michel Foucault's work is better because it is more rooted in reality. It suggests new ways to understand prisoners or mad people, for example. But much of his history is empirically wrong. What deconstructionists do often seems an intellectual game, though I imagine they don't see it that way.

NEG: When did you become interested in women's history?
KEDDIE: In 1969 or 1970 when I was compiling articles for *Scholars, Saints, and Sufis*[16] it suddenly occurred to me that I had done the whole book without having an article on women. I immediately approached B. J. Fernea who agreed, with Bob Fernea, to write an article for the book. This interest in women was part of the general atmosphere of the times. I had read Robert Briffault's *The Mothers*, about matriarchies, which almost nobody reads any more and is probably mostly inaccurate.[17] I had also read Simone de Beauvoir's book *The Second Sex*, when it first came out.[18] I had read Betty Friedan's book *The Feminine Mystique* when it first came out. I went out and bought a copy and thought it was great.[19] So I'd read some things on women, but I can't say that I brought them into my own work much until other people also became interested in working on women. Before that, like a number of other women, I would have felt

that a woman writing about women would be considered second class. One of the professors I knew at Berkeley assumed that I would be writing about women for my dissertation, and I was quite indignant. I don't think I was entirely wrong. I think writing about women was regarded as a second class thing to be handled only by second class people. In a conference I once brought up something about women and some man said, "Oh, I can see why *you* brought it up." Many people avoided the topic until there was a group that was willing to push against the barriers, to say "women are important." And there were not that many women historians around.

In the early 1970s I began to think women were something to pay attention to. When I saw how many interesting papers on women were being given at places like the Middle East Studies Association, I thought that the time had come to put together a volume on women in the Muslim world. Lois Beck also had this in mind. We were corresponding about something else, and it came up so we decided to edit the book together.[20] I got into the topic of Middle Eastern women early, but I have not done heavy primary research. As with a number of other subjects, I have had general ideas that have proved useful to other people. By the way, my true métier is as an editor. I do that better than anything else. I have recently co-edited, with Beth Baron, a new book entitled *Women in Middle Eastern History*.[21]

NEG: Has the rise of the Islamist movements affected your work?
KEDDIE: In my early article, "The roots of the ulama's power in modern Iran", I predicted that the power of the ulama is going to decline.[22] I wasn't alone in that. I have been writing about religion and politics since almost my first publication, so I had the background to analyse how social, political, and psychological factors have contributed to the new Islamic movements.

NEG: Could you assess the orientalist debate as of 1990?
KEDDIE: I think that Edward Said's book, *Orientalism*, was an important work around which to centre a debate and to make people think of the problems in Western approaches to the Middle East. I think that it is important to point out that Western scholars, coming in large numbers from colonialist countries, tended to have prejudiced attitudes toward orientals, as well as toward a lot of other people. The book is very well written. I think that has had some unfortunate consequences. I think that there has been a tendency in the Middle East field to adopt the word "orientalism" as a generalized swear-word essentially referring to people who take the "wrong" position on the Arab–Israeli dispute or to people who are judged too "conservative". It has nothing to do with whether they are good or not

good in their disciplines. So "orientalism" for many people is a word that substitutes for thought and enables people to dismiss certain scholars and their works. I think that is too bad. It may not have been what Edward Said meant at all, but the term has become a kind of slogan.

Then there is the interesting critique that some Arab leftists such as Sadik Jalal al-ʿAzm and others have brought forth, saying that Said has created a kind of monolithic Western orientalism, an essentialist entity, from which there was almost no deviation.[23] ʿAzm stresses what could be called the "essentialism" of Said. He points out that Said talks about orientalism as if it were the same thing from the Greeks to the present, and that he makes an entity of orientalism although he objects to people making an entity of the orient. I think that is an important critique. While Said's book is important and in many ways positive and informative, it may also be used in a dangerous way because it can encourage people to say, "You Westerners, you can't do our history right, you can't study it right, you really shouldn't be studying it, we are the only ones who can study our own history properly."[24] This is a trend among Middle Eastern intellectuals. It is not only founded on Said's book, but it does make use of it, even though Said himself does not take this position.

Said's book seems to have had more of an impact in other Asian fields than in the Middle East field. The problematic seems to be somehow more exciting to them, maybe in part because it doesn't get quite as directly involved in problems such as the Arab–Israeli dispute that polarize the Middle East field. Having said that, let me add that I think that the general ideas that people hold about orientalism would have been fairly similar even if the book had not existed. I don't believe that someone writes a book and then everybody changes their views. I am glad the book was written, and it has contributed to very important international and interdisciplinary debates, but it should be read along with its critics.

NEG: Could you assess the role of Gustave von Grunebaum?
KEDDIE: I think one of the really unfortunate things in our field – and maybe it is this way in all fields – is that the giants of the recent past tend to be largely forgotten as soon as they are dead if not before, especially if what they have written isn't what is now considered fashionable or central. There is also an optical illusion, in the sense that much of what these people have contributed is not recognized because it has entered so much into the field that people do not realize how novel a contribution it was. They are criticized when they are in error, but their achievements are forgotten. So Middle Eastern history has become a field without its own history. It is too bad. In my

field, who talks about Minorsky, a true giant? Who in the younger generation talks about Gibb? These people are much more important than most of the people who have criticized them. It is the same for von Grunebaum. Few people talk about him, though he was such a remarkable person. I don't mean only his intellectual work, although *Medieval Islam* is a truly great book, a kind of integrated cultural history.[25] He was somebody who could administer a major centre, building it up from nothing at UCLA, and at the same time carry on his scholarly work. Abdullah Laroui, a Moroccan historian, carried on a discourse critical of von Grunebaum, but he was very well aware that he was a great man and scholar. And von Grunebaum could appreciate and help scholars who criticized his work, and tried hard to get Laroui to stay at UCLA. Now there is no mention of von Grunebaum or the other scholars who have died in the past two or three decades, not even the true early giant, Ignaz Goldziher, the Hungarian-Jewish Arabist and Islamist. I think that is really mistaken.

NEG: Could you comment on Marshall Hodgson's work?
KEDDIE: I read his book when it was in the form of a manual for Chicago students. But the thing that got me really interested in Hodgson was his brilliant article on conceptualizing world history. He thought that it was best perhaps to divide world history into four major civilizational areas: the East Asian, the South Asian, the Middle Eastern, and the Western or European. Then he said if you wanted to take two of these four that would go together most closely in terms of their influences and culture, it would be the Middle Eastern and European. And I think that is absolutely true. Middle Eastern and European civilizations were both influenced by Greek logic and by monotheism. We are used to thinking of these two civilizations as enemies, but their cultural backgrounds have more similarities than do South Asian or East Asian civilizations.

NEG: Is the political activism of your early years reflected in your work?
KEDDIE: Clearly I am concerned about greater egalitarian justice for all groups in society, and that probably shows in my work. Even when I write about intellectual history I don't just talk about the self-development of the ideas of élite intellectuals. Somebody like Afghani is interesting because his ideas caught on with large groups of people, not so much in his own time but afterwards. Some elements in his thoughts are very important today.

I suppose my political point of view is now confused and skeptical. I think that is true for a lot of people. But I can be clear about what I want to fight against: war, prejudice, poverty, ignorance, disease, inequality, and unequal treatment.

NEG: What is your current project?

KEDDIE: I am currently working on a comparative historical study of Islamic militant movements, and for this I've travelled all the way from Senegal to Sumatra over a number of years. I have studied Islamic movements from the eighteenth century to the present. I am also putting together a work called, "Why has Iran been revolutionary?". And I am editing a new journal, called *Contention.* It addresses itself to debates in all fields of academic endeavour. It is written in comprehensible language, as people write for *The New York Review* or magazines like *Natural History* or *Science,* for people who are interested in knowing about the central issues in other disciplines or between disciplines. People are interested in scholarly debates. For example, in the *American Historical Review,* the section that my colleagues will read and talk about is the Forum where people write letters back and forth debating issues. I am getting a lot of enthusiastic interest, and prominent scholars like Eric Hobsbawm, Ernest Gellner, Paul Ehrlich, and David Landes are writing for us.

NEG: Could you comment on the current development of Iranian studies?

KEDDIE: On the one hand it is a rapidly growing field which is very encouraging; on the other hand, I see hardly any American students in it any more. This is not surprising, because they feel that they have to go to Iran in order to study the field and that is more difficult now. It is the fashion of our times to think one must travel to an area, though for historians this could be delayed until after the Ph.D. as it was for me. And look at many of the great nineteenth-century scholars who never went anywhere, yet they learned languages much better than we do. Someone has said in relation to Southern California that Iranian studies has become a kind of ethnic studies programme like other ethnic studies programmes. I think the mix of students is better. But there is a positive side to this Iranian majority because we have a large number of students who are doing very good work. They can combine what they know from their own culture with recent Western scholarship. Some of the Iranian scholars who were originally going into science or engineering have been traumatized by the revolution and have decided instead that they have to understand their own society. So they are Iran-oriented rather then Middle East-oriented. Ten years ago most Iranian students had difficulty with English, but now they have graduated from places like Beverly Hills High School and write better than 90 per cent of the American students. I also have had a few Japanese students, a Dutch student, and a few American and Israeli students. The students today are outstanding in the sense that many of them turn out publishable and published work even before their Ph.D. comprehensive examinations.

NEG: Do you have some advice for students who are only beginning to consider specializing in Middle Eastern history?
KEDDIE: I think they should go in two, apparently contrary, directions: on the one hand they should stress their language training much more than most of them do, in both the Middle Eastern languages and the European languages, and on the other hand they should keep up with main currents in European history because it is more developed. Then they can concentrate on the history of the Middle East. There is a kind of dichotomy among the younger historians, between their general theoretical outlook and the limited nature of the work they do. We are not seeing many big synthetic works. Maybe it is harder to do now, but we don't see the von Grunebaums, the Hodgsons, people coming up with new ideas for a real synthesis. Of course you can't encourage everybody to do that because not everybody can. I would like to see students concentrate more on material, technological, geographical, and ecological questions. Hardly any primary work has been done on them. Certainly political, socio-economic, and women's history are important, but many people are working in these areas. Almost no one is doing the kind of work pioneered by Richard Bulliet's *The Camel and the Wheel* and by Andrew M. Watson's *Agricultural Innovation in the Early Islamic World,* and we cannot really understand the rise and decline of Middle Eastern states without more such work.[26] Finally, in a period when the supply of Iranian history students is exceeding demand they should get training in subjects such as Pakistan, Central Asia, Russian and the Turkic languages, comparative women's history, religious studies, and other fields. This may lengthen their training, but it will increase their chance for employment.

Notes

1. Ahmad Kasravi, *Tarikh-i mashruta-yi Iran* (History of The Constitution of Iran) (Tehran: Amir Kabir Publications, 1951).
2. Nikki R. Keddie, *Roots of Revolution: An Interpretive History of Modern Iran* (New Haven: Yale University Press, 1981).
3. ———, "Religion and irreligion in early Iranian nationalism", *Comparative Studies in Society and History*, VI, 3 (1962), pp. 265–95.
4. ———, "Western rule vs Western values: suggestions for a comparative study of Asian intellectual history", *Diogenes*, 26 (1959), pp. 71–96.
5. Mangol Bayat, *Iran's First Revolution: Shi'ism and the Constitutional Revolution of 1905–1909* (New York: Oxford University Press, 1991); Janet Afary, *The Iranian Constitutional Revolution of 1906–11: Grassroots Democracy, Social Democracy, and the Origins of Feminism* (forthcoming, 1995).

6. Vladimir Minorsky, *Medieval Iran and Its Neighbours* (London: Variorum Reprints, 1982).
7. Nikki R. Keddie, *Religion and Rebellion in Iran: The Tobacco Protest of 1891–1892* (London: Frank Cass, 1966).
8. ——, *An Islamic Response to Imperialism: Political and Religious Writings of Sayyid Jamal ad-Din "al-Afghani"* (Berkeley: University of California Press, 1968).
9. ——, *Sayyid Jamal ad-Din "al-Afghani": A Political Biography* (Berkeley: University of California Press, 1972).
10. Ibid., "Religion and irreligion in early Iranian nationalism", pp. 265–95, and "Symbol and sincerity in Islam", *Studia Islamica*, XIX (1963), pp. 27–63.
11. ——, "The roots of the ulama's power in modern Iran", *Studia Islamica*, XXIX (1969), pp. 31–53.
12. See Albert Hourani, *Arabic Thought in the Liberal Age, 1798–1939* (New York and London: Oxford University Press, 1962); Elie Kedourie, *Afghani and ʿAbduh: An Essay on Religious Unbelief and Political Activism in Modern Islam* (New York: Humanities Press, 1966); Homa Pakdaman, *Djamal-ed-Din Assad Abadi, dit Afghani* (Paris: G.-P. Maisonneuve et Larose, 1969).
13. Nikki R. Keddie, "Is there a Middle East?", *International Journal of Middle Eastern Studies*, IV, 3 (1973), pp. 255–71.
14. ——, *Roots of Revolution*.
15. ——, "Material culture, technology, and geography: toward a holistic comparative study of the Middle East", in Juan Cole (ed.), *Comparing Muslim Societies: Knowledge and the State in a World Civilization* (Ann Arbor: University of Michigan, 1992), pp. 31–62, first published in *Comparative Studies in Society and History* (October 1984), pp. 709–35.
16. —— (ed.), *Scholars, Saints, and Sufis* (Berkeley and Los Angeles: University of California Press, 1972).
17. Robert Briffault, *The Mothers: A Study of the Origins of Sentiments and Institutions* (New York: Macmillan Co., 1927–52).
18. Simone de Beauvoir, *The Second Sex* (New York: Knopf, 1953).
19. Betty Friedan, *The Feminine Mystique* (New York: Norton, 1963).
20. Lois Beck and Nikki Keddie (eds.), *Women in the Muslim World* (New Haven, Yale University Press, 1978).
21. Nikki R. Keddie and Beth Baron, *Women in Middle Eastern History* (New Haven: Yale University Press, 1991).
22. "Roots of the ulama's power".
23. Sadik Jalal al-ʿAzm, "Orientalism and orientalism in reverse", *Khamsin*, 8 (1981), pp. 5–26.
24. Nikki Keddie, "The history of the Muslim Middle East", *The Past before Us: Contemporary Historical Writing in the United States*, ed. for the American Historical Association by Michael Kammen (Ithaca: Cornell University Press, 1980), pp. 131–56.
25. Gustave von Grunebaum, *Medieval Islam: A Study in Cultural Orientation* (Chicago: Chicago University Press, 1946).
26. Richard Bulliet, *The Camel and the Wheel* (Cambridge: Harvard University Press, 1975); Andrew M. Watson, *Agricultural Innovation in the Early Islamic World: the Diffusion of Crops and Farming Techniques, 700–1100* (New York: Cambridge University Press, 1983).

CHAPTER SEVEN

HALIL INALCIK

HALIL INALCIK, born in Istanbul *ca* 1916, specializes in the social and economic history of the Ottoman Empire. He studied at the Faculty of Geography, History, and Language in Ankara, and later at the School of Oriental and African Studies in London. For many years he was professor of Ottoman history at the University of Ankara. In 1972 he emigrated to the United States to take a position at the University of Chicago. He has been director of studies of the École des Hautes Études, Paris, and co-chairman of the First International Congress on the Social and Economic History of Turkey. He received an honorary doctorate from the University of Athens in 1987 and is a member of the American Academy of Arts and Sciences. He is founder and president of the International Commission on the Social and Economic History of Turkey, and honorary président, Committee for the Study of the Northern Black Sea Countries, Ukrainian Research Institute of Harvard University. He retired from the University of Chicago in 1986 and is currently organizing a history department at Bilkent University, Ankara.

Interviewed by Nancy E. Gallagher on 18 and 19 November 1989, in Chicago.

NEG: Can we begin with your family background?
HALIL INALCIK: I have two different birth dates, because in Turkey in the old days people used to change the birth dates of their children in order to get them into school earlier. You could change your identity card because there were no birth certificates. I later made inquiries about when I was born. Some of my mother's relatives remembered it was when the British bombed Istanbul. This was 1918. But it doesn't matter whether you are 73 or 71.

My family background is Crimean Turkish. Crimean Turks in Turkey don't distinguish themselves from the Turkish nation and don't like to be called Tartar. Since their mother tongue is Turkish, they are Turks. Besides, they joined the Ottoman Empire as far back as 1475 when the Crimea was annexed. My father came to Istanbul in 1905 from Bahçesaray, the capital city of the Crimean Khanate. My mother was from Istanbul. She was the daughter of a naval officer who served at Basra as an Ottoman naval commander.

NEG: Why did your father come to Turkey?
INALCIK: Some of our relatives had already come and settled in Istanbul. My aunt was married and living in Bursa, and family members from the Crimea often visited her. When the Russian–Japanese war broke out in 1905, my father did not want to be enrolled in the Russian army. Many immigrants came from the Crimea during this period. Because of my background I have always been interested in Crimean history and have written extensively about it.

NEG: Have you visited your father's place of birth?
INALCIK: No, but perhaps I shall be able to now.

NEG: Was your father an imam?
INALCIK: No, but my grandfather was a muezzin (one who makes the call to prayer) at the Mosque of the Khans in Bahçesaray. His son, my father, was a businessman. My father knew Russian, had some intellectual interests, and was a nationalist, a Turkish nationalist, of course.

NEG: What was his business?
INALCIK: In those days Western eau-de-Cologne was very popular in Turkey. He had a good business manufacturing and selling it. I remember his factory in Istanbul. Then he went bankrupt during the depression that followed World War I. In the 1920s economic conditions in Turkey were very harsh. He took up several businesses after that but with no great success. We were not prosperous in later years. My family was poor.

In 1925 we moved to Ankara where I attended primary school. It was a hectic period. Turkey was exhausted after the long war years which had started back in 1911. My father left Turkey for Egypt in 1929. He and my mother separated when I had just graduated from primary school. After that we had a hard time. My father died in Alexandria, Egypt, in 1934. A few years ago I went to Alexandria to find his tomb with no success. After forty or fifty years nobody in the bazaar remembered him.

NEG: Did you have brothers and sisters?
INALCIK: Yes, I have a sister in Turkey, still alive, two and a half years younger than I. She became an agricultural engineer.

I attended a modern primary school established by Atatürk. It was called *Ghazi Okulu*, Ghazi being Atatürk's title and *okul*, school. Then I went on to *Ghazi Enstitüsü* for secondary school. After that I was sent to Balikesir to attend a new high school – actually a teachers' school – established by Atatürk.[1]

I was lucky to be sponsored by a great scholar in legal history, another émigré from Russia, named Sadri Maksudi Arsal, a nationalist leader who taught legal history at the Faculty of Law in Ankara. My father was also a Turkish nationalist from Russia, and they were friends. We had actually lived in the same building since 1925. Arsal was a friend of our family for many years. I was twelve years old when my father left, and he was responsible for my admission to the teachers' school. He had spent some time in France before coming to Turkey. His daughter, Adile Ayda, who was six or seven years older than I, knew French very well. She eventually became a diplomat in the Foreign Office and in later years a noted literary figure. She taught me French, and when I finished high school, I was already able to read books in French.

NEG: Did you ever meet Atatürk?
INALCIK: He used to visit our school at the *Ghazi Enstitüsü*. Once he came to our class and asked me some questions. I have written an account of this great moment in my life, which is going to be published as an historical memoir.[2] Thus, I was exposed in primary and high school to the very intense nationalism of those years. This was during Atatürk's early years when Turkish nationalism was idealized as the basis of the new nation-state.

NEG: Were you influenced by pan-Turanism?
INALCIK: No, Atatürk was against pan-Turanism as a state policy. He believed in a Turkish national homeland in Anatolia and in the continuity of the Turkish-Anatolian culture. He did not seek a Turkish national identity in Central Asia but believed that Central Asia was the original homeland of the Turks, that Turkish civilization had spread from there.

When I went to the teachers' school in Balikesir, I was separated from my family. It was a disciplined life. Every morning at sunrise we were in class working like monks. These years, I believe, had a strong influence on my character and instilled in me a sense of purpose, especially nationalism. Turkish nationalism and identity conflicts were the dominant preoccupations at that time. We students believed that after independence and the defeat of Western imperialism we had to prove to Europe that all the negative features attributed to the name of Turk were not true. We had to find convincing arguments to establish a positive Turkish image in the world after the war. Atatürk then started his Westernizing reforms. He adopted the Swiss Civil Code in 1926. It was a revolutionary step to prove to Europe that Turkey was a secular European nation, with equal rights. That was the big challenge for every intellectual in Turkey in those days. The younger generation was under the strong influence of all these ideas and trends. Atatürk suffered from the negative Western image of the Turk, and he wanted to make the Turkish nation equal to all the Western nations. He believed that this was a matter of survival for Turkey. Most Turks continue to believe this. That is why Turkey today is so persistently endeavouring to become a member of the European Community.

In 1935, Atatürk established a Faculty of Geography, History, and Language, *Dil-Tarih-Cografya Fakültesi*, in Ankara to train experts to provide a scholarly basis for his thesis of Turkish history. He intended this to be the basis of the new Turkish national identity. He was, I believe, a far-sighted statesman. It was extraordinary that he was so passionately interested in history. He was seeking a Turkish identity different from the Ottoman or Islamic ones. He had already established an historical society in 1931, and then, as a corollary, he organized international congresses and invited European scholars to discuss the problems of Turkish history. The Faculty of Language, History and Geography was going to train young scholars to work and produce works that would match European scholarship. Atatürk was a man of positive thinking. He believed that the only way to improve the Turkish image in the West was to establish academic institutions to train Turkish scholars. I was one of the first students in his new university. In 1935 we took entrance exams, and they chose forty out of perhaps hundreds. From among these forty we have famous Turkish scholars such as the archaeologist, Tahsin Özgüç, and the medievalist, Osman Turan.

It was a coincidence that this academic expansion took place during the Hitler years, and many German scholars – Jews or others who didn't like Nazis – left Germany and came to Turkey.[3] Many of our professors were German. They were distinguished scholars such as the Turcologist, von Gabain, the Sumerologist, Benno Landsberger, the Hittologist, Hans Güterbock, the Sinologist, Wolfram Eberhard, the Indologist, W. Ruben, and the geographer, Herbert Louis. Reuter, later to become the mayor of West Berlin after World War II, was another professor in Turkey at the time. We were very fortunate to have these distinguished scholars as our professors.

NEG: Did they teach in German?
INALCIK: They taught in German, and interpreters and assistant professors helped them. Some learned Turkish. Hans Güterbock learned it so well that he could give his lectures in Turkish. There was a strong German academic influence in the years from 1935 through the Second World War.

NEG: Which professors were most influential in your formation?
INALCIK: Köprülü Fuat Bey [Mehmet Fuat Köprülü 1890–1966] in medieval history. In modern history, a young man who had just finished his studies in Germany – again the German tradition – his name was Bekir Sitki Baykal [d. 1987]. He was a very good man, and I am grateful to him, but my main supporter was always Mehmet Fuat Köprülü. I admired him deeply. He was a great scholar, an historian of Turkish culture, literature, and Sufi movements. He was just back from Paris when I entered the university. While in France he had come under the influence of the Annales school and had become interested in social and economic history. In 1931 he established the first journal on social and economic history in Turkey. It was called *Türk Hukuk ve Iktisat Tarihi Mecmuasi* (The Journal of Turkish Legal and Economic History). We were deeply influenced by this journal, which brought the views of the new French Annales school to Turkey. His new orientation took place during my undergraduate years. I became interested in the topic of institutions, the social origins of feudalism – a subject then being intensely discussed in France, the different interpretations of feudal institutions, and legal history, all of which influenced my later work.

In 1985 I wrote an article on the impact of the Annales school on Ottoman Studies.[4] So the first influence on my ideas was Atatürk's nationalism and the need to challenge Western literature on the Ottoman Empire. The second influence was French historiography which I learned from Mehmet Fuat Köprülü. Besides Köprülü's influence in bringing us French historiography, I myself could read all these famous authors: Marc Bloch; the Belgian scholar, Henri Pirenne; Henri Berr; and Lucien Febvre.[5] I recall now that years later when I met Professor Paul Wittek in London, he said, "It is an enigma for me how you were trained as an historian like any Western scholar. How did you have this background?"[6] He did not know about our university, our German professors, Fuat Bey, and my French. I presume that all this gave me a background and orientation that was different from that of my classmates.

In 1940 I finished college. Then I started a Ph.D., which I completed in two years, on "The application of the Tanzimat in Bulgaria and the reactions to it".[7] I was lucky to have found ten volumes of documents on the Bulgarian question in the Dolmabahce Palace. The documents had been collected for Sultan Abdul Hamid II and were the main source for my dissertation. In the dissertation, I concentrated on the conditions of the Bulgarian peasantry. I argued that the large Muslim landowners in the area of Vidin were the real cause of the peasant uprisings in the period 1840–50 rather than Balkan nationalism. My later interest in social and economic history was already visible in the dissertation.

NEG: Were you in the army during World War II?
INALCIK: Yes, I was in the army from 1943 to 1945, more than two years. I was very nervous in those days. Every moment we were expecting a German attack. We knew that the German war machine would annihilate the Turkish army in a short time. The Turkish army was poorly prepared for the challenge so there was great anxiety. We were like the American younger generation during the Vietnam War. I was lucky I wasn't in Thrace. Since I knew languages, I was stationed in Ankara, the capital. I was married during my military service, I lived in my house, and worked at the headquarters of the 28th division. I had free time so I translated Paul Ricaut's book on the Ottoman Empire.[8] I never finished it and later lost interest, but it is an important book. Thank you – you made me remember all those wonderful years.

I should tell you how I met my wife, Şevkiye Isil. We were in the same Arabic class at the university. I had begun to learn Arabic, and she was a regular student in Arabic. The teacher – do you believe in fate? – appointed me to help her. I knew Arabic better than she did; she did not even know the Arabic alphabet. This established a relationship which developed into marriage. She graduated and stayed on the same faculty as assistant professor of Arabic and later became the chair of the Arabic section, in oriental languages. Much later, in 1972 when I was contemplating coming to the United States, I told my wife I wouldn't accept the invitation to the University of Chicago if she did not want to come with me. She had published one book on Umayyad poetry, and we had both established careers in Turkey, but she sacrificed her career to come to this country with me.

Army life ended in 1945 and I returned to the Faculty of Letters, where I was an assistant professor and my main interest continued to be the same subjects that I had focused on in my doctoral dissertation. I concentrated on the nineteenth century, and I shifted to the Tanzimat reform period focusing on Westernization and modernization. Most of my writings were then on the reform period of the nineteenth century.

In 1949 I was sent to England for further study. This was another important leap in my life. At that time there was a regulation in the faculty that young assistant professors were sent to Europe or America for further training and experience. They could stay as long as two years. Now that period is shortened to six months, not enough for a real acquaintance with Western scholarship and the Western way of life. I met Paul Wittek in London. I worked in the British Museum and the Public Record Office archives. It was just after the war and life in London was hard: there was rationing of sugar, meat, and eggs. There was a real economic depression in 1949.

I remember passing by a Labour Party political celebration in 1949 at Hammersmith Palace. Anyone could enter by paying four shillings. I entered and saw that people were getting Mr Attlee's autograph, so I approached and got it too. Attlee, the prime minister, had won the elections against Churchill in 1945.

My main work was in the British Museum, so I went there regularly. I hated the London weather; it was cold, you could feel it in your bones even if you were indoors. The food was not very good for a Turk, used to eating good pilav . . . But I loved London, the empire was still intact. There were museums, the parks, Covent Garden, Albert Hall, promenade concerts conducted by Sir Malcolm Sargent. It was a great experience for me; I became "Westernized". In the British Museum, I went through all the Calendar of State Papers (the series of translations of documents from various archives), more than a hundred volumes. I found this collection the most interesting for me. The indexes helped me to find anything dealing with the Ottoman Empire. I filled book after book taking notes and copying documents. I had in mind to write a history of Ottoman–Western relations. In the meantime, I attended Professor Wittek's seminars, which he had the habit of holding once a week in the evening. I made friends with Bernard Lewis in this class. In the seminar mostly new publications were discussed. If one of us brought a paper and read it, the old man always made very incisive, sometimes cruel criticisms. I enjoyed and benefited greatly from these seminars. I especially admired Wittek's philological method and his strictness in interpreting the documents. I believe Wittek was the first Ottomanist to apply Western textual criticism to Ottoman texts. He evaluated early Ottoman Turkish archival documents and chronicles on the basis of textual criticism. He rendered a great service to Ottoman studies, which should be recognized. His work is epoch-making. Unfortunately, now the young generation – I don't know what is the motivation – almost all of them are attacking Paul Wittek as old-fashioned, even ridiculing his believing in the *ghazi* ideology as the most important and dynamic factor in the emergence of the Ottoman state, minimizing his method and his contribution. I believe all this is unfair. He was the pioneer in many ways in his approach to early Ottoman history. It is true that Wittek was a merciless critic, so most people disliked him because of his frankness and strictness. Perhaps he was a bit too aggressive, but I had such a great admiration for the old man. We were close friends. These London years had, I believe, a decisive influence on my personality, my approach to historical study, and my ideals.

When I returned to Turkey in 1952 I became a full professor at the University of Ankara by presenting a thesis on the close cooperation between the Crimean Khanate and the Ottoman Empire during and after the siege of Vienna, 1683–99. In 1953, to commemorate 1453, the quincentenary of the Ottoman conquest of Constantinople, we had to prepare a history of this epoch-making event based on the original Turkish documents. The main idea was not to remain dependent on what had been written by Westerners. So I worked in the archives in Istanbul. This changed my whole outlook on Ottoman history. I left the topic of Tanzimat reform and shifted my attention to the fifteenth century.

I was interested in social and economic history, preparing the results of my work on the *tahrir defteri*, the Ottoman provincial tax and population surveys. They are the most important archival sources for Ottoman social history. In 1954 I published the oldest of these registers, the *Arvanid Sancagi icmal* register, dated 1432.[9]

This was my first book. I could establish a map of Albania for the year 1432 on the basis of this register. Can you imagine that you could make a complete map of every village in Albania as it existed in 1432? One of my Albanian colleagues told me everyone knows my name in Albania because he can find his village in the document I published.

My main orientation in those years was to subject to a critical examination all that had been written on Ottoman history. One example of this was my review of the history of Mehmet the Conqueror by Franz Babinger.[10] Since I was working on Mehmet the Conqueror myself, I tried to consult all the documents of this period that were in the archives. Of course that was impossible, but I was well initiated into the documents. I thought I had a better picture of the Conqueror's reign than Babinger.

NEG: Had Babinger worked in the Ottoman archives?
INALCIK: No. One year before his book appeared, he came to Istanbul. Then we were good friends. He knew that I was also working on Mehmet the Conqueror. I must add that Babinger expected the Turks to help him by opening the archives, because he was working on the history of the Conqueror. But he was disappointed, and he left Turkey in bitterness. I guess this bitterness affected his work.

NEG: How did you learn to read the Ottoman documents?
INALCIK: Remember that I was born an Ottoman, in 1916 or 1918. In my primary school education we were trained in the old Arabic alphabet until 1928 when the alphabet was changed to the Latin characters. I also had some Ottoman culture in primary school. I remember that we recited the Quran in class. We were taught Persian and Arabic grammatical rules for the Turkish language, so it was not too hard for me to adapt and learn the official language used in the Ottoman chanceries. I was lucky to combine this Ottoman background and the new epoch, the republican nationalist period. Later on I studied Arabic and Persian, so it wasn't very difficult for me to decipher these documents in old Ottoman Turkish. This kind of background is crucial.

I am currently embarked on a very ambitious project to publish about 1,000 documents from the *qadi* [court] records of Bursa, which I have studied since 1948. I found them lying on the floor in the dust in one of the darkest rooms of the Bursa museum, a former *medrese* [school]. They were in a bad condition, but proved to be among the oldest and most valuable documents in Turkey. They date back to the 1460s and are particularly valuable because Bursa was a very important trade centre in those days. One day when I was in that room at the museum working hard on the documents an American couple showed up. It was William Langer, the noted professor of European diplomatic history, and his wife. Our acquaintance started there. I guess he appreciated my zeal to work on these dirty, dusty volumes. In 1954, I began to publish a selection of the documents. So far I have carefully edited and published 400 of them in *Belgeler*, the journal of the Turkish Historical Society; but no one, I must confess, can pretend to decipher and understand everything in these documents.

Our work is different from that of our colleagues who specialize in European history because we don't have corpora of documents already deciphered and carefully published. The German scholars, for example, already have the documents in the *Monumenta* series at their disposal; they are deciphered, and almost every problem is solved.[11] As one of my colleagues said, we look like those people who go through the desert making their own roads. We place the stones ourselves and then walk on them. We find and publish the documents ourselves, and then we interpret them.

NEG: How do you select the documents to publish?
INALCIK: They pertain to the topics I am interested in. I am interested in social, economic, and administrative history, not so much in diplomatic or political history. When I was studying the nineteenth century I focused at first on diplomatic history, especially on the

Eastern Question, so I used diplomatic documents. I do not minimize the importance of diplomatic history, but it didn't attract me very much. Now, the social and economic structures, the background of the events seem more important to me. I have a confession to make. When Atatürk's Faculty of History, Geography, and Languages was opened, I never thought I was going to be an historian. I was more interested in literature. Perhaps if I had not been led into this profession, I would be a novelist. Now I realize that this gave me an advantage. It is my belief that the historian must have a vivid imagination to recreate the past. You have to interpret the little evidence that is available. I don't mean you have to indulge in inventing things, but rather that the power of imagination is essential in interpreting the sources. Anyway I am still interested in literature: I write verses in the old Ottoman style.

NEG: Could you comment on your relationship with Mustafa Akdag, the well-known leftist historian then at the faculty?
INALCIK: Mustafa Akdag and I were classmates in high school, but he joined the university two or three years later than I. Later he published interesting articles on Ottoman social and economic history. I did a lot of thinking and studying before I wrote a review article on his first major work on Ottoman social and economic history.[12] Actually, Akdag brought up important questions, which made me think. This is a great service, I believe, even if his formulations were not always correct. He sometimes exaggerated things, but in the last analysis he had a positive impact on Turkish studies. He was also a student of Mehmet Fuat Köprülü. He took his main ideas primarily from Köprülü. But I must add that the world economic crisis of 1930–31 had a strong impact on Turkey and on Turkish intellectuals in general. Atatürk and many intellectuals became interested in socialism and economic matters in general. We students were also interested in economic problems and in socialism. This was the 1930s, and Akdag was strongly influenced by these ideas. Throughout Turkey, the local historians and the high school history teachers were also interested in social or popular movements in their regions, and they dug up the local *qadi* records on such topics. There are many publications on social movements during the 1930s. The People's Houses (*Halkevleri*) were very active, they published books on local history, popular movements, brigandage, and so on. Akdag's main intellectual interest emerged in this atmosphere. I tried to take a less emotional approach to these questions rather than interpreting all popular movements in Ottoman history in Marxist or radical terms. Take, for instance, the *celali* [rebel] movements. Akdag thought the *celali* movements were popular movements against the landowners and

were part of a class conflict. I didn't share this view because the full evidence was not there. I thought that it was primarily the depredations of troops whom the state had employed during the wars. When the war was over the troops were released from service and to survive they became brigands.[13] Likewise in fifteenth-century France, after the Hundred Years War, the *Companies* became brigands across France, and they ruined the country. The *celali* disturbances were very similar to this, being caused by unemployed soldiers plundering villages and cities. They had no social awareness; they did not represent a social movement. Akdag's interpretation was anachronistic. So I tried to be a more prudent student, trying to stick to the documents, to the evidence. Akdag became very popular in the 1970s, because he believed that he was the historian of radicalism in Turkey. He was a kind of hero. He was dean of the faculty. He met the students in the open and encouraged them, saying to them, "You are in the forefront of the socialist movement." He became very much involved in politics. Our fields of interest paralleled each other, but he followed another direction. I tried to become more of an historian; I was never interested in politics, not even in administration. I remembered the Turkish proverb, "You cannot carry two water melons under one arm" (*bir koltuğa iki karpuz sığmaz*). After all, there is so much to do as an historian.

NEG: How did you happen to come to the United States?
INALCIK: In 1953 I was invited to be a visiting professor at Columbia University for one year. This was my first visit to America. Fuat Köprülü was the Turkish Minister of Foreign Affairs at the time, and his friend Tibor Halasi-Kun, the senior professor of Turcology at Columbia, had come to this country from Ankara. Halasi-Kun was a Hungarian scholar who had taught at the faculty in Ankara. Because of a change in the atmosphere in Turkey, all these German and other foreign professors began to leave Turkey for America. Tibor was one of them. He came to Columbia University to establish Turkic studies. Köprülü knew him from the faculty where they had been colleagues, so he supported him and gave him matching funds to establish a Turkish position at Columbia. With these funds, Turkish studies were started seriously in the United States. Tibor was a philologist and needed an historian. I was on good terms with him, and he asked me if I could join him and teach Ottoman history at Columbia University. I said, "Yes, why not?" After my London visit, my English was good enough to teach, and I decided to spend one year in New York.

My first strong impression was in King's Crown Hotel on 115th Street. It was early September and very hot and humid. I suffered, and there was a Coca Cola vendor downstairs. I took perhaps ten or twelve

Coca Cola bottles into my room every day, so from the first day my strongest recollection is of Coca Cola.

Eisenhower had just left as president of the university, upon his election as president of the United States. At Columbia my close colleagues were: Jay Hurewitz, Shaykh Ikram from Pakistan, and Tibor Halasi-Kun. It was a pleasant atmosphere; I enjoyed the life in New York.

After a year I returned home. I visited the U.S. about twelve times between that time and 1972 when I came for good. By then I had been a visiting professor at Columbia, Princeton, and the University of Pennsylvania. In 1956 I had a Rockefeller fellowship which enabled me to spend a year at Harvard. There I attended classes on American constitutional history and opening up the West. Intellectually, I benefited from my visit to America. I realized that American history was a field with modern problems such as the study of banking, industrialization, the impact of railroads, and the opening of the West. All these problems were new and different to me and made an impact on my approach to history. The classes were taught by the famous professors at Harvard. I got to know William Langer, whom you will recall I had first met in the Bursa museum. He asked me to revise the chapters on Ottoman history in his *Encyclopedia of World History*.[14] There also I met Speros Vryonis, the well-known Byzantine historian. My daughter attended primary school in Cambridge and learned English in that year.

I wrote the *Ottoman Empire and the Classical Age* at Princeton in 1967.[15] I wrote it in Turkish, and Norman Itzkowitz translated it into English. Colin Imber later translated the last chapter on culture. I still have difficulty writing in English. Whatever I write needs to be edited by an English speaker.

NEG: Why did you decide to leave Turkey?
INALCIK: In the 1970s there were continuous student riots in Turkey that were very disturbing for researchers and university teachers. In the hallways of the university, gunshots were heard, students burst into classes and told the students to attend demonstrations outside, they would insult the teacher ... I was very disturbed at the time and wanted to find better conditions to continue my work outside Turkey. In 1972 the University of Chicago invited me to teach Ottoman history. They invited me as a university professor and promised to give me the best conditions to continue my research projects, so I chose to come here. There was already a good basis for Turkish studies in Chicago, the university library was excellent, there was a Turkish programme, and Turkish literature and languages were taught. I was very happy in Chicago. I was able to continue my research work in a

stimulating atmosphere. I offered courses for many years on Ottoman social and economic history, and there was no interference in my programme so I could concentrate on it. My students, some of them now professors in various places, were, I believe, influenced by this type of approach to Ottoman studies, putting emphasis on archival work, on concentrating on and analysing the documents. They mostly focus on urban, economic, and social history.

NEG: Could you explain your theory of the Ottoman agrarian social structure?
INALCIK: This is a theory which I have developed in my classes at the University of Chicago during the last ten or twelve years. Prior to that I had written an article on agrarian taxation, "Raiyyet rusumu" (peasant taxation).[16] In it I developed the idea of what I called the *çift-hane* system as the basis of the Ottoman agrarian social system. I have recently read papers at conferences on this theory of the Ottoman agrarian structure.[17] I focused on social stratification in the country-side and emphasized the importance of peasant family labour on state-owned lands. Over 90 per cent of the population of the empire was part of this system of small peasant family production. It was the basis of the Ottoman economy and society. I believe that this theory, which is based on the documentary evidence, will explain not only the peasants' conditions in the countryside, but also the Ottoman social and political structure, its basic principles of government. In other words, with this framework, I can describe and explain the basic economic and social system of the Ottoman Empire. I anticipate that the *çift-hane* model will take the place of all those inspired by Marx, Weber, and others. It will answer questions raised by social historians or sociologists who rely on Marxist models such as the so-called Asian Mode of Production. Their interpretations follow too rigidly the Marxist theory that attempts to explain the social structure of Asiatic empires on the basis of the usurpation of the surplus production of the peasantry. I believe that if Marx were alive he would find this *çift-hane* model more suited to his general theory since it offers a formulation based on the analysis of documents. It explains the social formation not on sheer usurpation but on a specific articulation of the forces of production. I believe that this *çift-hane* theory is my main contribution after so many years of research in the archives.

NEG: Could you comment on the recent interest in "world history"?
INALCIK: We are grateful to the historians of our time who attempted to write world history: A. Toynbee, W. McNeill, and F. Braudel. They rendered a great service to Ottoman history, in general, by drawing attention to the economic and political importance of the Ottoman Empire in world history. Before that, Ottoman history was coloured by

the "Eastern Question" approach of the nineteenth century. Many scholars believed that everything the Ottoman Turks did was brutal and did not take the pains to see how this empire was able to build up a society that lasted more than five centuries. Now, thanks to these great historians, the Ottoman Empire is receiving more serious attention, and more people are going to the authentic sources, the Ottoman archives. So we are very grateful to these prestigious world historians for understanding the place of the Ottomans in history. We should not forget another recent trend started by sociologist Immanuel Wallerstein, and the research group he organized at the State University of New York at Binghamton.[18] Their work on the Ottoman Empire within the "capitalist world economy" is a fresh approach of major importance.

It is a pity that the place of Ottomans in world history has not yet been fully recognized in universities in this country, and that chairs or positions already created have been abolished. Here in Chicago, when I retired, no appointment was made to replace me for Ottoman history. Nevertheless, I believe that Ottoman history will be in the near future one of the major disciplines in the university curricula. With Ottoman studies, you will have a more in-depth view of Byzantine history for its last two centuries, for Balkan history for its six centuries, under Ottoman rule, and for Middle East history for its five centuries under Ottoman rule. Without the Ottoman archives you cannot write the history of the Arab world for the last four centuries, not even for the twentieth century. Without the Ottoman archives, for instance, you cannot understand how the Saudis rose in Arabia. The history of the countries from the Danube to the Indian Ocean can only be understood through Ottoman studies. When Middle East centres consult me about hiring a young scholar, my first question is whether he or she knows Ottoman Turkish and can use the Ottoman documents because without the use of the Ottoman archives he or she cannot produce a really original work. Even Ottoman newspapers are important. Newspapers were first published in Istanbul in the 1860s.

NEG: Have you read Orientalism *by Edward Said? Could you comment on it?*
INALCIK: I must confess I did not finish reading the whole book. But I am aware of the controversy. I am glad you asked this question. It is true that European academic interest in the Middle East began in the nineteenth century or before with pragmatic concerns. After all, the first European specialists in Turkish were the *Jeunes de langues* who worked for the consular services translating Ottoman and Arabic documents. But even during the Age of Imperialism, we cannot deny that in Europe there were universities that were autonomous. True, at

the same time there were institutions in Europe that were closely influenced by their governments. But there always existed independent, scholarly work by European orientalists. We still are dependent on their solid scholarship and their erudition. It was these scholars who produced the best Persian, Arabic, and Turkish dictionaries. They published texts without which no serious work can be done even today. So I think that it is an exaggeration to claim that European orientalism is altogether affected by the imperialists' concerns and influences, or that they were all biased against Islam, Arabs, or Turks.

I have already expressed my concern about how Turkish history has been distorted. Of course there was a Eurocentric approach, even by orientalists. It is also an exaggeration to say that the orientalists were too narrow, that they were strictly philologists, that they could not present the historical past in its entirety, that they were compartmentalized, or that they would take a text and analyse it without having an historian's broad perspective. There were many great scholars – among them, Ignaz Goldziher, Vasilii Barthold, Louis Massignon, Carl Brockelman, Theodor Nöldeke, Carl Becker, H. A. R. Gibb, and Paul Wittek – we owe them so much.[19] The rather unfair attacks against them originate from proponents of certain narrow and biased doctrines. If a thing is not presented within the framework of a particular doctrine or a model it is not valid for them. Actually they suffer for lack of a solid basis of facts and documents from which to make a sound interpretation. What they say is sometimes purely speculative. A scholar must first work in the archives, discover solid sources, and interpret them using our modern notions of social and economic history without necessarily depending on a particular doctrine.

I consider Marx, like Max Weber, to be a great sociologist. Without literally following the doctrine of Marx or Weber, we definitely can benefit in our approach to Ottoman history from these two great theoreticians.

In the last twenty or thirty years, periphery-centre theory and prosopography have become fashionable. True, these new approaches also give a perspective that is important for historical understanding, but I consider it essential to work with the documents, to never alienate ourselves from the historical solid ground. But at the same time in choosing our topics and in our interpretations, we have to answer the questions raised by these social theorists. The history of the Ottoman Empire definitely requires these new approaches to be more than a chronology. But I have to say once more that the perspectives Marx and Weber had on the Ottoman Empire are rather misleading. Weber, as you will see in my forthcoming article, "Comments on 'Sultanism': Max Weber's Typification of the Ottoman Polity", was strongly influenced by the jingoistic newspaper articles of his time on the Eastern Question.[20] He didn't have a deep understanding of Ottoman history, and what he wrote consisted of certain general impressions he had formed about Ottoman society. Neither Marx nor Weber themselves claimed their theories to be final. Some Ph.D. candidates take them too seriously and blindly follow a particular model and try to fake things for the sake of theory. If we depend on theories and abstractions neglecting the concrete, the unique in history, what we are presenting is not history. Some of the recent works on the Middle East are too dependent on models which are sometimes pure fantasy.

I also do not believe in comparison in history. The so-called comparative history is useful as long as it leads to a focus on essential points to understand the history of a particular society, but to draw conclusions by comparing an incomplete, biased Ottoman history with an incomplete, biased Chinese history seems to me absurd. Comparing two unknowns only leads us to fantasy. In other words, sociologists or social historians draw by comparison formulae applicable to all empires, but if the basic knowledge and interpretation are not solid, what is the use of comparison? So the historian must do his task and cling to it. He must try first to draw the objective facts from solid sources. Of course you can never reach absolute objectivity in anything. What I mean by objectivity is to find the facts and make an honest analysis of what the documents say. Perhaps the sociologists can then make better and more reliable comparisons and formulations, but I still believe this is not *history*.

NEG: How do you deal with the question of Ottoman decline?
INALCIK: Decline means when an institution no longer serves the purpose for which it was originally created. Only in this case can you speak of decline. The capitulations, for example, continued but no longer served their original purpose. So decline or deterioration happened in the capitulary regime. There was a decline in the Ottoman state's original system which collapsed at the end of the sixteenth century. The classical Ottoman state changed fundamentally. Shaken by the change, contemporaries went back to the origins of the institutions to identify the "decline". But as an historian I interpreted the "decline" as a transformation or adaptation to the new conditions for survival.

Modernization in Europe was so rapid when compared to the Ottoman Empire that though the empire made efforts to adjust, it could not catch up. Ottoman culture was traditional like that in India or China. The Ottomans could make changes in the army, the bureaucracy, and the fiscal organization but not in the culture. The first half of the seventeenth century was a time of crisis, and the eighteenth century a period of adjustment which continued until World War I when the empire was faced with a total collapse. So for survival Atatürk decided to adopt without condition Western culture. Today there is a dramatic clash between the traditional and modern in Turkey and in other Islamic countries.

NEG: Do you see a continuity between the Ottoman Empire and modern Turkey?
INALCIK: After the collapse of the Ottoman Empire the rising new nations considered their life under the Ottomans to be a dark age and blamed the Ottomans for their shortcomings. I can understand why the Christian peoples of the Balkans might nurture such a notion, but the Arabs too turned against the Ottoman Turks. One of reasons they have for repudiating their Ottoman past has been the identification of the Ottoman Empire with a particular ethnic group, the Turks. They learned to call it the "Turkish" Empire, a term borrowed from Western literature. This term gives the wrong idea about the Ottoman Empire. The Ottoman Empire was primarily a kind of commonwealth, a dynastic state. It was founded by Turks and its language was Turkish, but all the peoples included in it – Turks, Arabs, Greeks, Slavs, Albanians – contributed to its rise and final formation. Recently certain national movements sought to use this mistake in terminology for their claims against Turkey believing that the Turkish Republic is a continuation of the "Turkish Empire" even after the abolition of the sultanate. There also are certain groups in Turkey itself which still continue to identify the Turkish nation state with the Ottoman Empire forgetting the fact that the empire ended in 1922 when the sultan left Turkey. Atatürk, the founder of the nation-state of the Turks, fought against the sultanate like any other new nation which gained its independence from the empire. Some people believe, and I think rightly, in a cultural continuity. The new Turkey considers itself culturally a continuation of the Ottoman Empire. But with the formation of the Turkish Republic there was a decisive political rupture with the Ottoman Empire. The correct interpretation of Ottoman history in Turkey and in the West depends on our understanding of this key point.

NEG: You have mentioned women only very occasionally in your works. Could you comment on the study of women in Ottoman history?
INALCIK: Fortunately, in the last ten years, women in the Ottoman-Turkish society have received a growing interest. In 1993 Leslie Peirce published her study on harem women and their political role, based on documents from the Topkapı Palace archives. In the same year an

exhibition on "Women in Ottoman-Turkish Society" was organized at the Topkapı Palace Museum. The Ottoman kadi court records, which have been exploited by Ronald Jennings, Suraiya Faroqui, Amnon Cohen, and others, contain a rich documentation on women's history.[21]

NEG: Has the Islamic resurgence had an influence on Ottoman studies in Turkey?
INALCIK: There is now a greater interest in the Islamic heritage. This has contributed to the expansion of studies on the Ottoman-Turkish past because the faculties of theology and history have recently been producing researchers able to read the old manuscripts and documents. Now the sources are more extensively exploited.

NEG: Have you considered returning to Turkey now that you have retired?[12]
INALCIK: In 1992, Bilkent University in Ankara offered me a position with the task of organizing a history department. I accepted this rather challenging offer and moved to Ankara. You would think it is unwise to accept such a responsibility at my age, but I am enjoying it. I donated my library of over 3,000 books to the Library of Bilkent University now open to the public.

NEG: What are your impressions of American students of Ottoman Studies?
INALCIK: I am surprised and gratified that students in this country learn oriental languages so well. They are competent to read the sources in Arabic, Turkish, and Persian and have become distinguished young scholars who produce original works. Among my students are those who mastered the Ottoman language within two years. Some of them are attracted too much by doctrines and models. But most of them contribute solid empirical work. They are mostly concentrating on social and economic history. My hope is that in the near future when we have more empirical studies it will be possible to make solid syntheses and interpretations on Ottoman history, with emphasis on social and economic structure and change. This is the general trend in recent historiography. So I am very hopeful.

NEG You do not agree with the idea that only Turks can do Turkish history?
INALCIK: No. I am convinced that Western universities, with their autonomous, independent, scholarly tradition, train very capable scholars in our field. There is good cooperation with our colleagues in Turkey. A recent, very promising development is the improved access to the Turkish archives. I may be allowed to say that this is partly the result of an effort I pursued for many years. We organized a conference on the Turkish archives in Istanbul five years ago and

invited Turgut Özal, then prime minister. The change dates from that time. Big sums were allocated to modernize the Turkish archives, hundreds of young people were hired and trained as archivists, and many new collections have been made available to researchers.

In Europe, during the last thirty or forty years following the Second World War, Ottoman studies suffered an eclipse, but it is coming back quite vigorously in France, Germany, and England. *Turcica,* the best review on Ottoman studies, is prepared in France. In Munich they have a well-trained, productive, young group of Ottomanists. Nor must we forget England where major universities have good programmes in Ottoman history and are turning out very able young scholars. So all this gives great hopes for the future of Ottoman Studies.

Notes

1. For further information see Roderic H. Davison, "Westernized education in Ottoman Turkey", *Essays in Ottoman and Turkish History, 1772–1923: The Impact of the West* (Austin: University of Texas Press, 1990), pp. 166–79.
2. The account of Atatürk's visit to the author's school will be published in the Turkish magazine, *Turquoise.*
3. For further information on the German migration to Turkey, see Laura Fermi, *Illustrious Immigrants: The Intellectual Migration from Europe: 1930–41* (Chicago: University of Chicago Press, 1968), pp. 66–70 and pp. 359–64, and Donald Fleming and Bernard Bailyn, *The Intellectual Migration: Europe and America, 1930–1960* (Cambridge: Harvard University Press, 1969).
4. Halil Inalcik, "Impact of the Annales School on Ottoman studies and new findings", in Inalcik (ed.), *Studies in Ottoman Social and Economic History* (London: Variorum Reprints, 1985), pp. 69–96.
5. Marc Bloch, *Feudal Society* (Chicago: University of Chicago Press, 1961); Henri Berr, *History and Historiography* (New York: MacMillan, 1932); Henri Pirenne, *Medieval Cities: Their Origins and the Revival of Trade* (Princeton: Princeton University Press, 1925); Lucien Febvre, *Life in Renaissance France* (Cambridge: Harvard University Press, 1977).
6. Paul Wittek, *The Rise of the Ottoman Empire* (London: Royal Asiatic Society, 1938).
7. Halil Inalcik, *Tanzimat ve Bulgar Meselesi* (The Tanzimat and the Bulgarian Question) (Ankara: Turkish Historical Society, 1943).
8. Paul Rycaut, *Histoire de l'état présent de l'empire Ottoman* (Colon: Chez Pierre du Morteauv, 1676).
9. Halil Inalcik, *Suret-i defter-i sancak-i Arvanid* (The Register of the Province of Albania) (Ankara: Turkish Historical Society, 1954).
10. Franz Babinger, *Mehmed the Conqueror and his Time*, ed. W. C. Hickman, translated R. Manheim (Princeton: Princeton University Press, 1978); Halil Inalcik, "Mehmed the conqueror (1432–1481) and his time", *Speculum*, 35 (1960), pp. 408–27 (review article).
11. Herbert Grundmann, *Monumenta Germaniae historica, 1819–1969* (Munich: Monumenta Germaniae historica, 1979).

12. M. Akdağ, "Türkiyenin iktisadi vaziyeti" (Turkey's economic situation), *Belleten*, 5 (1949), pp. 497–571 and 55 (1950), pp. 319–418.

13. Halil Inalcik, "Military and fiscal transformation in the Ottoman Empire, 1600–1700", *Studies in Ottoman Social and Economic History*, pp. 283–337.

14. William Langer, *An Encyclopedia of World History* (Boston: Houghton Mifflin Co., 1948).

15. Halil Inalcik, *The Ottoman Empire, the Classical Age, 1300–1600* (New York and London: Praeger, 1973).

16. ——, "Osmalilarda raiyyet rusûmu", *Belleten*, 23 (1959), pp. 575–610.

17. ——, "The emergence of big farms, *çiftliks*: state, landlords, and tenants", *Studies in Ottoman Social and Economic History*, pp. 105–26. For a fuller exposé of the *çift-hane* system, see "Village, peasant, and empire" in ——, *The Middle East and the Balkans under the Ottoman Empire* (Bloomington: Indiana University Press, 1993), pp. 137–60.

18. Immanuel Wallerstein, *The Capitalist World-Economy: Essays* (New York: Cambridge University Press, 1979) and *Mercantilism and the Consolidation of the European World-Economy, 1600–1750* (New York: Academic Press, 1980).

19. Ignaz Goldziher, *Muhammedanische Studien* (Halle a.S.: M. Niemeyer, 1889–90); Carl Barthold, *Turkestan down to the Mongol Invasion*, translated by T. Minorsky (London: Luzac, 1968); Louis Massignon, *La passion de Husayn ibn Mansur Hallaj: martyr mystique de l'Islam* (Paris: Gallimard, 1975); Theodor Nöldeke, *Geschichte des Qorans* (Göttingen: Verlag der Dieterichschen Buchhandlung, 1860); Carl Becker, *Christianity and Islam*, translated by H. J. Chaytor (London and New York: 1909); Carl Brockelmann, *History of the Islamic Peoples*, translated by Joel Carmichael and Moshe Perlmann (New York: G. P. Putnam's Sons, 1947) H. A. R. Gibb, *Modern Trends in Islam* (Chicago: University of Chicago Press, 1947); Wittek, *The Rise of the Ottoman Empire*.

20. Halil Inalcik, "Comments on 'Sultanism': Max Weber's typification of the Ottoman polity", *Princeton Papers in Near Eastern Studies*, 1 (1992), pp. 49–72.

21. Leslie P. Peirce, *The Imperial Harem: Women and Sovereignty in the Ottoman Empire* (New York and Oxford: Oxford University Press, 1993); Ronald Jennings, "Women in early seventeenth-century Ottoman judicial records: The Sharia court of Anatolian kayseri", *Journal of the Economic and Social History of the Orient*, 18 (1975), pp. 53–114; Soroya Faroqui, "Town officials, *timar*-holders, and taxation: the late sixteenth-century crisis as seen from Çorum", *Turcica*, 18 (1989), pp. 53–82; Amnon Cohen, *Economic Life in Ottoman Jerusalem* (New York and Cambridge: Cambridge University Press, 1989).

ABDUL-KARIM RAFEQ, born in Idlib, Syria, on 21 April 1931, specializes in the history of the Arab provinces under Ottoman rule. He is professor of history at the University of Damascus and is currently visiting professor and Chair of Middle Eastern Studies at the College of William and Mary in Virginia. He has also taught at the University of Chicago, the University of California, Los Angeles, and the University of Pennsylvania. He has trained numerous scholars to work with Syrian court records to uncover new information on social and economic history.

Interviewed at the University of California, Los Angeles, and at the University of California, Santa Barbara, on 14 November 1990 by Nancy Gallagher.

NEG: Shall we begin with your early years?
RAFEQ: I was raised in the town of Idlib, a small town about 60 kilometres to the west of Aleppo. At that time it had about 10,000 inhabitants. Most people owned small plots of land and earned their living from their olive trees and from their employment in town. My parents had two small pieces of land: a vineyard which belonged to my father and an olive grove which belonged to my mother. We used to spend the summer in the vineyard which was nearer to town and had fig trees, a cistern containing rain water, and a cottage with a spacious concrete terrace where we sat in the evenings.

My father was a cloth merchant; he had his own shop in the *suq* [market]. He used to travel to Aleppo and Beirut to buy wholesale cloth, mostly made in Europe, which he retailed in his shop largely for credit to individuals. On special days he used to go to weekly fairs that were held in the region. His handwriting was the best in the locality, and many neighbouring shop owners would come to him to get help with writing. The land was a source of additional revenue for us.

During World War II my father lost his business, and we were broke for a period of time. There was rationing, and we survived by selling olive oil produced on our land. I am reluctant to sell that land now because it keeps my parents' memory, and because we lived off it in the distant past.

I was brought up in a family atmosphere that was very caring. I am most grateful to my parents for my upbringing. They gave me the best education available and were examples of piety, kindness, and sincerity. They taught us never to tell lies, to be kind to people, and to cooperate with them. I have one brother who studied law and is now a school teacher in Aleppo. I have two sisters, both older than me, one married in Idlib, the other in Aleppo.

I attended elementary and intermediate [junior high] school in Idlib. At the end of the intermediate school one had to sit for the government examination (*Brevet*) to be able to continue one's studies. Those who passed the examination had to go to Aleppo to enrol in a secondary school. I enrolled at the American College there, which originally had been established in Gaziantep (Aintab) now in Turkey, but had moved to Aleppo in 1939. The college prepared the students from all over the region for the government *baccalauréate* programme and also for its sophomore programme. A number of my colleagues who graduated from the college had distinguished careers later on. I may mention the name of one of them, the well-known film producer in the United States, Mustafa Akkad, who was my classmate. Many others became medical doctors or engineers.

I stayed in Aleppo for three years, during which time I passed the examination of the Syrian Baccalaureate that the college prepared its students for in the freshman year. The following year I finished the sophomore year. With a Syrian Baccalaureate, I was admitted to the Syrian University in Damascus in 1951. It was only a few years after the evacuation of the French and Syria's attainment of independence, and the new national government was rapidly expanding the educational system. Syria already had a faculty of medicine and a faculty of law dating to the time of Faysal's Arab nationalist government [1918–20]. These faculties had become the Syrian University (later the University of Damascus) in 1923. In 1946 the government established the Faculty of Arts and the Faculty of Sciences. The university aimed at preparing young people in these two faculties to teach in the secondary schools because the teachers at the time were few and mostly old. At the time, however, students were more interested in studying medicine or engineering. To encourage them to join the faculties of arts and sciences to become teachers, the ministry of education created the Higher Institute for Teachers which selected students from all over the country on the sole basis of merit, provided them with adequate funds to live and study at the University of Damascus, and trained them in the field of study they had chosen for themselves. I chose to study history. I was interviewed by the Higher Institute's committee and accepted. About one hundred students from all over Syria were selected every year to study for five years at the expense of the government. It took four years to obtain the Licence (Bachelor of Arts) and an additional year for the diploma in education. These students formed the backbone of the educational system in Syria.

Constantine Zurayk was president of the Syrian University when I was a student. He also taught courses in the history department. He later became vice-president of the American University of Beirut. Students at that time often demonstrated against the military dictatorship of Adib Shishakli. When government troops tried to storm the outer gate of the University, President Zurayk himself stood at the gate to stop them. Students from the various political parties active at the time were grateful to him for his stand.

I was recently asked to contribute an article for a *Festschrift* for President Zurayk. The article was published both in Arabic and in English. The English title is "The social and economic structure of Bab al-Musalla (al-Midan), Damascus, 1825–1875".[1] Bab al-Musalla was the quarter where Zurayk was born. When socio-economic and communal riots had erupted in the nineteenth century, that quarter had demonstrated communal solidarity among its religious communities. Zurayk emphasized this communal solidarity and coexistence in his call for Arab nationalism.

NEG: Were you influenced by the political activities of that era?
RAFEQ: I never belonged to any political party, but I identified and still identify as an Arab. I believe in the Arab nation and in Arab culture and its continuity through the ages. I consider myself an Arab before anything else. If you ask me what is your religion I would rather tell you that I am an Arab. I identify with my country and I bear its culture. I was raised there as were my parents and my ancestors. Generations of people were raised together in a common Arab culture that they shared and contributed to no matter to what religion they belonged. All the people cherished common ideals and a common history, and this is the most important thing.

Arab nationalism was and still is strong in Syria. The simple fact that students studied the history of the Arabs implied a certain solidarity with the other Arab states. The university was very political during the 1950s. Each political group acted freely. There was the Syrian Socialist Nationalist Party, the Communist Party, the Muslim Brothers, and the Baath Party. The parties displayed their newspapers and publications freely, and their members were very active. The aim of the nationalist parties was to bring the Arab states together for the welfare of the Arab people.

In 1956 I graduated from the University of Damascus and became an instructor there, giving courses and preparing myself for my specialization in modern Arab history. In 1958 I was chosen to go to the University of London to study for the Ph.D. in modern Arab history. Two of my fellow students were given scholarships to study in Spain and Egypt, and all three of us ended up teaching in the history department of the University of Damascus.

I went to London shortly after the union between Syria and Egypt was announced. The Egyptian cultural attaché in London who then represented the new United Arab Republic used to invite Syrian, Egyptian, and other Arab students to celebrate Evacuation Day, Syria's national holiday commemorating the French evacuation of Syria on 17 April 1946. The United Arab Republic was a source of pride not only for the Syrians and the Egyptians, but for all the Arabs. At the time, it seemed a dream come true, and even though it was dissolved a few years later, it showed that unity could be achieved if the Arabs learnt from their mistakes.

When I arrived in London the first thing I wanted to do was to go back to Syria. I was on my own in a foreign country for the first time. But I got used to life there and I remained for five years. I was exposed to students from Egypt, Iraq, Sudan, Saudi Arabia, and other countries and made friendships which I still maintain. It was good to meet with so many Arabs, and this opened new horizons for me.

After passing a qualifying examination, I registered for the Master of Arts programme and was then recommended for the Ph.D. programme. My adviser and the supervisor of my dissertation, Professor Peter Holt, was most helpful to me. I was also fortunate to study with other distinguished professors such as Paul Wittek, then the senior scholar in Ottoman studies, Harold Bowen, an expert in Arab–Ottoman institutions, Bernard Lewis, a leading authority on the Middle East, who taught late Ottoman and Islamic history, and Ann Lambton, who taught medieval Islamic history. The School of Oriental and African Studies was acknowledged worldwide as the major institution for oriental studies. I also had a good opportunity to study European history at the University of London with the best professors in the field. I attended for a year the lectures of Professor Eric Hobsbawm who is one of the leading authorities on the history of Europe during the nineteenth century. I learned much from him, especially from his writings on primitive rebels and bandits, which I could compare with similar phenomena in eighteenth-century Syria. His other books have also been a source of inspiration for me in my research and in my occasional teaching of European history at the University of Damascus.

A weekly seminar at the School of Oriental and African Studies in the University of London was held for graduate students and faculty. It was presided over by Bernard Lewis, professor of Near and Middle Eastern history. Scholars from other British universities, sometimes from abroad, used to be invited to make contributions to the seminar. Albert Hourani came down from Oxford and gave a lecture on the Urabi revolt in Egypt. Mr Hourani was not only easily accessible but was most encouraging to me. He helped me locate sources and gave me advice on a number of issues. His article entitled "The changing face of the Fertile Crescent in the eighteenth century" was what made me decide to write on the ʿAzm family.[2] The title of my dissertation was the "Province of Damascus between 1723 and 1783" when the ʿAzm family was in power. The ʿAzms, like the Zayadina in Upper Galilee, the Jalilis in Mosul, and the mamluks in Baghdad, demonstrated provincial assertiveness in a century of Ottoman decline.

I wrote my dissertation for the most part in the huge reading room of the British Museum. For source materials, I used the Levant Company archives in London and the French consular dispatches from Syria. The French consuls of the eighteenth century left detailed and fairly accurate accounts of the political and economic situation there. The consular reports are found in the Archives Nationales (National Archives) in Paris and in the Chambre de Commerce (Chamber of Commerce) in Marseille. I also used to go to the University of Tübingen in Germany to consult the voluminous collection of Arabic manuscripts, many of which were chronicles or biographical dictionaries dealing with the history of Syria during the Ottoman period. They had been acquired in the nineteenth century by Prussian consuls to Syria for the royal library of the king of Prussia in Berlin. In World War II the manuscripts were moved from Berlin to Tübingen for safe keeping. I also consulted travellers' accounts and secondary studies based on Ottoman sources.

My dissertation was recommended for publication by the examining committee at the University of London, and through a generous grant from the University of London was published in Beirut in 1966.[3] Few studies on the Arab provinces of the Ottoman Empire had been published at that time. My book served as a useful source for Syrian Ottoman history. When Professor P. M. Holt published his work on Egypt and the Fertile Crescent, he was kind enough to refer to my work on Syria.[4]

NEG: How did you come to specialize in modern Arab history?
RAFEQ: The University of Damascus had already sent a colleague to London to specialize in medieval Islamic history. Another colleague was sent to France to study ancient Near Eastern history. So the university needed a specialist in modern Arab history. Modern Arab history for us begins with the Ottoman conquest of the Arab lands in 1516. I chose to focus on Syrian history, but I could have chosen to write on the history of any other Arab country. I thought that writing at first on Syrian history could be a stepping stone for studying Arab history at large at a later time. The coming of the ʿAzm family to power in Syria in the eighteenth century is in itself part of an Arab phenomenon that appeared at that time and which represents a major departure from the practice of the two preceding centuries when only Turks were appointed as governors. A new relationship developed in the eighteenth century between the centre and the Arab provinces and indeed the non-Arab provinces as well. The ʿAzms were referred to by the local chroniclers as Arabs because they spoke Arabic and had lived in Syria since at least the middle of the seventeenth century. They were also praised by a contemporary Damascene chronicler, who was a Greek Orthodox priest, for their tolerance towards the religious minorities in Syria, which fits in with traditional Arab tolerance.

NEG: What were your research foci after you finished your dissertation?
RAFEQ: After I finished my dissertation I was appointed assistant professor of history at the University of Damascus. I started teaching in 1963, developing my own notes and my own way of teaching. My dissertation covered only a part of the syllabus. In our under-developed field of Ottoman studies, Ottoman rule in the Arab provinces was earlier dismissed in local historiography as the Age of Darkness. No one was interested in it because not much was known about it. Also the dark picture largely emanates from the clash between Arab nationalism and Turkish nationalism early in the twentieth century. The attempt by the Young Turks to impose their Turkification methods on the Arabs caused much animosity between the parties and eventually brought about the Arab Revolt against the Turks in 1916.

I started expanding my dissertation to cover Ottoman Syria since its conquest by the Ottomans and to include other Arab provinces. Within five years I was able to write the history of geographical Syria and of Egypt from the Ottoman conquest until the Napoleonic invasion. This history was published in 1968 in a book titled *Bilad al-Sham wa Misr, 1516–1798* (Syria and Egypt, 1516–1798).[5] The book was based mostly on Arabic chronicles, European archival materials, and other publications dealing with Ottoman history at large. It is used as a textbook in a number of Arab universities because it filled a lacuna in Arab–Ottoman studies.

Six years after the publication of this book, I prepared another study which dealt with the history of all the Arab countries under Ottoman rule. It came out in book form in 1974 under the title of *al-ʿArab wa al-ʿuthmaniyyun, 1516–1916* (Arabs and Ottomans, 1516–1916).[6] The book is not arranged country by country. It rather studies the changing relationship between the Arab provinces and the Ottoman Empire and how these provinces reacted to the weakness and decline of the Empire and then to the reforms in the nineteenth century. In addition to Syria and Egypt, the book included Iraq, the Hijaz, Yemen, the Gulf, and also North Africa. It is divided into four sections each of which begins with a brief study of the situation in the Ottoman Empire at the time. The book begins with an introduction devoted to the study of the rise of the Ottoman Empire and its clashes with the Safavids and the Mamluks.

The first section deals with the sixteenth century, when the Ottomans were at the peak of their power in Europe. The second section surveys the symptoms of weakness in the Ottoman Empire which started to appear after the death of Sultan Sulayman the Magnificent in 1566. The third section surveys the main factors behind the decline of Ottoman power in the eighteenth century. It then focuses in detail on the reaction of the Arab provinces to this decline. The fourth section deals with the impact of industrial Europe on the Ottoman Empire and the Arab provinces in the nineteenth century. *Al-ʿArab wa al-ʿuthmaniyyun* is also used as a textbook in a number of Arab universities. The focus of the book underlined the need for an Arab view of history which looks beyond local and regional histories. The study of Arab history as a whole under the Ottomans also highlights the need for comparative studies with other parts of the Empire, such as the Balkans and Anatolia.

My research later on centred on the study of the economic and social history of Ottoman Syria, for which I used the court records. I studied *miri* (state) land and *waqf* (endowed) land and pointed to the exploitation of these lands by influential groups, mainly the military.[7]

NEG: Could you explain how you came upon the Syrian court records?
RAFEQ: Until the mid-1960s very few people were aware of the historical importance of the court records of Syria simply because they had not yet been brought from the different courts in the major cities, classified, and placed in a central archive. When this was done, access to the records became easier, and more people came to know about them and their usefulness for research. Jon Mandaville of Portland

State University was the first person to survey the court records of Syria and Palestine and to publish an article describing their types, numbers, and contents.[8] The earliest court records in Syria are those of Hama and date from 1535. The records from Aleppo begin in the 1540s, those of Damascus in the 1580s. It seems that the earlier records from Damascus had been lost. The records of Jerusalem date from 1530 which make them the oldest of all the Syrian records. The Muslim courts were the only official courts that functioned under the Ottomans prior to the nineteenth century. They registered, among other things, deeds of sale and lease contracts, transactions of loans and credit as well as contracts of marriage and divorce. They also inventoried, in a special court, the estates of deceased persons. When the new European-style courts were established in the second half of the nineteenth century, the Muslim courts were limited to dealing with basic Islamic cases bearing on matters of marriage and divorce, minors and guardians, and for a limited period religious endowments, until the government took over the administration of *waqf.*

The establishment of the Centre for Historical Archives in Damascus in the late 1960s, which grouped together all the court records and other state documents, greatly facilitated scholarly research. Foreign researchers are given the same facilities to use the archives as those given to Syrian and Arab researchers. To alert the community of scholars at large to the usefulness of the records, I published two articles in the mid-1970s describing the records and updating the information about their numbers which had been augmented with new acquisitions.[9] Other articles which I published in Arabic helped acquaint our graduate students with the importance of these records.

NEG: Is it necessary to use the Ottoman archives for the study of the Arab provinces under Ottoman rule?
RAFEQ: The Ottoman archives are extremely important for certain areas of research. They are useful, for instance, for studying administration, finance and taxation, agricultural products, and demography. They also provide important information on land tenure, affairs of tribes, caravan trade, and the relations between the centre administration and the provincial governors. However, to reconstruct the details of everyday life in the Arab cities and to examine the relations between the urban and the rural regions, the Syrian court records provide unique information. Also, in matters concerning the successions of individuals, the Syrian probate inventories constitute a mine of information on these and related issues. It is important in this respect to indicate that almost 99 per cent of the court records are written in Arabic.

NEG: How did you come to write the monograph on Gaza?

RAFEQ: This monograph was originally conceived as a paper to be submitted to the Third International Conference on the history of Syria, which was held at the University of Jordan in Amman in April 1981. The conference, one in a series on the history of Syria jointly sponsored by the University of Damascus and the University of Jordan, had as its theme that year the history of Palestine. The Syrian archives had the only existing register from the court of Gaza. The register was rich and varied in its information, and became the basis of my monograph, *Gaza: an Urban, Social, and Economic Study, 1273–1277 A.H./1857–1861 A.D.*[10] Professor Charles Issawi translated excerpts from the monograph and included them in his work *The Fertile Crescent, 1800–1914: a Documentary Economic History.*[11] Later on, on the basis of the same Gaza register, I wrote another paper entitled "al-Fiʔat al-ijtimaʕiyya wa masadir al-tharwa wa al-sulta fi Ghazza fi awakhir al-khamsinat min al-qarn al-tasiʕ ʕashar" (Social groups and sources of wealth and power in Gaza in the late 1850s) which I contributed to another *Festschrift* for Constantine Zurayk which was devoted to studies on Palestine.[12] The Gaza monograph is the second one that I wrote for an international conference.

NEG: Could you describe your experience teaching in other Arab countries and in the United States?

RAFEQ: I taught for two years, from 1969 to 1971, as part-time visiting professor at the University of Jordan. I was one of a number of Syrian professors who commuted from Damascus to Amman. Teaching in Amman was a new experience for me. Classes were limited in size, and attendance was obligatory for students. In Damascus, we had large numbers of students at the time, and attendance was not obligatory nor indeed was this possible given the large number of students. I also taught on a part-time basis, together with a number of colleagues from the University of Damascus, at the Lebanese University in Beirut during the period between 1972 and 1974. We were involved there in graduate studies. At the time, Beirut was a major centre for the publication and the distribution of books. Having access to new books was one of its many attractions.

In 1977 I was invited by Thomas Naff, then director of the Middle East Center at the University of Pennsylvania, to teach modern Arab history for a year as part of the Fulbright exchange programme. Naff and I had been classmates at the School of Oriental and African Studies. The invitation came at the right moment. My mother, who had been living with my wife and I in Damascus after the death of my father, died suddenly in 1976. Being very much attached to her, I felt I needed to go away for a while. My wife, Thérèse Laktineh, a graduate of Damascus University with a B.A. in geography and a diploma in education, was teaching in a public school in Damascus. We had a one-year-old son, Sam'an. My family accompanied me to Philadelphia, and my wife managed to take leave of absence from her teaching job. We spent a pleasant and rewarding year in Philadelphia.

In 1981 I accepted an invitation from the University of Chicago, where for two years I taught modern Arab history. My wife and three young children accompanied me to Chicago. The University of Chicago is a leading institution in many fields. Arab history had not been taught there on a regular basis since William Polk had left in the early seventies. I profited from the new research being done in economic and social history. The university library was rich with source material. The students were anxious to study modern Arab history. The students, mostly college graduates preparing for the M.A. or the Ph.D. degree, were highly motivated and were anxious to study modern Arab history. I liked their questions and scholarly performance, though our field is very politicized and can be highly charged. It needs patience, understanding, tolerance, and above all compassion.

I was next invited to teach at the University of California at Los Angeles for the spring quarter of 1984. An excellent programme in modern Arab history had been launched there through the efforts of Afaf Lutfi al-Sayyid Marsot and her colleagues. I am currently visiting professor at the College of William and Mary in Virginia, where I hold a chair for the teaching of Arab and Middle Eastern studies endowed by William Bickers, a former professor at the American University of Beirut, and his wife, Annie Bickers.

I have tried to teach students to study modern Arab history in the context of Ottoman and European history and the wider social and economic background. This approach has been well-received by students, especially Arab students, who were anxious to depart from the traditional method of memorizing events.

One result of the new approach to the teaching and writing of history is the publication since the early 1980s by the University of Damascus of a historical journal, *Dirasat tarikhiyya* (Historical studies). This journal has become a scholarly forum to which Arab historians from all over the Arab world have contributed. Its aim is to establish the foundations of a historical school based on scholarship and objectivity which will contribute toward a better understanding of Arab history and culture. I am a member of its editorial board and I have published many articles in it.[13]

NEG: Has the Annales school influenced your approach to history?
RAFEQ: Yes. I was acquainted with this school through the *Annales*

journal and through the writings of historians who formulated and contributed to its methodology. The works of Fernand Braudel tower high in this respect. I became interested in the various aspects of everyday life, social networks, and spatial dimensions which influenced events. In Syria, the law-court records and the probate inventories are excellent sources for this kind of research.

The influence of the Annales can be seen throughout my work. In one article I dealt with financial relations between urban and rural social groups, and with social banditry and militant Sufi religious movements, both forms of social and economic protest against exploitative ruling authorities.[14] In another, I studied the travel agents, organized in *ta'ifa*s (corporations), who took care of the pilgrims' voyages to the holy cities. I was able to describe in detail the one way or round trip fare, the amount of luggage allowed with each passenger, the fees requested for food, drinking water, and extra luggage, and the seating of pilgrims on the backs of camels.[15] In another article, I dealt with preparing and fighting wars: the procurement of guns and the manufacture of gunpowder, troops' recruitment and pay, and their motivation, slogans, and performance on the battlefield. These are important questions that can decide victory or defeat.[16]

NEG: Have you been able to bring women into your studies of society and economy in the Arab provinces?
RAFEQ: Not at first because there were other priorities. I thought we first needed a comprehensive, well-argued study outlining the region's political history. That did not exist because Arab history during Ottoman rule was not studied adequately until very recently. I devoted the first ten years of my teaching and research to writing the general history of the Arabs under Ottoman rule from 1516 to 1916.[17] Then I started to study the infrastructure of Syria's economy and society.

I have just begun to focus on women. In a study based on one of the earliest court registers from Hama dating back to 1535, I examined patterns of marriage and divorce in Hama and its countryside. Using data and tables, I showed which quarters in the city intermarried with each other or with the neighbouring villages, and also which villages intermarried with each other.[18] In the article on social groups, I found women were deeply involved in the real estate market and in loans and credit.[19] In two other studies based on the probate inventories in Syria, I dealt with the bequeathments of women and men.[20] I examined the estates of women, the number of times each woman was married, the number of children she had, and the ratio of females to males in the households of the deceased. Of special importance were the patterns of monogamy and polygamy. In an article published recently, I dealt with public morality in eighteenth-century Damascus and the role which female intriguers, procuresses, and prostitutes had played in certain quarters in undermining public morality in association with unruly troops.[21] The court records, like the probate inventories, yield tremendous information on women during the Ottoman period. A woman's dowry upon marriage, for instance, can be traced throughout the centuries. These records still need to be studied.

NEG: Could you comment on the debate over orientalist scholarship?
RAFEQ: Edward Said's book, *Orientalism*, has been translated into Arabic, and the debate has continued for a long time in the Middle East, where many people subscribe to his ideas. The book was well-timed because people in the Middle East were disillusioned with the West which had coerced them and ruled them for generations. The overall picture which Said contributed was that orientalism emerged at the same time as European imperialism and that many orientalists were in the service of the imperialists. Edward Said himself recognizes the good work done by a number of orientalists. They promoted many disciplines, focused attention on the merits of Arab–Islamic civilization, and brought to light the Arabs' contribution to world civilization. Many examples serve to illustrate this trend, but that does not mean that all orientalists worked to serve imperialism. Volney, for example, was a very shrewd and tactful Frenchman who described intelligibly the conditions he witnessed in Egypt and Syria during his three-year journey in the early 1780s.[22] Napoleon Bonaparte in preparing to invade Egypt in 1798 read Volney's account of his travels, but Volney apparently did not write it for this purpose. Some orientalists were merely interested in exposing only the negative aspects of Middle Eastern civilization. All human cultures have negative aspects. Objectivity and fairness dictate that one study the negative alongside the positive. I think that the last word on orientalism has not been said.

NEG: Could you comment on current trends in the writing of Syrian and modern Arab history?
RAFEQ: More and more researchers, Syrians, Arabs, and non-Arabs, are becoming interested in the study of Syrian and modern Arab history, especially the Ottoman period. Students in the West and in Syria are studying the history of Aleppo, Damascus, and Hama, and doing good, objective work. Furthermore, many of these scholars are addressing major social and economic issues which place their studies in the best tradition of modern historiography. Historians in other Arab countries are also addressing similar issues relating to their

countries. This new scholarly approach will eventually make it possible for Arab historians to combine efforts and produce an in-depth study of Arab history with emphasis on its social and economic aspects.

NEG: Could you describe your current work?

RAFEQ: I am currently interested in developing my own research on the economic and social history of Ottoman Syria. One topic that has occupied me for some time is the organization and functioning of the craft corporations (*ta'ifas*) in Ottoman Syria and the integration of the religious communities in them. In the work ethic that permeated and dominated the craft organizations, merit was more important than religious affiliation, especially in the *ta'ifas* of mixed membership. Muslims, Christians, and Jews shared in the membership of many *ta'ifas* and maintained a smooth relationship among themselves. Representatives from all three communities, or from two communities when membership was limited to them, went side by side on joint delegations to the Muslim court to notify the judge of their common decisions. Despite certain political and social limitations imposed by mostly alien rulers, the communities were fully integrated in the traditional economy and society. Sales transactions of residential property in the Syrian cities, as revealed in the court records, indicate the mixing of residences of the various communities. No community lived in a ghetto-like situation. In fact, during the three centuries that preceded the impact of industrial Europe and the domination of the world capitalist economy in the nineteenth century, which caused socio-economic and communal riots, no such riots occurred at all.[23]

Another topic which has interested me of late is the way the ulama and Arab Muslim intellectuals identified themselves under Ottoman rule prior to the spread of Arabism and nationalism.

NEG: Do you have any advice for students considering specializing in Middle Eastern history?

RAFEQ: I encourage specialization in Middle Eastern history, because there is so much to be done. The Ottoman period is still undeveloped. Arabs and non-Arabs can together contribute to this field in the best traditions of modern historiography. Multi-disciplinary training is an asset enabling the scholar to ask the right questions and arrive at the right conclusions. A knowledge of the appropriate technical language of the relevant sources needed for research is a primary prerequisite for the scholar. Finally, there is need to reconsider some of the hasty conclusions which have been drawn with regard to our history. We must interpret the sources cautiously and abstract our models and theories from within local history and avoid forcing preconceived ideas upon it.

Notes

1. Abdul-Karim Rafeq, "The social and economic structure of Bab al-Musalla (al-Midan), Damascus, 1825–1875" in George N. Atiyeh and Ibrahim M. Oweiss (eds.), *Arab Civilization, Challenges and Responses, Studies in Honor of Constantine K. Zurayk* (Albany: State University of New York Press, 1988), pp. 272–311.

2. Albert Hourani, "The changing face of the Fertile Crescent in the eighteenth century", *Studia Islamica*, 8 (1957), pp. 89–122.

3. Abdul-Karim Rafeq, *The Province of Damascus, 1723–1783* (Beirut: Khayats, 1966).

4. P. M. Holt, *Egypt and the Fertile Crescent, 1516–1922* (Ithaca, New York: Cornell University Press, 1966), p. 106.

5. Abdul-Karim Rafeq, *Bilad al-Sham wa Misr, 1516–1798* (Syria and Egypt, 1516–1798) (Damascus: Atlas, 1967).

6. ——, *al-ʿArab wa al-ʿuthmaniyyun, 1516–1916* (Arabs and Ottomans, 1516–1916) (Damascus: Alif Ba, 1974).

7. See, for example, ——, "Aspects of land tenure in Syria in the early 1580s" in Abdeljelil Temimi (ed.), *Les provinces Arabes et leurs sources documentaires a l'époque Ottomane* (Zaghouan: Centre de recherches ottomanes et Morisco-Andalouses, 1987), pp. 153–63; "Cities and countryside in a traditional setting: the case of Damascus in the first quarter of the eighteenth century", in Thomas Philipp (ed.), *The Syrian Lands in the eighteenth and nineteenth century* (Berliner Islamstadia, Bd. 5).

8. John Mandaville, "The Ottoman court records of Syria and Jordan", *Journal of the American Oriental Society*, 29, 3 (1966), pp. 311–19.

9. Abdul-Karim Rafeq, "Les registres des tribuneaux de Damas comme source pour l'histoire de la Syrie", *Bulletin d'Etudes Orientales* (French Institute in Damascus), XXVI (1973), pp. 219–35, and "The law court registers of Damascus with special reference to craft corporations during the first half of the eighteenth century" in Jacques Berque et Dominique Chevallier (eds.), *Les Arabes par leurs Archives (XVIième–XXième siècles)* (CNRS, Paris, 1976), pp. 141–59.

10. ——, "Ghazza: dirasa ʿumraniyya wa ijtimaʿiyya wa iqtisadiyya min khilal al-wathaʾiq al-sharʿiyya, 1273–1277" (Gaza: a socio-economic and urban study, 1857–1861) (Damascus: n.p. 1980).

11. Charles Issawi, *The Fertile Crescent, 1800–1914: A Documentary Economic History* (New York and London: Oxford University Press, 1988), pp. 443–5.

12. Abdul-Karim Rafeq, "al-fiʿat al-ijtimaʿiyya wa masadir al-tharwa wa al-sulta fi Ghazza fi awakhir al-khamsinat min al-qarn al-tasiʿ ʿashar" (Social groups and sources of wealth and power in Gaza in the late 1850s) in Hisham Nashshaba (ed.), *Studia Palaestina: Studies in Honour of Constantine K. Zurayk* (Beirut, 1988), pp. 83–126.

13. Twelve of these articles are reprinted in one volume, Abdul-Karim Rafeq, *Buhuth fi al-tarikh al-iqtisadi wa al-ijtimaʿi li bilad al-Sham fi al-ʿasr al-hadith* (Studies in the economic and social history of modern Syria) (Damascus: n.p. 1985).

14. ——, "al-Fiʾat al-ijtimaʿiyya wa mulkiyyat al-ard fi bilad al-Sham fi al-rubʿ al-akhir min al-qarn al-sadis ʿashar" (Social groups and land ownership in Syria in the last quarter of the sixteenth century), *Dirasat tarikhiyya*, Damascus, nos. 35, 36 (March–June 1990), pp. 111–44.

15. ——, "New Light on the transportation of the Damascene Pilgrimage during

the Ottoman Period" in R. Olson (ed.), *Islamic and Middle Eastern Societies: A Festschrift in honor of Professor Wadie Jwaideh* (Brattleboro, Vermont: Amana Books, 1987), pp. 127–36.

16. ——, "The Local Forces in Syria during the seventeenth and eighteenth centuries" in V. J. Parry and M. E. Yapp (eds.), *War, Technology, and Society in the Middle East* (New York and London: Oxford University Press, 1975), pp. 277–307.

17. *al-ʿArab wa al-ʿuthmaniyyun*.

18. Abdul-Karim Rafeq, "Mazahir iqtisadiyya wa ijtimaʿiyya min liwaʾ Hama, 1535–1536" (Economic and social aspects of the province of Hama, 1535–1536), *Dirasat tarikhiyya*, nos. 31–32 (March–June, 1989), pp. 17–66.

19. ——, "al-Fiʾat al-ijtimaʿiyya wa mulkiyyat al-ard".

20. ——, "Mazahir sukkaniyya min Dimashq fi al-ʿahd al-ʿUthmani" (Population data from Damascus in the Ottoman era), *Buhuth*, pp. 217–40; "Dirasa sukkaniyya li Dimashq wa Halab fi ʿam 1277 A.H./1861 A.D. min khilal sijillat al-tarikat" (Demographic Study of Damascus and Aleppo in 1277/1861 based on the probate inventories in *Studies in History and Literature in Honour of Nicola N. Ziadeh*, ed. Ihsan Abbas, Shereen Khairallah and Ali Z. Shakir. Hazar Publishing, London, 1992, pp. 95–105.

21. ——, "Public morality in eighteenth-century Ottoman Damascus", *Villes au Levant: Hommage à André Raymond, Revue du Monde Musulman et de la Méditerranée*, nos. 55, 56 (1990), pp. 180–96.

22. C.-F. Volney, *Travels through Egypt and Syria, in the Years 1783, 1784, and 1785* (New York: David Longworth, 1798).

23. See, for example, Abdul-Karim Rafeq, "New light on the 1860 riots in Ottoman Damascus" in Axel Havemann and Baber Johansen (eds.), *Die Welt des Islams*, Festschrift in honour of Professor Fritz Steppat, XXVIII (1988), pp. 412–30; ——, "Craft organization, work ethics, and the strains of change in Ottoman Syria", *Journal of the American Oriental Society*, 111.3 (1991), pp. 495–511; and ——, "Craft organizations and religious communities in Syria (XVI–XIX centuries)", *La Shiʿa Nell'Impero Ottomano* (Accademia Nazionale Dei Lincei, Fondazione Leone Caetani, no. 25: Rome, 1993), pp. 25–56; ——, "Ottoman historical research in Syria since 1946", *Asian Research Trends: A Humanities and Social Science Review*, 2 (1992), pp. 45–78.

SUGGESTIONS FOR FURTHER READING

ALBERT HOURANI

Arabic Thought in the Liberal Age, 1798–1939 (New York and London: Oxford University Press, 1962).

Europe and the Middle East (Berkeley: University of California Press, 1980).

The Emergence of the Modern Middle East (Berkeley: University of California Press, 1981).

A History of the Arab Peoples (London: Faber and Faber, 1991; Cambridge, Mass.: Harvard University Press, 1991; New York: Warner, 1991).

Islam in European Thought (New York and Cambridge: Cambridge University Press, 1991).

CHARLES ISSAWI

The Arab World's Legacy: Essays by Charles Issawi (Princeton: Darwin Press, 1981).

An Economic History of the Middle East and North Africa (New York: Columbia University Press, 1982).

"The Middle East in the world context: a historical view" in Georges Sabagh (ed.), *The Modern Economic and Social History of the Middle East in its World Context* (Cambridge: Cambridge University Press, 1989), pp. 1–28.

"Technology, energy, and civilization: some historical observations", *International Journal of Middle Eastern Studies*, 23 (1991), pp. 281–9.

Issawi's Laws of Social Motion (Princeton: Darwin Press, 1991).

ANDRE RAYMOND

Artisans et commerçants du Caire au XVIIIième siècle (2 vols., Damascus: Institut français de Damas, 1973–4).

The Great Arab Cities in the Sixteenth–Eighteenth Centuries: An Introduction (New York: New York University Press, 1984).

Grandes villes arabes a l'époque ottomane (Paris: Sindbad, 1985).

"The economic crisis of Egypt in the eighteenth century" in A. L. Udovitch (ed.), *The Islamic Middle East, 700–1900: Studies in Social and Economic History* (Princeton, N.J.: Darwin Press, 1981), pp. 687–707.

"Cairo" in Albert Hourani, Philip S. Khoury and Mary C. Wilson (eds.), *The Modern Middle East* (Berkeley: University of California Press, 1993), pp. 310–37.

AFAF LUTFI AL-SAYYID MARSOT

Egypt and Cromer: A Study in Anglo-Egyptian Relations (London: John Murray, 1968; New York: Praeger, 1968).

Egypt's Liberal Experiment: 1922–1936 (Berkeley: University of California Press, 1977).

Egypt in the Reign of Muhammad Ali (New York and Cambridge: Cambridge University Press, 1984).

A Short History of Modern Egypt (New York and Cambridge: Cambridge University Press, 1985).

"Popular attitudes towards authority in Egypt", *Journal of Arab Affairs*, 7, 2 (Fall 1988), pp. 174–98.

MAXIME RODINSON

Mohammed (London: Allen Lane, The Penguin Press, 1971; New York: Pantheon Books, 1971).

Islam and Capitalism (London: Allen Lane, The Penguin Press, 1974; New York: Pantheon Books, 1974).

Marxism and the Muslim World (London: Zed Press, 1979; New York: Monthly Review Press, 1981).

The Arabs (Chicago: University of Chicago Press, 1981; London: Croom Helm, 1981).

Europe and the Mystique of Islam (Seattle and London: University of Washington Press, 1987).

NIKKI KEDDIE

An Islamic Response to Imperialism: Political and Religious Writings of Sayyid Jamal ad-Din "al-Afghani" (Berkeley: University of California Press, 1968).

Women in the Muslim World, coedited with Lois Beck (New Haven: Yale University Press, 1978).

Roots of Revolution: An Interpretive History of Modern Iran (New Haven: Yale University Press, 1981).

Women in Middle Eastern History: Shifting Boundaries in Sex and Gender, coedited with Beth Baron (New Haven: Yale University Press, 1991).

"Material culture, technology, and geography: toward a holistic comparative study of the Middle East" in Juan Cole (ed.),

Comparing Muslim Societies: Knowledge and the State in a World Civilization (Ann Arbor: University of Michigan, 1992), pp. 31–62.

HALIL INALCIK
The Ottoman Empire: the Classical Age, 1300–1600 (London: Weidenfeld and Nicolson, 1973; New York: Praeger, 1973).
The History of Mehmed the Conqueror, by Tursun Beg, translated by Halil Inalcik and Rhoads Murphey (Minneapolis: Bibliotheca Islamica, 1978).
The Ottoman Empire: Conquest, Organization, and Economy (London: Variorum Reprints, 1978).
Studies in Ottoman Social and Economic History (London: Variorum Reprints, 1985).
The Middle East and the Balkans under the Ottoman Empire (Bloomington: Indiana University Turkish Studies, v. 9, 1993).

ABDUL-KARIM RAFEQ
The Province of Damascus, 1723–1783 (Beirut: Khayats, 1966).
"The local forces in Syria during the seventeenth and eighteenth centuries" in V. J. Parry and M. E. Yapp (eds.), *War, Technology, and Society in the Middle East* (New York and London: Oxford University Press, 1975), pp. 277–307.
"Economic relations between Damascus and the dependent country-side, 1743–71" in A. L. Udovitch (ed.), *The Islamic Middle East, 700–1900* (Princeton: Darwin Press, 1981), pp. 653–85.
"Work organization, work ethics, and the strains of change in Ottoman Syria", *Journal of the American Oriental Society,* 111, no. 3 (1991), pp. 495–511.
"Ottoman historical research in Syria since 1946", *Asian Research Trends: A Humanities and Social Science Review,* 2 (1992), pp. 45–78.

INDEX

al-'Azm, Sadik Jalal 145

Baath Party 173
Babi movement 139
Babinger, Franz 158
Baer, Gabriel 6, 16, 63
Bakriyya (Sufi order) 99
al-Baquri, Shaykh 103
Barakat, Bahi al-Din 95, 100
Barkan, Ömer, Lûtfi 79, 89
Baron, Beth 144
Barthold, Vasilii 165
Baykal, Bekir Sitki 155
de Beauvoir, Simone 143
Becker, Carl H. 9, 165
Beck, Lois 144, 149
Beeston, A. F. L. 34
Ben Gurion, David 25
Berkeley (University) 132, 133, 134
Berque, Jacques 13, 14, 39
Berr, Henri 155
Bilad al-Sham wa Misr 1516–1798
    (Syria and Egypt, 1516–1798)
    176
Bilkent University 151, 168
Binder, Leonard 36
Bloch, Marc 3, 60, 69–70, 155
Boupacha, Jamila 124
Bowen, Harold 174
Braudel, Fernand 3, 10, 60, 163,
    181
Briffault, Robert 143
Britain in Egypt (study) 99
"British Politics in Tunisia from 1830
    to 81" (Raymond) 77
British Society for Middle East
    Studies (BRISMES) 83
Brockleman, Carl 165
Bulliet, Richard 148
Bursa *qadi* records 159

Cahen, Claude 3, 5, 70, 73, 79, 137,
    142
Cambridge History of Islam, The 12
Camel and the Wheel, The 148
Camus, Albert 71
"Case for Lebanese Independence,
    The" (Issawi) 53

Centre Nationale de la Recherche
    Scientifique (CNRS) 77, 83, 113
"changing face of the Fertile
    Crescent in the eighteenth
    century, The" (Hourani) 175
çift-hane model 163
Clapham, J. H. 60
Cohen, Marcel 112
"'Comments on 'Sultanism': Max
    Weber's Typification of the
    Ottoman Policy" (Inalcik) 165
"Congress for Cultural Freedom,
    The" (conference) 37
Congress of Orientalists, Cambridge
    1954 4
Columbia University 161
communism 74, 109
communist party 69, 113, 173
    French communist party 109
    Lebanese communist party 116
    Tunisian communist party
comparative history 166

Damascus, French Institute in 77,
    115–6
Dane, Edmund 62
"Decline of the West in the Middle
    East, The" (Hourani) 31, 94
deconstruction 60, 143
Derrida, Jacques 60
Description de l'Egypte 87
Digard, Jean-Pierre 142
Dozy, Reinhardt 62

Eberhard, Wolfram 154
Ecole des Langues Orientales 112
*Economic History of Iran, 1800–1914,
    The* (Issawi) 57, 65
*Economic History of the Middle East,
    1800–1914, The* (Issawi) 57, 65
*Economic History of the Middle East and
    North Africa, The* (Issawi) 57, 64,
    65
*Economic History of Turkey, 1800–1914,
    The* (Issawi) 57, 65
economics in Egyptian history 100
Economics of Middle Eastern Oil, The
    (Issawi) 7